Society and God

Society and God

Culture and Creed
from a Philosophical Standpoint

William Charlton

Ⓒ
James Clarke & Co

James Clarke & Co
P.O. Box 60
Cambridge
CB1 2NT
United Kingdom

www.jamesclarke.co
publishing@jamesclarke.co

Hardback ISBN: 978 0 227 17700 6
Paperback ISBN: 978 0 227 17699 3
PDF ISBN: 978 0 227 90697 2
ePub ISBN: 978 0 227 90698 9
Kindle ISBN: 978 0 227 90699 6

British Library Cataloguing in Publication Data
A record is available from the British Library

First published by James Clarke & Co, 2020

Copyright © William Charlton, 2020

All rights reserved. No part of this edition may be reproduced, stored electronically or in any retrieval system, or transmitted in any form or by any means, electronic, mechanical, photocopying, recording, or otherwise, without prior written permission from the Publisher (permissions@jamesclarke.co).

Contents

Acknowledgements   vii

    1. A Philosophical Standpoint   1
    2. Does Society Exist?   9
    3. Social Life, Egoism and Altruism   21
    4. What Is Religion?   37
    5. The Divine Virtue of Faith   48
    6. Natural Science and Creation   59
    7. Atomism and Holism in Soteriology   78
    8. The Christian Soul   95
    9. Life After Death   107
    10. Questions of Life and Death   123
    11. Sex and Natural Law   136
    12. Education and Multiculturalism   158

Bibliography   179
Index

Acknowledgements

The book brings together work I have done since the publication of *Being Reasonable About Religion* in 2006. I have greatly benefited from discussing the topics with members of the Newcastle philosophy group organised by Mary Midgley and later by Michael Bavidge, with my friends, and above all with Anne Charlton, whom I must thank for unfailing support and encouragement. Some of the material appeared in an earlier form in articles in *The Heythrop Journal*, *New Blackfriars*, and *Philosophy*, and I am grateful to the editors of these journals for allowing me to work up and reuse this material.

1
A Philosophical Standpoint

There are two reasons why a philosopher should discuss society and God together. One is practical and obvious. In various parts of the world today the worship of God is thought to impede the smooth running of society. In China both Muslims and Christians of various denominations are still being imprisoned and 're-educated'. In the democratic West, we are told, opinion polls reveal that half the population believes that over the course of human history religion has been the primary cause of war between nations, of oppression within them and of unhappiness to individuals. Two questions seem to emerge in informal discussions. Is belief in God, on the whole, good or bad for society? And is it possible to have a society in which several different religions co-exist comfortably with each other and with people of no religion?

The other reason, though this is not widely recognised, is that society presents something of a problem to those theologising about God. Christianity, and the same goes for Judaism and Islam, is supposed to provide a system for relations between God and human beings; but does God deal with us as individuals, or in and through societies?

Let me take these reasons in turn.

In 2015 a commission set up by the Woolf Institute in Cambridge published a report on 'Religion and Belief in British Public Life' which made a number of recommendations summarised on pages 80-5 for 'living with difference' which included creating 'a shared understanding of the fundamental values underlying public life', 'measures to reduce selection of pupils and staff on grounds of religion' in 'schools with a religious character', replacing 'the requirement for schools to hold acts of collective worship' by 'a requirement to hold inclusive times for reflection', and obliging the British Broadcasting Corporation to include in its *Thought for the Day* 'speakers from non-religious perspectives such as humanists'. The Report began with a promise to say what religion is, but made no attempt to fulfil that promise. Perhaps the Commissioners thought that everyone knows the difference between religion and non-religion, and would agree that humanism is not a religion. Probably many people are equally confident that they know what society is, and share the opinion once associated with Margaret Thatcher that there is really no such thing – that the world really contains only numbers of many, many individual human beings. If, however, people are confused or mistaken about society and about what religion is, discussion of the two questions I mentioned just now is bound to be futile, and, if it actually seems to be futile, or to generate more heat than light, that may be because the participants in the discussion are confused or mistaken about these things.

Who can tell us what religion or society is? 'Sociology' means the systematic study of society, so should we consult sociologists? 'Biology' means the systematic study of life, but a biologist who is asked 'What is life?' is likely to feel caught on the wrong foot. Biologists will readily provide examples of life: plants, animals, perhaps microbes; not so readily a definition. Arithmetic is about numbers, but until the end of the nineteenth century no arithmetician was able to say what a number was. Physics for us is the paradigm of a natural science, but, if you ask a professor of physics what a science is, you may not get a ready answer. Most people would say that psychology has to do with the mind, but asking a psychologist what the mind is may be unfruitful. These very general questions can be answered up to a point by any intelligent person; beyond that, they fall to philosophers. Many natural scientists today might refer us to the philosopher Karl Popper for an account of what science is. Natural science itself began when the philosopher Aristotle tried to define nature. Frege, the first person to produce a definition of number, did so as a philosopher, not an arithmetician.

What, then, is philosophy? Universities contain departments of philosophy, and those in English-speaking countries are sometimes criticised for the time they devote to the analysis of concepts instead of to the enlargement of our knowledge of the world; but it is only by the analysis of the concepts which words like 'nature', 'life' and 'science' (and 'philosophy' itself) are used to express, that these very general questions can be answered in a systematic way. Philosophers, provided that they have some knowledge of human history and of cultures other than their own, are specially qualified by their training to carry this analysis through.

Tim Crane in *The Meaning of Belief* recognises that the concept we use the word 'religion' to express is problematic and comparatively recent, and he brings to bear on it the techniques of analytical philosophy which I try to use here. Although he holds that religion has, so to speak, a social dimension, he does not discuss society as such; nor, I think, does he bring out the extent to which our thinking about religion is shaped by the role of Christianity in European history.

In the chapters that follow I first discuss society and the part it plays in all rational life. Against the liberal tradition in political thought, I argue that human beings are essentially social beings, that they need society for all that we count as rationality. Only in Chapter 4 do I come to what today we mean by 'religion'. I argue that our concept is taken from Christianity, that Christianity is our paradigm. Such has been its influence on European history that we assume that every society up to now must have had a religion, and we apply the label 'religion' to whatever in societies other than our own most resembles Christianity. Since Christianity is in fact the offspring of Athens and Jerusalem, combining elements of Jewish and Greek culture, we should not expect to find close matches for it outside Europe, but we look for them.

H.J. Rose observes in his article on religion in *The Oxford Classical Dictionary* (p. 758): 'No word in either Greek or Latin corresponds to the English "religion" or "religious"'; nor does any word in any non-European language. When atheists and humanists speak of religion, Christianity is what they primarily have in mind, and, when people today discuss problems that religion may cause society, they often have in mind problems caused by Christianity. Christians in fact, in societies with European languages, despite their sectarian divisions, form the principal sub-society that has a culture in competition with secular liberalism. Even current discussions of threats from Islam are conducted with regard to teaching derived by Christians from the Jews about sheltering and helping alien refugees.

Religion causes problems for society because any sub-society which has a different culture from that of the larger society within which it exists will cause problems for the larger society. The concept of religion, however, and the concept of belief which, as we shall see, enters into it, are confined to European culture. People from other cultures may concede to speakers of European languages that they have a religion, if not religious beliefs, but, even if they are monotheists, neither concept is part of their thinking and, when they form sub-societies within states with a European culture, it is reasonable to attribute any threat they seem to pose more to their culture as a whole than to religion. The general concept of religion is provincial and unhelpful.

The second reason for a philosophical discussion of society and God is more theoretical than practical. Philosophers since the seventeenth century have taught what I dispute in Chapters 2 and 3, that language and society are products of human intelligence, and theologians have not questioned this. They have thought of the Judaeo-Christian God as dealing with human beings as rational individuals. It has occasionally been noticed that the Old Testament represents God as dealing with a society, the Jewish nation, and some theologians, for instance, Karl Rahner, have recognised that we are essentially social, but I do not think any theologian has considered the implications of this fact about us for the presentation of Christian teaching generally. That is something a sympathetic philosopher can attempt. In Chapters 6 to 9 I argue that the view we take on whether we are essentially social beings ought to make a difference to how we understand the three doctrines upon which all Christians are agreed, those of the Trinity, redemption by Christ and life after death.

* * *

In writing, then, about society and God, and concentrating on Judaeo-Christian monotheism, I hope, on the one hand, to make clearer how religion as we conceive it can cause problems within a society, how tensions between religion and politics arise and why they are hard to reduce, and, on the other, to offer a fresh view of some central doctrines of Christianity. I could not do the second without arguing that we are essentially social. I might argue that we are essentially social without discussing Christian dogmatic beliefs. These do, however, have implications, which I shall try to bring out, for life in society, and they are integrally bound up with the traditional moral principles of Christianity, which are themselves a set of social customs. Furthermore, if we want to understand the tensions that now exist in Western states because of religious and other ethnic sub-societies within them, Christianity has played so large a part in creating Western culture that we cannot afford to ignore any beliefs that are integral to Christianity.

Christians, like everyone else, have beliefs about how the world is, which (thanks to their legacy from ancient Athens) they formulate in creeds, and customs concerning the three central occurrences in human

1. A Philosophical Standpoint

life, birth, procreation and death. I look at both; but first, while discussing society, I look at the notion of belief itself. In Western society we talk much about beliefs, but we seldom consider why that is so or what we mean. The best the Woolf Commission, p. 14, could do in the way of explaining it was to say:

> In international legal documentation the equivalent of the English phrase *religion and belief* is in French *la religion et les convictions*. The French word *convictions* has connotations of firmness, weight, intensity and commitment, and refers to something which is fundamental in someone's sense of values, self-worth and identity. To count as a belief so far as the law is concerned a point of view or *une conviction* must 'attain a certain level of cogency, seriousness, cohesion and importance, be worthy of respect in a democratic society and . . . not incompatible with human dignity'.

The quotation is from a publication in 2015 by Peter Edge and Lucy Vickers (*Review of Equality and Human Rights Law Relating to Religion or Belief*, pp. 15-6) and, if they are right, we cannot expect to find our concept of belief in societies which do not share our conceptions of seriousness, democracy and human dignity. Crane in *The Meaning of Belief* (pp. 14-16) attempts a philosophical analysis. 'What makes a belief *a belief*,' he tells us 'is the same in every case', and he lists as 'the features that philosophers identify as essential to belief: . . . accessibility to consciousness, the connection to action and the aim at truth . . . *belief aims at truth*'.

Discussions of consciousness and truth are peculiar to Western philosophy. So, I shall claim, are the general philosophical concepts of belief, which we extend to cover practical principles or 'convictions', and our concept of religion, which relies upon it.

Christian 'beliefs', both doctrinal and practical, are often said to depend on faith, and, as a preliminary to looking into their content, in Chapter 5 I ask what faith is and how it relates to practice. Christians call faith a virtue, and a virtue distinct from charity; I argue that the two are aspects of a single thing.

I then turn to the doctrinal beliefs Christians formulated long ago in creeds, and consider how today they are best understood. The first, of course, is that there is one God, 'creator of Heaven and Earth'. Christians took from the Jews the idea, alien to Greek and Roman thinking, that the whole natural order has its source in a person who does not himself belong to it. The gods whom we know from Greek and Latin literature were conceived as important parts of the natural order. In Greek mythology they are not creators but themselves generated by processes analogous to human procreation: Hesiod was the first writer to attempt anything in the way of cosmology, and his work is correctly called *Theogony*, the Generation of the Gods. The question whether we are essentially social does not bear on this primary belief, but another does: how should we conceive creation?

We all have a concept of skill or craftsmanship. We are able to bring vases into being by acting on clay, houses into existence by assembling bricks, wine by treading grapes. Theologians have tended to model creation on the causal action of skilled craftsmen, to think that God made the universe in the way a potter makes a pot; and this does appear to be a cosmological speculation comparable to the theory that the universe just popped up in a big bang a finite time ago, and the theory that it had no beginning but has existed for infinite time. In Chapter 6 I argue that we need not understand creation as causation and that a decision on whether the universe was created should be sought in the same sort of way as decisions in a court of law.

A second central doctrine of Christianity is that Jesus of Nazareth was the Son of God. This is not a piece of genealogy; it is bound up with the idea that he is our Redeemer. The earliest creeds present that doctrine in terms of incarnation, resurrection and a divine Trinity. Christians say they believe in God the all-powerful Father, and in Jesus Christ, his only Son, 'conceived through the Holy Spirit and born of the Virgin Mary', who was crucified, was buried and rose from the dead. Today, while Christians still recite these creeds, at least in the West theologians and preachers put more emphasis on the unconditional love of God for every human being than on the miraculous conception of Jesus and his actual return from the dead. In Chapter 7 I contrast what I call atomistic and holistic views of the Incarnation and of God's redemptive activity. The holistic approach which I favour (unlike the view of creation I propose in Chapter 6) involves accepting the view of human nature advocated in Chapters 2 and 3.

Debates about whether or not we are essentially social are a comparatively recent phenomenon. Since before Christianity started thinkers have asked whether each of us is one thing or a conjunction of two, a body and a soul. Plato was the first person to distinguish our physical qualities from our mental or psychological powers and activities. His distinction caught on and became current in Greek thinking. It does not appear in the Old Testament or in the Gospels. Plato himself argued that physical and mental properties belong to different *things*, and that a

1. A Philosophical Standpoint

human being consists of a body which has only physical properties and a soul that has mental powers. Jews who were not influenced by Greek thought took it that a human being is just one thing, a psychosomatic unity. Both ideas have been current among Christians, and which they favour inevitably affects their thinking about a life after death. I show how this comes about in Chapters 8 and 9.

From these doctrinal beliefs I proceed in Chapters 10 and 11 to practical convictions about matters of concern to all societies, birth, death and sex. These conflict with the convictions of some, though by no means all, non-Christians, and they are not agreed by all Christians.

Among Christian denominations, Catholics have stood out in claiming that traditional Christian teaching about sex can be defended by basing it on natural law. Bad arguments for a position not only fail to support it; they discredit it. In Chapter 11 I first describe some of the changes which have taken place in theories of natural law since Classical times, and argue that no natural law theory will do the work required.

I then contrast two general approaches to ethics. One is to found the difference between right and wrong upon law. It is right to do what law commands, wrong to do what law forbids. The first books of the Bible are books of law; in Western Europe emphasis on law increased from the twelfth century, when law was codified in the law school of Bologna, down to the eighteenth, when the German philosopher Kant came near to founding a religion of rule-worship. In contrast to this approach, Plato and Aristotle declared that no legislative skill whatever could formulate a law that says what is best and most right for all people at all times. To act rightly in particular situations, they held, we need good practical judgement, for good practical judgement we need good moral character, and good moral character is acquired by controlling our emotions and reacting rationally to circumstances. This approach was rediscovered in the thirteenth century when translations of Aristotle's writings reached Paris and Oxford, but it did not prevail over law-based thinking, which became increasingly popular as the Enlightenment brightened. It was tried again in the twentieth century when English-speaking philosophers started reading Aristotle and Plato in Greek, but the so-called 'virtue ethics' which resulted found little favour with theologians trained in Continental philosophy. Nevertheless, it accommodates the idea that we are essentially social beings, and I suggest that it provides a better way of defending traditional Christian moral principles than natural law theory.

A philosophical standpoint is not one of neutrality. On the issues I discuss I have my own views. I should not write about them if I had not and, in Chapters 2 to 4 and 12, where the issues are, it seems to me, straightforwardly philosophical, I put them forward. I argue that we are essentially social, and that a multicultural society, though preferable to civil war and the persecution of sub-societies, is fundamentally unstable. In Chapters 5 to 11, which deal with specifically Christian ideas about the world and how we should live, I do not write as if I had no opinion on whether they are right or wrong, and I do not believe any philosopher ever has. Certainly, Bertrand Russell, John Mackie, Antony Flew, Elizabeth Anscombe, Richard Swinburne and Alasdair MacIntyre have left their readers in little doubt about where they stand. In a passage to which I shall recur, John Stuart Mill suggested that teachers, when they come to 'disputed topics', should not consider 'the truth or falsehood of opinions' but confine themselves to 'the matter of fact that such and such an opinion is held on such grounds, by such authors, or schools, or churches'. Mill was speaking of teachers, not philosophers; but it would be strange if a teacher who came to an urgent 'disputed topic' such as global warming or gender showed no interest in the truth or falsehood of opinions, and dealing with religious beliefs in this way would give a clear message that the teacher thought them all false. On the other hand, philosophy is not apologetics. Apologists for any set of ideas inherent in a culture do well to draw on philosophy, but I confine myself here to saying how I think someone defending Christian ideas can best do so; I am not trying to convince a jury, but offering a counsel's opinion on how a case can best be presented.

Nor is a philosophical standpoint that of one specialism among others. Ours is an age of specialisation. We have many separate academic subjects, physics, biology, history, economics, philosophy, theology, and, more recently, sociology, linguistics, cognitive science – every year they multiply. Anything important that requires thought has many different aspects which raise questions for different disciplines, history, science, philosophy and so on. The relation between society and Judaeo-Christian monotheism has such a plurality of aspects. In this book I try to treat them together. That may seem overambitious. We are apt to refer the questions that come up to the appropriate experts for them to pursue separately; but the lack of contact between experts in different fields ought to breed misgivings about this strategy. If you want to pass an examination in theology, history or even philosophy, you must read specialised books, but, to form a responsible opinion on any of these important subjects, you must take a comprehensive view. A crucial function of philosophy, I believe with Mary Midgley (*What is Philosophy For?*), is to help people to do that.

2
DOES SOCIETY EXIST?

'There is no such thing as society; there are only individuals.' What does this mean? Not that there are no societies. The world is full of societies. In England we have the Royal Society for the Prevention of Cruelty to Animals. That is a society for the purpose its name proclaims. We have societies for leisure activities, like the Middlesex Cricket Club, and for leisured inactivity, like Boodle's Club. We have partnerships in medicine and law, for the pursuing of those professions, and business companies that exist to provide goods and services for profit. These are societies with limited specific purposes. There are however also societies for no specific purpose, societies in which people simply live. Sovereign states like France and the United States are societies of this kind, and so are certain ethnic or cultural communities that exist within sovereign states: tribes and clans, extended families and even nuclear families consisting only of a breeding couple. Since these are societies in which people just live more or less closely together, I distinguish them from societies for limited purposes by calling them 'societies for life'. Life is not a specific, limited objective; it is a condition of pursuing any specific objective whatever. It is of societies for life that people have said they are nothing over and above the individuals that make them up; and what is meant by this is explained very clearly, if rather heavily, by John Stuart Mill in *A System of Logic* (6.7.1):

The laws of the phenomena of society are, and can be, nothing but the laws of the actions and passions of human beings united together in the social state. Men, however, in a state of society, are still men; their actions and passions are obedient to the laws of individual human nature. Men are not, when brought together, converted into another kind of substance, with different properties: as hydrogen and oxygen are different from water, or as hydrogen, oxygen, carbon and azote are different from nerves, muscles and tendons. Human beings in society have no properties but those which are derived from, and may be resolved into, the laws of the nature of individual man. In social phenomena the Composition of Causes is the universal law.

The behaviour of people, Mill means, in a family, a community or a sovereign state can be explained entirely in terms of the laws which (as he puts it in *Essays on some Unsettled Questions in Political Economy*, p. 134) 'appertain to man as a mere individual, and do not presuppose, as a necessary condition, the existence of other individuals except, perhaps, as mere instruments or means'.

What laws are these? Today many philosophers hold that everything that happens, including all human thoughts and actions, must have physical causes, and be explainable in the same way as the movements of billiard balls on a table, the movements of the planets in the sky, and the interactions of atoms and sub-atomic particles. We are affected by the action of other things upon our bodies, and especially of light on our eyes and sound on our ears. This action causes changes in our brains, which have a highly complex structure determined partly by our genes and partly by what happens to us as we grow up; and the changes in our brains cause movements in our limbs. The brain-events also, in some fashion not yet fully understood, cause conscious experiences. They make us feel sensations and desires and think that we see and hear things. However, the real explanation of these feelings and thoughts and of all we do lies in the physical action of our surroundings upon our bodies, and the whole chain of interactions proceeds according to the laws of physics.

When Mill spoke of the 'laws of the nature of individual man', he did not mean the laws of physics. He meant psychological laws correlating what people think or know and what they want with how they act. They are summarised in the first words of Jeremy Bentham's *An Introduction to the Principles of Morals and Legislation*:

2. Does Society Exist?

> Nature has placed mankind under the governance of two sovereign masters, *pain* and *pleasure*. It is for them alone to point out what we ought to do, as well as to determine what we shall do.... They govern us in all we do, in all we say, in all we think: every effort we can make to throw off our subjection, will but serve but to demonstrate and confirm it.

Mill followed Bentham, who himself followed Hume, Locke and Hobbes. These thinkers were agreed that all our behaviour is self-interested; that we act or refrain from action to obtain what is good for ourselves and avoid what is bad. This belief is far from intuitively evident, and they probably took it unconsciously from the Christian doctrine, much emphasised by some Protestant reformers, that human nature is fundamentally depraved. They also agreed that what is good for ourselves is pleasure, what is bad pain; and that pleasure and pain are either bodily sensations or states of mind that play an equivalent role in our lives.

We, and perhaps all sentient beings, are so constituted physically that we experience sensations of pain, itching, thirst and nausea and also pleasant bodily feelings of warmth, coolness, sexual excitement, and so forth. We have these feelings independently of society, and animals that did not have them would not long survive, nor would they breed. Liberal thinkers took it as a law of individual human nature that we do what we think will cause or prolong pleasant feelings and end or prevent feelings that are painful or otherwise unpleasant. In fact, that is less a law of nature than a tautology. We call a sensation 'pleasant' precisely if we want to experience or prolong it, and we call a sensation 'painful' precisely if we want to avoid it or get rid of it; that is part of the meaning of the words 'pleasant' and 'painful'. It seems that we also, independently of society, take pleasure in exercising our abilities. That is to say, not that the exercise gives us pleasant sensations – it may give us unpleasant – but that we enjoy walking and running, even when not seeking food or avoiding predators. Walking and running are bodily skills; but, independently of society, we can have rather more intellectual skills, for instance, at making likenesses or catching fish, and people enjoy fishing even after they have caught all the fish they need to end their hunger. On the other hand, prolonged exertion can produce exhaustion, pain or boredom, and, when this happens, we cease acting. These laws of nature – that we act to obtain pleasant sensations or to get rid of unpleasant, and also to obtain enjoyment in exercising our abilities, but cease acting to avoid exhaustion, pain and boredom – these laws hold, of course, only for the most part, and only when there is no strong reason to the contrary. We don't act to obtain pleasure or private enjoyment if in so acting we should incur pain – again, unless there is an overriding reason to discount the pain.

Those who say that there is no such thing as society believe that all human behaviour can be explained in this way. They think that individual human beings, independently of society, are sufficiently intelligent to work out plans for future pleasure and enjoyments, future deliverance from pain and boredom. They discern, also, that it will be to their long-term advantage as individuals to form a society with rules binding the members to do some things and refrain from doing others. Otherwise, says Hobbes in a famous passage (*Leviathan*, 1.13):

> In the nature of man we find three principal causes of quarrel. First, competition; secondly, diffidence; thirdly, glory. [Competition, he means, for the same food, drink, women and the rest, fear of other people and desire for fame, conquest and power] . . . Whatever, therefore, is consequent to a time of war, where every man is enemy to every man; the same is consequent to the time wherein men live without other security than what their own strength and their own invention shall furnish them withal. In such a condition there is no place for industry, because the fruit thereof is uncertain; and consequently no culture of the earth; no navigation, nor use of the commodities that may be imported by sea; no commodious building; no instruments of moving, and removing, such things as require much force; no knowledge of the face of the earth; no account of time; no arts; no letters; no society; and, which is worst of all, constant fear and danger of violent death; and the life of man solitary, poor, nasty, brutish and short.
>
> It may peradventure be thought [Hobbes goes on] there never was such a time, nor condition of war, such as this. [However, he tells us] The savage people in many places of America . . . live at this day in that brutish manner.

Individuals, then, in order to get out of this brutish condition, enter into a contract with one another by which they give up their natural right to act as they please and form societies with rules. These rules, however, will work on them according to the laws of individual human nature. Locke receives the torch of Enlightenment from Hobbes and puts the point explicitly. Having argued that good and evil 'are nothing but pleasure and pain', he says in a passage (*An Essay Concerning Human Understanding*, 2.28.6.) to which I shall return in later chapters:

> Since it would be utterly in vain to suppose a rule set to the free actions of man without annexing to it some enforcement of good and evil to determine his will, we must, wherever we suppose a law, suppose also some reward or punishment annexed to that law. It would be in vain for one intelligent being to set a rule to the actions of another if it was not in his power to reward the compliance with, and punish deviation from his rule, by some good or evil *that is not the natural produce and consequence of the action itself* [my italics].

Hobbes' picture of what he called 'the natural condition of the nature of individual mankind' has not escaped criticism over the centuries, but I think that many people today believe that it is fundamentally sound – that human beings form societies out of intelligent self-interest, and that all human behaviour is still governed by 'the laws of the nature of individual man'.

In fact, Hobbes' picture is fundamentally flawed by his theory of language. Human rationality depends upon language, and language depends upon society. Hobbes and Locke imagined that language started with a solitary man introducing signs to record the ideas in his mind. Speech consists, says Hobbes (*Leviathan*, 1.4): 'of names or appellations, and their connection; whereby men register their thoughts; recall them when they are past; and also declare them to one another for natural utility and conversation; without which there had been amongst men neither commonwealth nor society nor contract.'

Hobbes says that language preceded society, and without it human beings could not have formed societies. Of the origin of speech, he says: 'The first author of speech was God himself, that instructed Adam how to name such creatures as he presented to his sight.'

In attributing speech to God, however, he might have had his tongue in his cheek, and he would have agreed with what Locke says (*An Essay Concerning Human Understanding*, 3.2.1-2):

> Man, though he have great variety of thoughts, and such from which others as well as himself might receive profit, yet they are all within his own breast, invisible and hidden from others ... The comfort and advantage of society not being to be had without communication of thoughts, it was necessary that man should find some external sensible signs whereby those invisible ideas which his thoughts are made up of might be made known to others. ... The use men have of these marks being either to record

their own thought for the assistance of their own memory or, as it were, to bring out their ideas and lay them before the view of others, words in their primary and immediate significance stand for nothing but the ideas in the mind of him that uses them.

The word 'snake', for example, on this view of language (which goes back to some ill-judged words of Aristotle in *De Interpretatione*, 16a3-8) does not stand for snakes but for an idea, a mental likeness of a snake. If God had wanted to teach it to Adam, he would have had to excite his own idea of a snake in Adam – perhaps by showing him a real snake.

This theory of language is discredited among philosophers today. People do write their thoughts in diaries or elsewhere, but they are not only using words current in their society, but also able to read and write. Is it credible that people could have literacy before they had society? Suppose I go for a walk on the moors, and want to remember the flowers and birds I see. If I merely make up the sounds 'ptarmigan' and 'tormentil', not only must I remember these sounds, something harder, perhaps, than to remember the specimens themselves; I must remember which applies to which. Instead of composing sounds in my head I might do pastel drawings. These might remind me of plants or birds I have seen, so might specimens I picked or shot, but neither a picture nor a specimen is a word.

It is unrealistic to suppose that the project of making signs to record thoughts could occur outside society. People actually learn words in a social situation. Children find that people around them are making sounds or signs in order to get them to do things or to stop doing things, they also see that particular signs are customary in particular situations or obtain particular effects. A sign can be a word for a snake, for example, only with a group of people who use it when they want members of the group to know that a snake is present; a sign can be a word for a movement like sitting down only among people among whom it is customary to use it when they want members of the group to sit down.

Language depends upon society; and all rational thought depends upon language. Without language we might learn that some things give pleasure and others cause pain: and perceiving honey we might want to eat it, perceiving nettles we might wish to avoid them. We could not, however, have the thought that a period of sunshine was the *cause* of snow's melting into water, or that it was *for the reason* that there were salmon up the river, or *for the purpose* of catching one, that someone went down to the pool. Distinguishing these things and bringing them together in the mind is inseparable from distinguishing them and combining them in various ways in *speech*; we need forms of thought corresponding to conjunctions

2. Does Society Exist?

like 'because' and 'in order that'. Hobbes himself acknowledges that without society there could be 'no account' of time. Grasp of temporal relations depends on grasping the meaning of conjunctions like 'before' and 'after'. Indeed, without language we should not distinguish between moving a distance, say, a mile, and moving for a time, say, twenty minutes; and, without making these distinctions, we should have no general concepts of time and space at all. Generalisation also depends on language; without words like 'all' and 'this' or constructions for universal and particular predication, we could not have thoughts about all birds distinct from thoughts about what is true of particular birds. Without general beliefs, without grasp of temporal relations, without understanding of causal processes and purposive behaviour, there could be no rational thinking at all, let alone what would be necessary for non-social individuals to work out the advantages of a social contract.

Why did the thinkers of the European Enlightenment think that human beings could exist and think rationally independently of society? Is that a natural assumption? Plato in the *Republic* speculated about the origin and purpose of political institutions. He did not, however, like Rousseau in Part 1 of his *Discourse on the Origin and the Bases of Inequality among Men*, paint a romantic picture of 'the natural state of man', when the earth was 'covered with immense forests', and men lived 'dispersed up and down in these forests', with the individual man:

> satisfying his hunger at the first oak, and slaking his thirst at the first brook; finding his bed at the foot of the tree that afforded him a repast; and, with that, all his wants supplied.... Everyone lived where he could, seldom for more than a single night; the sexes united without design, as accident, opportunity or inclination brought them together, nor had they any great need of words to communicate their designs to each other; and they parted with the same indifference.

Plato says (*Republic*, 2, 369 b-c):

> Society [the *polis*] came into being, I think, since it turns out that we are not each of us self-sufficient, but in need of many [sc. people, or perhaps things].... And so one person brought in another for one necessity or another, and being in need of many things they gathered many people together to help each other and share, and to that union we gave the name '*polis*' ... what makes a *polis* is our needs.

Plato then goes on to build up a society with members, corresponding to the needs of human individuals: first, food, then housing, then clothes, and he argued that, to meet these needs, there will have to be people engaged in various branches of food production, builders and weavers and other craftsmen, traders and retailers and so forth. These speculations were not, like those of Enlightenment thinkers, presented to explain how as a matter of history states arose, but what as a matter of practical necessity they must contain, and Plato's ultimate purpose was to use the structure of a society as a model for the internal complexity of individual human beings. He does not suggest that there ever actually existed a population of dispersed, stateless individuals without language. He does, in *Statesman* (271-2) describe a Rousseau-esque state of affairs in which the earth provides men with food in abundance without any effort on their part, and they live in the open without clothes and talking with animals. Plato, however, is explicit that this is not history but myth, idle fantasy that no one takes seriously, and, far from commending this happy way of life, he says it would keep men as unreflective children. I come back to his *Statesman* in Chapter 12.

Aristotle at the beginning of his *Politics* (1, 1252b22-24) says that in ancient times people lived 'dispersed', *sporades*, like the race of Cyclopes in Homer's *Odyssey* (Book 9). Homer's Cyclopes, however, have language and call on each other for help, and Aristotle probably envisaged the kind of society without literacy or law-enforcement that still existed in parts of the world in 1984, when Joseph Pestieau documented its presence in *Guerres et Paix Sans État*.

The Epic of Gilgamesh begins with an account of a solitary forest-dweller, Enkidu, made by a goddess out of a rock in the image of the semi-divine Gilgamesh. Enkidu has no clan; he lives with wild beasts in the forest and eats the same food as they. Gilgamesh, however, is told of his existence, and sends a temple priestess to trap him and show him the power of women. She seduces him, and under her influence he becomes god-like and exchanges life among the animals for human life. She teaches him human ways and brings him to the society ruled by Gilgamesh. *The Epic of Gilgamesh* was not known to Enlightenment thinkers, though if it had been, this episode might have caught their fancy. However, whereas Enkidu fits Rousseau's idea of a primitive man, he is represented in the *Epic* as unique, and as coming into being in a world where people already have language and live in cities with kings, temples and priestesses.

If there is any assumption it is natural to make about prehistory, it is that we can have no more factual knowledge about it than about life on another planet. Hobbes in his theory of language refers to Adam, and Enlightenment thinkers probably derived their idea of the origins of society and language from the Bible. In the story of Adam and Eve human life starts from a single human being created out of earth. He has no parents, let alone any precedent society, he lives naked in a garden 'with all his wants supplied', and he is able to give names to animals. Then a woman is produced miraculously out of his body, like Athene out of Zeus' head, and all other human beings are descended from her. However sceptical Enlightenment thinkers became about Christian theology, this provided their preconception. In fact, the Jewish thinkers from whom this story comes, and who may well have been acquainted with *The Epic of Gilgamesh* or similar Mesopotamian stories, were not speculating about the origins of human society. Rather, as Joseph Fitzpatrick argues persuasively in *The Fall and the Ascent of Man*, they were trying to make their hearers or readers imagine the transition from the life of animals to that of human beings. The 'death' with which Adam is threatened if he eats from the tree of practical knowledge is the death of the child at maturity and the birth of the adult. By seventeenth-century Western Europe, however, a good quantity of factual knowledge had accumulated about the past, and, since the time of Bede, educated people had seen the Bible as a possible source of prehistoric knowledge. The Reformation in Germany and England and the spate of printed books reaching private hands encouraged people to look in the Bible for the answers to contemporary factual questions about the past and about cosmology. Enlightened thinkers cut out the supernatural but used whatever else about the natural world they read.

I said earlier that language depends upon society and intelligent life depends upon language for its forms of thought, for generalisation, historical ordering, and various kinds of understanding and explanation. It also depends upon language and society for most of the content of its thought. As individuals we will come to recognise the animals and plants which are important for life and have some knowledge of activities or processes that are important for life, like eating, drinking, breathing, running, and swimming. Anyone who has language will have words for these things. Their meaning can be explained ostensively, and words for them can easily be translated from one language to another: 'horse' means the same as *cheval*, *equus*, and *hippos*. If, however, we turn from words like these to psychological terms, words for mental processes and states, the situation (as I argue in 'Is the Concept of the Mind Parochial?') is different. Modern English contains the word 'snobbish'. It signifies a trait of character. It is hard to explain what it means, or to find equivalents for it in other languages. We can point to people we think snobbish, and mention particular speeches, actions and reactions that betray their snobbery, but this may not convey what we mean by snobbery to someone from an alien society. Yet the concept of snobbery is important in our practical thinking; we are averse to it, try to avoid it in ourselves, are repelled by it in others. The Classical Greeks had a word *aidôs* which seems to cover both what we call 'modesty' and what we call 'shame'. They respected it and *aidoioi*, people with it. We in our society cannot be sure we grasp it. The Greeks also had a word *thumos*, which seems to have covered two things that seem to us quite different: anger and what we colloquially call 'dash' or 'go'. *Thumos* plays a big part in Plato's philosophy of mind and political thinking; we have no equivalent concept today. The fact is that intelligent human life is an infinitely varied continuum, and different societies pick out different particular elements within the continuum to form concepts which their members can use to guide their relations with one another. It is with words as it is in painting. A painter is faced with a continuum, and out of the continuum he picks out elements, significant objects or shapes or contrasts of colour, on which he concentrates to make an intelligible picture.

The difficulty is not limited to rather specific psychological terms like 'snobbish', 'perceptive', 'subtle', 'arrogant', 'smarmy', 'aloof', 'imaginative', 'delicacy', 'pedantry', 'vulgarity', 'officiousness'. It is the same with our broadest psychological terms. Every language has a different vocabulary of love. No English word captures exactly either of the Greek words *erôs* and *agapê*. In English we have the word 'mind'. The French have no equivalent; they must make do with *esprit* and *âme* which have no exact English equivalents. We use the word 'belief'. There is no French word which corresponds to 'belief' in all its uses – neither *croyance* nor *conviction* does that. We call any false opinion a 'belief' and speak of 'the belief that today is Tuesday' when it is actually Wednesday. Our conviction that everyone has beliefs and that beliefs form an important class of mental states is a consequence of European history. Plato drew a distinction between mental and physical activities and states. There is no such distinction in Homer's work or even in fifth-century literature. From Plato we have inherited a dualistic conception of human beings as a combination of the mental and the physical, and a desire to anatomise both. It is not safe to assume, however, that societies uninfluenced by ancient Greece, either primitive societies in equatorial forests or civilised societies in Asia and the Far East, have our conception of intelligence or put our emphasis on belief.

If our psychological concepts depend upon society, still more do our social and political. The solitary individual in the woods is a fiction. Even in small primitive societies (by a primitive society I mean one without literacy or a police force) there are social roles and offices, chiefs, doctors, hunters, and being male or female, old or young, is itself a social role. Even animals like dogs and horses have roles in human societies. These roles differ from society to society. European anthropologists look for matches of their own social roles in other societies: priests, doctors, lawyers, soldiers, and so forth. That is provincial of them. (Provincialism is a concept which only we possess and which we are unwilling to apply to ourselves.) We need look to nothing more remote than the mediaeval West to find the roles of priest and civil servant imperfectly differentiated. In other societies priests and doctors overlap. Some years ago, when visiting Central Sulawesi, I thought that the Salvation Army, the main Christian denomination there, was filling both roles. Relationships between members of more or less extended families are not conceived solely in terms of biology; rights and duties are attached to sexual partners, parents, grandparents, brothers, sisters, cousins, older and younger siblings, parents of sexual partners and so on, and the rights and duties vary from society to society. Much of our practical thinking is thinking about what we owe to members of our family and can expect from them.

That different societies should have different social and political concepts is not surprising, but we might assume that people's concepts of the same natural phenomena should be the same everywhere. Reflection shows that such an assumption would be rash. By far the most important natural phenomena, on which all life depends, are the relative movements of the Earth and the Sun. Relatively to the Sun, the Earth turns on its axis once a day and goes round in a circle (or near-circular ellipse) once a year. The circular revolution causes the seasons, which in turn govern the growth of fruit and cereals, and the rotation causes night and day, light and darkness. These effects vary enormously in different parts of the globe. Inevitably, then, people in different latitudes have different concepts of day and night and of what Europeans call spring, summer, autumn and winter. You must conceive day and night differently depending on whether you live near the Equator or near one of the Poles. Not only is June in the Northern Hemisphere like December in the Southern, but in some parts of the world food production depends on a rainy season, in others a mild autumn, in some parts drought is the enemy to be feared, in others snow. In the prosperous West the population is not conscious of these differences, because houses have heating and cooling systems installed and the same food is in the shops all year round. However, this is a recent development. The concepts of day and night, light and dark and the seasons which were formed in

Europe before we had these conveniences are still embedded in our literature and linger in our thinking. Perhaps in time, if our society grows increasingly rich and urban, they will be modified. It is hard, however, to believe that people will ever regard natural phenomena and react to them otherwise than as social beings.

3
SOCIAL LIFE, EGOISM AND ALTRUISM

We are not, then, just individual living organisms. Society is not a mere appearance like a rainbow but a reality. In what does it consist? The difference between a society and an aggregate of people is that a society has rules; if not written laws, at least customs which function as unwritten rules.

Customs are essentially social; we acquire them from others. In that respect they differ from habits, which we can form as individuals. They also differ from conventions. Conventions, such as shaking hands when you greet someone, are also social; they require agreement by others; but they are recognised to be arbitrary and they can therefore be changed easily. Rules of language are based on convention. It is a language-rule that the word 'snake' signifies an animal of a particular kind; English-speakers need not think it a *better* word than, say, *ophis*, but for speech it is necessary to agree upon some word. Similarly arbitrary are some rules of society, like the British law that motorists should drive on the left. The right might be as good or better; still it is good for road-users in a society to agree on one side or the other. However, most of a society's customs are not like this.

As I said in Chapter 2, some societies, like a law firm, a tennis club or a society for the protection of birds, have specific purposes. Their rules and customs are shaped partly by their purposes. Other societies have no specific purpose, they are societies, as I put it, for life. Sovereign states are of that kind; so are ethnic and religious communities within sovereign states, and tribes, clans, extended families and even nuclear families. Societies for specific purposes, of course, can exist only within societies for life. It is societies for life that are necessary for rational life and thought. Sovereign states are a civilised development, but for rational life all that is needed is a society large enough and stable enough to have a language and customs. The customs of a society for life concern all the varied parts of life: eating, dress, birth, death, social interactions. Though not based directly upon economic or scientific knowledge, they are not arbitrary, nor do they grow up by chance. They develop together, interacting with each other and with the social and political concepts, and even with the psychological concepts and the concepts of natural phenomena, prevalent in the society. They are not an aggregate, like a pile of pebbles; they are like living organisms in a wild area, forming a natural eco-system. The whole is what we call a 'culture'. Both customs and concepts are shaped by the history and geography of the society; and they are tested pragmatically over time. In general, therefore, they make economic and biological sense. Though they may be altered in response to changing circumstances and new knowledge, a society must already have elaborate customs before the activity of legislation can emerge, and an individual can evaluate a custom only against a background of other customs that are unquestioned.

If a society exists for a specific purpose its rules apply to members only when they are pursuing that purpose, practising law, concerning themselves with birds, using the club. The rules of a society for life are rules with regard to which the members live. They apply to members, therefore, at all times, in whatever activities they are engaged. The members are individuals, and they must, and do, pursue their aims as individuals – avoidance of pain, hunger and other unpleasant sensations, enjoyment of pleasure and so forth. Societies have customs regulating the pursuit of these aims, prohibiting members from impeding each other in pursuit of them. Up to a point such rules will be the same in every society. There could hardly survive a society in which killing other members is not restricted. In all societies, members hold against each other a right to life and the pursuit of their individual aims; but these rights are conditional, and the conditions under which these rights are given, and under which members hold them against other members, differ from society to society. In every society there is personal property, such as clothing and tools, but, whereas in primitive societies individuals do not appropriate land, in advanced societies they usually do, and there are laws governing the appropriation and defining the rights of proprietors.

3. Social Life, Egoism and Altruism

The Greeks in Classical Antiquity drew a sharp distinction between nature, on the one hand, and, on the other, law or custom. Nature is the same everywhere; law and custom vary from society to society. The notion of law, however, became ambiguous in two ways. Besides recognising laws of society, drawn up by legislators or voted upon by assemblies, people started to talk of laws of nature. At first laws of nature were conceived as admitting exceptions. What was natural was what, independently of us, happens *for the most part*. However, as time went on people in the West developed a notion of natural necessity and of laws of nature which, like laws formulated by legislators, admit of no exceptions. For the understanding of what society is, we must grasp a fundamental difference between laws of nature like the law of gravity and the laws of human societies. We cannot obey or disobey laws of nature; we can obey or disobey laws of society. Laws of nature say what actually happens independently of our choices whereas laws of society say what members of the society ought to do or refrain from doing.

That is one ambiguity. Second, the Romans established an empire covering the whole Mediterranean world which was successful largely because of its legal system: Roman law brought peace and justice to all its ethnically diverse citizens. It was formulated, however, in Latin, and Latin has a single word, *ius*, which means both law and right. The French *droit* has a similar ambiguity. To English speakers the notions of law and right are quite distinct, though laws and rights are related in various ways. To speakers of French or Latin the notions are not. This ambiguity is important because over the centuries Western thinkers have moved, without realising it, from relying upon law to relying upon rights. From thinking that rights are granted and sanctioned by laws and depend upon them, they have moved to thinking that laws are based on the right of every individual to choose how he or she wants to live. I shall come back in Chapter 11 to these shifts in Western thinking about law generally and about natural law in particular.

We live as social beings in living with regard to the laws and customs of our society. That is not quite the same as living in obedience to them. Some of us often disobey the law, for instance, in motoring, and often depart from what custom prescribes. We are still, however, living with regard to our laws if, when we break them, we are conscious of doing so, and do so reluctantly or with misgiving. Customs of a society for life are unwritten rules, prescribing what in that society is thought right or good and forbidding what is thought bad or wrong – good or bad not always or absolutely but for the most part and other things being equal. Living with regard to social custom, even when we depart from it, involves sharing the judgement that what it requires is on the whole right.

This is hard to grasp, since as children of the Enlightenment we are brought up to think that we obey the law (which is custom codified) only because it is in our interest to do so; only by obeying the law can we avoid punishment and enjoy the security and conveniences of civilisation. Some law-abiding behaviour may be explained like this. When I am driving, I might slow down at a speed limit sign or refrain from parking in a forbidden space, not because I think I am driving too fast or because the space seems unsuitable, but simply in order to avoid a fine. My reasoning is: 'The sign says I should slow down; if I don't do what it says, I may be fined; so, I'd better slow down.' In general, however, living with regard to the law is not like this. The premise that disobeying the law is costly does not enter into our thoughts as a premise. Even when what a law prescribes is arbitrary, such as driving on the left, we think it sensible to have such a law; we think that most of what our laws prescribe is good in itself, and what they forbid, bad or wrong.

To think this is to be disposed to see situations in a certain way. If it is customary in my society to refrain from reading other people's letters, then for me to think this custom good is for me to take the fact that a letter is addressed to someone else as at least a *prima facie* reason for not reading it. Consciousness that it is addressed to someone else takes the form of reluctance to read it. If it is the custom to treat persons of a certain ethnicity with scorn, and perceiving you to be of that ethnicity I automatically treat you with scorn, I think the custom good. If it is the custom to teach girls of five to read, then I think this custom good if, realising that my daughter is five, I want her to be taught to read; I am conscious of her age as a practical reason for teaching her or having her taught. In some societies it has been the custom for people to care for family members who have become old and dependent. In such a society being conscious that your father is blind you feel it necessary to care for him: necessary not in order to avoid prosecution for neglect, but necessary independently of any consequences. That we ought to follow custom is not a premise in the reasoning of a social being; rather it is a principle of it. From the premises that Oedipus was her father, blind and homeless, Antigone inferred that she had to take charge of him, and that was seen as rational in archaic Greece. Far from following custom out of fear of punishment, when it came to burying her brother Antigone did what custom ordained despite knowing that she would suffer if she did. Being disposed, in circumstances in which custom requires us to act in a certain way, to see those circumstances as a reason (even if not an overriding reason) for so acting, is what it is to think the custom good.

3. Social Life, Egoism and Altruism

If we cannot accept this account of rational behaviour for social beings, it is because the only rules for rational inference we admit are rules for theoretical reasoning, that is, for reasoning that is deductive. Mathematical reasoning is deductive, and, using it as our model for rationality, we feel that practical reasoning from what is the case to how we should act is by itself invalid, and that to become valid it must be bolstered by premises like 'We ought to obey the law' or 'We ought to do what will give us pleasure and prevent pain.' In Chapter 11 I return to the difference between premises and rules of inference and develop what I say here.

We sometimes act against the rules of our society in order to pursue our interests as individuals, but we may also do so out of disinterested concern for another person or even for another living organism. We can make the well-being of another person an end in itself, independently of any benefit that may come to us as individuals or as social beings. Not only are we essentially social; we are also essentially altruistic. Scientists sometimes restrict the word 'altruism' to behaviour injurious to the agent. Richard Dawkins in *The Selfish Gene* (p. 4) defined it as something's behaving 'in such a way as to increase another entity's welfare at the expense of its own', and Edward O. Wilson in his *Sociobiology* (p. 578) as 'self-destructive behaviour performed for the benefit of others'. For these thinkers, bees are paradigmatic altruists since they defend the hive by stinging and stinging is fatal to themselves. I use the word to include disinterested action even when it does no harm to the agent.

People who say that there is no such thing as society, will also say that there is no such thing as altruism. We do what benefits others, they will say, only in order that they may help us in return, or simply because beneficence gives us a good feeling: in the last analysis all our behaviour is selfish.

This opinion is now sometimes supported by appeal to the theory of natural selection. This is not the theory that human beings and other species that exist in the world today are descended from different species that existed in the past and had less internal complexity. That is the theory of evolution. Natural selection is proposed as the mechanism by which earlier species evolve into later and simpler organisms into more complex. The mechanism, it is said, is chance: random changes in replication of genetic structure. Organisms replicate themselves, a process which can be fully explained by the laws of physics; but occasionally the replication is imperfect, and, when that happens, the variation in structure may give the organism a greater likelihood to survive and replicate itself. The variation is handed on to its descendants, and accumulation of such variations over many generations results in a new species. If human beings arose that were genuinely altruistic, they would be unable to compete for survival successfully against human beings that helped others only when it would produce a benefit to themselves, only if the others were likely to return the favour; consequently, their natural altruism would be eliminated by natural selection.

Precisely how does this theory about how evolution occurs (a theory not free from difficulty, though nothing better is at present on offer) support the view that we always do what seems to us likeliest to benefit us as individuals? We sometimes think we are acting purely to benefit a friend, and people do seem ready to forego pleasure, to endure pain and even to give up their lives for others. It is not pretended that we really act in order to replicate our genetic structure by having children, or in order to give rise to new species. Most people have no idea of replicating their genetic structure, much less of doing so in the hope that there will be the kind of imperfect replication the theory postulates. What is suggested is something like this. Our desires and objectives are illusions caused by processes in our brains: they are representations projected by these processes somewhat like images projected on a cinema or computer screen. Our belief that these desires provide the real explanation of our actions is mistaken. Our actions really have a purely physical explanation, are really determined by physical interactions between the rest of the world and our complex brains. However, the illusion somehow helps us to replicate, so it has been 'naturally selected'.

It will be seen that the real work in this modern argument against the possibility of altruism is done not by the claim that natural selection is the mechanism of evolution, but by the claim that all our actions have a purely physical explanation. That was not the reasoning of Hobbes, Adam Smith, Mill and other Enlightenment philosophers. They, as I said in Chapter 2, believed that all our actions can be seen as ultimately selfish, as having the *aim* of benefiting us as solitary individuals.

Adam Smith's *Theory of Moral Sentiments* begins with the claim that 'sympathy' or fellow feeling is among the 'original passions of human nature', and, by the 'original passions of human nature', I think he means feelings we have by virtue of our physical make-up. We are apt to picture in ourselves the feelings of others and, imagining them, we 'feel something which, though weaker in degree, is not altogether unlike them'. This gives rise to the 'social and benevolent affections' of generosity, humanity and kindness, and apparently altruistic action has the aim of satisfying these 'social passions'. Natural selection has been used to prove egoism only in recent years, and to succeed it must prove too much: it must prove not only that there is no altruism but that there is no egoism either, since egoism consists in acting *to* benefit yourself. The thought that we always act to benefit ourselves is as illusory as the thought we sometimes act to benefit someone else.

If we reject this fairly incredible theory of our consciousness of intentional action, it remains groundless cynicism to deny that we sometimes act out of genuinely disinterested concern. Those who invoke natural selection to rule out altruism perhaps think that, if we ever acted altruistically, our genes and our physical make-up would make it necessary for us to do so always and in every situation, but that is again falling back on physicalism. Sometimes we act selfishly, sometimes we just follow custom, and sometimes we act disinterestedly. Or it would be better to say that rational life is a mixture of selfishness, respect for society and altruism, that it always has, so to speak, these three dimensions, but that in different situations one is often particularly salient.

Given, however, that altruism is a real possibility, is there a genuine difference between acting altruistically and acting out of respect for the customs of your society? Certainly, they complement each other. Personal concern for those to whom we have duties reinforces the social sense of duty. Conversely, social life promotes altruism. In gregarious mammals like elephants, wolves and bats we find the rudiments of our kind of altruism. Observation of vampire bats has shown that the females especially form individual friendships and are willing to risk their lives by regurgitating food a friend needs. Elephants will show concern for the young of other species. In all human societies language gives members clear insight into each other's thoughts and desires and they discuss the persons and animals they care for among themselves. If you fail to go to the rescue of a drowning child or to come to the aid of anyone severely injured because it would involve some personal inconvenience, you can expect to incur censure and possibly prosecution. The United Kingdom has strict laws against cruelty to animals and the British Highway Code requires motorists to 'show consideration for other road users'. Forms of autism in which a person's capacity for disinterested concern is diminished are considered sufficiently unnatural to be counted as illnesses.

Although sharing in social life and being concerned for others naturally go together, they are distinct. We have concern for animals with which it is impossible to have society, because they are not intelligent enough, like butterflies, or because they live in an environment impossible for us, like giant squids. We feel for others within our society as individuals, not just as fellow members. Concern for another individual within our society is one of the strongest motives for acting against its laws; it is the stuff of the greatest dramas and tragedies. We can also, of course, be caught between conflicting customary requirements, but societies have ways of resolving such conflicts, and they are different in feel from a conflict between what is demanded by law or custom and what is needed by an individual for whom we concerned.

The feelings we have as social beings differ from those we have as altruists in two ways. In the first place, as social beings we have a range of good and bad feelings concerned with our position in society which have no parallels in our lives as altruists. As Hobbes observed, there is a desire for dominion over others, for power. There is also shame, and fear of disapproval, contempt or exclusion by others. The desire for sexual conquest is an emotion we experience as social beings, distinct from sexual desire, which we experience as individuals. As individuals we desire relief from hunger, thirst, cold and so forth, and we may desire money as a means to this relief; we may also desire it to help those for whom we have disinterested concern; but desire for wealth as such is a social emotion, as is shame at poverty, and these emotions are strongest in societies like those of the modern West where economic growth is viewed as an end in itself and people are respected for being rich. Envy too and longing for vengeance are social feelings. Our emotional attitudes towards other human beings involve beliefs about them which depend heavily upon concepts peculiar to our society such as the psychological and social or political concepts I mentioned a moment ago: we think of people as holding social roles and ranks, and as having good and bad characteristics labelled in our language.

Besides these social feelings directed towards individuals we have feelings concerning our society as a whole. We are dismayed by threats to its survival such as plague, famine and war, and we rejoice when such threats disappear. We also compare our own society with others. We can feel pride in its superiority or shame at its inferiority, and people aiming at political power within a society may try to fan fear of foreigners and to awaken in its citizens a desire for dominion over other societies.

As altruists we rejoice in the happiness of those for whom we have concern, and feel distress and pity when things go badly with them. It is obvious that these feelings are not only different from the social feelings I have just mentioned but often incompatible with them. There is also a difference in quality. The sensations we have as individual organisms are entirely determined by our bodily make-up. They are gut feelings. The feelings we have as social beings are partly determined by this, though they also depend on the concepts and customs peculiar to the particular society in which we live. Those customs, however, are customs according to which we live as organisms that are born, breed and die. They often concern those events. Living with regard to them is beneficial to us as animals of a particular species. Our feelings as altruists are modified by our bodily make-up, but they are determined primarily by our understanding of what is good and bad for the other people or animals for which we are concerned.

We have concern for other human beings as individuals but also as social beings and as themselves altruists. We see their circumstances as significant for them in all three ways. The Good Samaritan was conscious of the wounded man's needs as an individual organism. Charles Dickens in *Our Mutual Friend* describes the efforts of those who feel concern for Bella Wilfer to make her more dutiful and altruistic. However, while circumstances which are significant for people we care for have practical significance for us, our sense of another person's danger or need is different in quality from our sense of our own – the feeling that your friend must conquer his lust for his daughter is different from your feeling that you must conquer your lust for yours. Our motivations as altruists can be strong enough to overcome our desire to do what society or our own safety requires, but we experience these feelings more or less independently of our own bodily makeup and even our society's rules. Suppose that I belong to a society which forbids eating certain food, for example, shellfish. You may yourself have no scruples about what you eat, but, if you invite me to dinner, as an altruist you may take care to provide something other than shellfish; my horror of crab weighs with you, though you do not share it.

Not only do our feelings as social beings differ in quality from our feelings as altruists; there is a difference also in our beliefs. As social beings, we want our beliefs about what is the case and what is good and bad to coincide with those of other people in our society; and the strength with which we hold such beliefs is proportional not only to the evidence in favour of them but to their currency among those around us. As altruists we consider what those for whom we are concerned believe and desire; and our reading of their minds is more or less independent of how others, we think, read their minds, and also of whether others share their beliefs and desires. I can act on the belief that you admire and trust someone that is generally distrusted and despised. As social beings, even as members of a family, we may be relatively insensitive to the peculiar beliefs and desires of those around us. However, our beliefs about what they think can give us strength at certain moments to act against the laws and customs of our society, and may contribute in the long run to new ways of social thinking. I return to the character of our beliefs about the thoughts and aims of other persons in Chapter 5. That altruistic behaviour is relatively independent of the agent's bodily needs and social situation has a bearing I shall consider in Chapter 9 upon religious beliefs about a life after death.

In Chapter 2 I argued that rational life depends upon language and language on society, and in this chapter I have argued not only that we are essentially social beings but that we are essentially altruistic. How does this view of human nature compare with others? It is manifestly inconsistent with the view that all rational behaviour is ultimately selfish, but plenty of people both in the recent and in the remote past have been dissatisfied with that. Some people felt that World War I showed the depths of irrationality to which humanity can sink, and Wilfred Trotter in *Instincts of the Herd in Peace and War* argued that, in addition to the instincts for self-preservation, nutrition and sex recognised by the psychologists of his time, human beings have a gregarious instinct to come together and act as one. This gregarious or, as he sometimes called it, this '*social*' instinct accounts, on the one hand, for our suggestibility, for our predilection for believing what we are told to believe or what we see others believing, independently of any rational grounds, and, on the other, for altruism, which Trotter identified rather vaguely as unselfishness. It has, he claimed, evolutionary value in that a group can find a use for individuals with characteristics that would be weeded out in competition with other individuals; and it operates more continuously than the three previously recognised instincts and in a different way.

Trotter was not himself a professional psychologist, and he wrote in a readable but satirical style; perhaps for these reasons his ideas received less attention than they deserved and after a brief period of popularity were forgotten. Far more influential in the long run was Freud. In *The Ego and the Id* he distinguished three elements in the human mind or psyche, the Id, the Ego and the Superego. The Id, of which we are unconscious, is the seat of bodily passions or gut feelings. The Ego is the part of the mind or self of which we are conscious and which is the seat of rationality. The Superego, which is generated in children by parental repression of their Id-ish impulses, provides the Ego with an ideal of what we should be and performs some functions Catholics attribute to conscience.

Protestants sometimes identify conscience with practical judgement. Bishop Butler in his second 'sermon upon human nature' (*Works*, Volume 1, p. 31) says it is the faculty:

in every man, which ... pronounces determinately some actions to be in themselves just, right and good; others to be in themselves evil, wrong and unjust: which, without being consulted, without being advised with, magisterially exerts itself, and approves or condemns him the doer of them accordingly.

Catholics, however, and Freud was brought up a Catholic, often give conscience a narrower function, that of judging whether what we want to do is really consonant with the laws of God and the teaching of the Church. For Freud the Superego acts upon us as a kind of censorious monitor and restraining influence. It has a social character, keeping close watch on our behaviour towards others, and could not exist within Rousseau's solitary primitives. Freud's tripartite division of the psyche is often compared with the division Plato proposed in his *Republic*. I shall come to that in a moment.

Another essay in metapsychology which has been compared with Plato's is W.H. Sheldon's classification of personality-traits in *The Varieties of Temperament*. His empirical studies showed that traits ranging from love of risk and chance to untroubled sleeping are not distributed in a random way but come in groups. The grouping marks out three temperaments. Some people have a temperament he calls 'viscerotonic'. They like relaxation, comfort, sociability, food, and affection, but are rarely drunkards and relatively uninterested in sex. Somatotonic people like physical exercise and adventure, they are direct and ruthless and have vigour and push. Cerebrotonic people are mentally intensive, secretive and subjective but find a protective sanctuary in universities in which the people of their sort compete more successfully than they would elsewhere. Colin Strang, in his paper 'Tripartite Souls, Ancient and Modern', proposed matching these three temperaments with the three parts of the psyche which, according to Plato, are present in the psyche of every individual, though one will be pre-eminent in one person and another in another. Plato gave his parts names which are usually translated the 'calculating', the 'spirited' and the 'desiring'. There is a good match between the cerebrotonic temperament and Plato's calculating man and between the somatotonic temperament and the man dominated by his 'spirited' part – the Greek word *thumoeides* Plato uses has no satisfactory English referent. The man Plato thinks is dominated from his desiring part only partly resembles Sheldon's viscerotonic man, since Plato's desiring man has a strong sexual drive, whereas Sheldon finds this more characteristic of cerebrotonics like university teachers.

Karen Armstrong in her Introduction to *Fields of Blood* (pp. 4-5) notes that:

> Each of us has three brains which coexist uneasily. In the deepest recesses of our grey matter we have an 'old brain' which we inherited from the reptiles that struggled out of the primeval slime 500 million years ago. . . . Some time after mammals appeared they evolved what neuroscientists call the limbic system, perhaps 120,000 years ago. . . . [D]uring the Palaeolithic age human beings evolved a 'new brain', the neocortex, home of the reasoning powers and self-awareness.

The 'old brain', she says, equips us with aggressiveness and 'self-centred' impulses; the limbic system gave sentient creatures 'the capacity to cherish and care for creatures other than themselves', and the neocortex enables us 'to stand back from the instinctive primitive passions'. These brains are not the homes of Plato's three parts of the psyche – Plato has a different story about their location in *Timaeus* (69-72) – but they correspond to them and perhaps provide conditions necessary for their functioning.

Plato was a brilliant psychologist – he could be said to have created the subject – and the different interpretations that have been proposed in recent years of what he says show that he is still rewarding to read. My distinction of three dimensions of rational life ('Trisecting the Psyche') is derived from his trisection of the psyche but I do not claim that it fits it more perfectly than either of the threefold distinctions offered by Freud and Sheldon. Plato places gentleness and concern for others in his 'Calculating' part, and seems to deny rationality to his 'Spirited' and 'Desiring' parts. I allow us to be rational and calculating in pursuing our interests as individual organisms and gratifying the Id-ish passions which, Plato, like Freud, detects in our dreams, and which he locates in the Desiring part. In the course of his life Plato becomes less confident of the power of reasoning, comparing and measuring to control our lives, and depends increasingly on the Spirited part to help the Calculating by tenacious fidelity to custom and law. To that extent he anticipates Freud's conception of the Superego. However, he also gives the spirited part traits that belong to Sheldon's somatotonic temperament, quickness, pugnacity and ruthlessness, which can be injurious to society, and he places increasing emphasis on the importance of temperament. In the *Republic* he wants us to bring the three parts of our individual psyches into harmony, and this corresponds closely to bringing into harmony the parts of our nature as egoists, social beings and altruists, but in the *Statesman* he recommends a balance between state-officers of gentle, reflective, cerebrotonic temperament and officers of active, assertive, risk-taking, somatotonic temperament – as we should say, between doves and hawks.

Those who maintain that there is no such thing as society may do so in order to oppose the idea that the good of a society is something over and above the good of the individuals that make it up. They do not deny that there is such a thing as the common good: the phrase 'the common good' is frequently on the lips of public figures of every kind, and nobody questions whether it designates something for which both governments and individuals should work. Mill, however, (in *Utilitarianism*, Chapter 4) says: 'Each person's happiness is a good to that person, and the general happiness, therefore, a good to the aggregate of all persons.' The common good of a society, whether individual members aim at it or not, is the sum of the private goods of its members. The Second Vatican Council (in *Gaudium et Spes*, s. 26) defined the common good, in words that would not displease Mill, as 'the sum total of social conditions which allow people, either as groups or as individuals, to reach their fulfilment more fully and more easily', and added: 'The social order and its development must constantly yield to the good of the person.'

Most people speak as if they agreed. Growth of a society's economy is taken to contribute to the common good because, according to liberal economics, it 'trickles down' to benefit even the poorest members, and literacy and numeracy in the society are said to contribute to the common good, not because without them it would be impossible to run a society of many millions, but on the grounds that they benefit individuals.

There are two persuasive reasons for taking this view of the common good. There is the rather academic argument that what is good must be good for some living thing, that only living things can be benefited; and that a society is not a living thing. There is also the disturbing fact that political leaders have justified odious and repressive measures by appeal to a good of the society or the race that somehow takes precedence over the good of individuals. Trotter was an offender here; his common good, for which we should all strive, is the next evolutionary leap: the emergence of individuals as united in action and committed to their society as bees and ants, while retaining our present brain-power and 'capacity of varied reaction' (p. 61). In Chapter 12 I suggest that evolution need not produce a society in which individuals are subordinated to the whole in this way.

On the other side it may be pointed out that a society can be wiped out by enemies or die out naturally and this is plainly bad for it; its continuance, therefore, must be good for it, and good also for its members, inasmuch as, for beings that are essentially social, any society is better than none.

It is true that a society is not a living thing. There is, however, something that stands to a society as life stands to an individual, namely the living of its members with regard to its laws and customs. We all aim at this, not because we hope to derive some benefit to ourselves as individuals, but because we are social beings and it is good for us as such to share in social life. Homer says:

> Nothing is stronger and better than this,
> Than when two people, minds thinking alike,
> Hold fast to a home, husband and wife.
> (*Odyssey*, 6.182-4)

What Homer calls 'two people, minds thinking alike' ('*homophroneonte noêmasin*') we call 'sharing the same values.' The nuclear family is a society, though a small one.

In general, then, the peaceful, unimpeded living of the members of a society in accordance with its laws and customs is a common good. It is not something separate, however, from the good of the individuals who make it up, but, since the individuals are essentially social, it is part of that good; it is the social dimension of their lives. As such, it is threatened by enemies trying to destroy the society from outside, and by population decline through famine, plague or infertility. Military strength, economic growth and high rates of literacy and numeracy do not so much contribute to social life as counter these threats to it.

However, social life within a society is threatened from inside by disagreement about what social life should be, about how it is best to deal with birth, procreation and death, and about how to do other things like eating, dressing and washing. I said earlier that for rational life all that is needed is a society large enough and stable enough to have a language and customs. Such a society can be quite small: a tribe or a village. So small a society, if it had no dealings with other societies, would probably have no enforcement of its customs, let alone members with the social role of enforcing custom, and the members would all know each other. In a frequently cited article, 'Neocortex Size as a Constraint on Group Size in Primates', R.I.M. Dunbar argued that the size of the primate brain corresponds to the number of other individuals an individual knows and interacts with, and, in 'Co-Evolution of Neocortex Size, Group Size and Language in Humans', of which I say more later, he calculated that the human brain cannot store the necessary information about more than about 150 people. The smallest viable society for rationality would be about that size.

If Dunbar is right, it is impossible for the members of a larger society all to know each other. In Mondragon, where in place of ordinary capitalism a successful economy was established based upon worker-owned cooperatives, it was found that the largest productive unit that works well has about 500 members. Aristotle said that a city-state should not have more than 5,000 citizens – and he had in mind adult male citizens with full civil rights. In a society of 150 people or even 500, individuals not liking a custom can (space permitting) go elsewhere and found a separate society, rather as female vampire bats allegedly do if the local males are disagreeable. However, in a society of 5,000 it is likely that laws will have to be enforced, and before Aristotle's time enforcing them was a recognised social role. Some Classical Greeks were at first reluctant to give up self-rule, and a system was evolved in which the offices were held by all citizens together or by all citizens in turn, the turns being decided by lot. This system broke down, and, though David van Reybrouck in *Against Elections* records some recent pleas for its revival, it is understandably unattractive to those who have been elected to office on 'merit'. Most countries have a system (roughly speaking, that commended by Plato in his *Laws*, 6) in which every few years the whole population elects a small number of persons, perhaps only one, to whom it is left to appoint legislators, judges and executive officers.

Today (though some remote tribes or villages may not know it) we all belong to societies with many millions of members. We do not need Dunbar to tell us we cannot know more than a fraction of our fellow-citizens, and we positively demand efficient enforcement of the law by police, judges, gaolers and other officers. We belong, as Nicholas Boyle has put it in a recent article, 'Truth Telling, the Media and Society' (*New Blackfriars* 98, 2017, pp. 19-33) not just to societies but to 'mass-societies'.

Few, given the choice, would prefer going back to a primitive society of 150 members to living in a mass-society. Boyle suggests that the coercion in mass-societies is rendered tolerable by allowing all members to vote in elections. Even before universal suffrage came in, however, if the coercion was felt to be 'fair', there was no demand for more freedom. It does not bother us that we know only a minute proportion of the individuals that make up our society, that even the people who actually control our day-to-day lives are quite unknown to us – the people bringing food from distant places, providing paid employment, passing laws, making war or peace, and organising social services. Nobody complains of this and Boyle suggests that the media provide compensation for our ignorance. On television, in the papers, or by radio, they familiarise us with a few people, heads of state, outstanding athletes and entertainers, whose names and faces we recognise, and whom we feel we know as we feel we know the fictional characters who appear in soap operas. This gives us the illusion of knowing what goes on in our globalised world and even of having some control of it, in the way in which the members of a primitive society really know what goes on, and have some control of what goes on, within its narrow limits.

Boyle may be right about this. However, even primitive societies split up into smaller societies. A pupil from Nigeria, I hope not counting on my credulity, told me that in her fairly remote part of the country actual languages proliferated, that new languages might develop within a village. Dunbar gives us reason to expect this in any society of more than 150 members, and, despite the anaesthetising influence of the media and regular elections, sub-societies for life do appear in mass-societies. These can present a threat to the social life of the main society quite independently of the external threats of plague, famine and war. It is here that society and religion can come into conflict, here, despite any contribution it makes to public health, economic growth, education or even science, that religion can actually threaten the common good.

4
WHAT IS RELIGION?

The word 'religion' comes from the Latin *religio*, but it has changed its meaning over the centuries. To the ancient Romans *religio* chiefly meant fear of the preternatural; in the Middle Ages it meant the consecrated life of nuns, monks and friars. In More's *Utopia*, however, published in 1516, it is used in its modern sense. Utopus, the ruler who gave Utopia its name, was able to conquer the country because the inhabitants were 'fighting assiduously among themselves about religions' ('*de religionibus inter se assidue dimicasse*', *Utopia*, Book 2, chapter *De religionibus*, p. 264). It was perhaps when wars afflicted Europe at the time of the emergence of nation-states that *religio* was pressed into service to say what some of the fighting was about. Today in the West the word 'religion' is in constant use. People think that what they mean when they write it or utter it is clear and unproblematic: it signifies an easily recognised natural phenomenon, like mosquitoes or sleep. Anthropologists assume that every society in the past had a religion, and writers for the general public speculate on why that is and whether it will be the same in the future. Surveys show that many people in Western countries now say they have no religion. Could religion disappear from world altogether? Might it be just a passing phase in the history of mankind?

Is it really so clear, however, what today we mean by 'religion'? In the last century a number of attempts were made to define it. William James in *The Varieties of Religious Experience* (1902, p. 31) said it is 'the feelings, acts and experiences of individual men in their solitude'. Karen Armstrong perhaps shows the influence of James in *Fields of Blood* (p. 2): 'In the West we see "religion" as a coherent system of obligatory beliefs, institutions and rituals, centring on a supernatural God, *whose practice is essentially private* [my italics].'

James' suggestion is astonishing. It is as social beings, not as solitary living organisms, that people think, feel and act as Christians, Jews, Muslims, and adherents to other recognised religions. Rousseau's 'religion of man', that is, of man, in general, is as mythical as the presocial human beings whose religion he supposed it to be. If we fail to see the essentially social character of religion, we shall never understand why it is so important to people and so divisive.

Bertrand Russell in *What I Believe* (1925, p. 5) said God and immortality are 'the central doctrines of the Christian religion', and continued, 'It cannot be said that either doctrine is essential to religion. . . . But we in the West have come to think of them as the irreducible minimum of theology.' Although he himself disavowed religion, Julian Huxley in 1927 wrote a book entitled *Religion without Revelation* and defined religion as 'the reaction of the personality as a whole to its experience of the Universe as a whole'(p. 137). Stephen Clark in a recent article, 'Atheism Considered as a Christian Sect' (2015, pp. 277-303), argued that atheistic humanism with its commitment to truth, reason and human perfectibility is so much the product of European Christian culture that it is not just a religion but a Christian sect.

Russell was on the right scent. By 'religion' 'we in the West' actually mean Christianity, and anything that sufficiently resembles it for us to slap the same label onto it. That, in effect, is what William P. Alston says about the word in *The Encyclopaedia of Philosophy* (1967). Until recently Christianity was very much a reality for the West. In some countries, including England, it was established by law; in all it was taught to children and children were regularly forced to say prayers and herded into churches. It is our paradigm for a religion. It has a number of salient features. It is highly social both in organisation and in practice. Christians belong to churches, denominations, parishes, congregations, and these associations have bishops, priests, pastors and similar officers. There are communal prayers, processions and other rites, and special buildings, cathedrals, parish churches and chapels, where these rites are celebrated. There is a sacred book, the Bible. There are prophets, reformers and other notable introducers of new ideas and practices. There are beliefs concerning a personal God and life after death which provide a rationale for Christian practices; and their beliefs

4. What Is Religion?

and practices are deeply important to Christians. Most of these features are easily discernible in Jewish life as known from the Bible and in Classical Greece and Rome. So, we say that the ancient Jews, Greeks and Romans all had religions.

This concept of religion which so perfectly fits Christianity is comparatively recent. The ancient Greeks had no word to express it. They had a word for worship, *thrêskeia*, but worship was not connected with belief. Devotion to the Olympian gods carried with it neither theoretical beliefs about the universe nor practical principles about how people should behave. The ancient Jews noticed that other societies worshipped different gods, but they did not think of their own adherence to the God of Abraham as a matter of religion but rather of race. They distinguished themselves from other nations, and classified differences in worship between themselves and the Greeks as ethnic. As a nation they had their distinctive laws and customs, but had no concept to enable them to separate their religious customs from their non-religious. The recent change in translating the Bible from using 'nations' or 'peoples' to using 'pagans' for the Greek *ethnê* is misleading. The word 'pagan', which originally signified a country-dweller or rustic, acquired its current religious meaning only after Christianity had spread through the Mediterranean world; a word was then wanted to distinguish Jews and Christians, who were mostly found in towns, from everyone else. There was still no word meaning exactly what we mean by 'religion' in the Middle Ages. Aquinas, writing in 1267-72, discusses various ways of understanding *religio* in *Summa Theologiae* (*ST*) (2a 2ae, Q. 81) and favours identifying it with a disposition to give due worship to God; but in Question 186 he narrows it to life in vows of poverty, chastity and obedience. Everyone was conscious of the division between Christian and Muslims, but it was thought of as chiefly ethnic; Muslims spoke of Christians as Greeks, Romans and Franks, though Christians also spoke of differences in faith. William Caxton at the end of his 1470 translation of Voragine's *The Golden Legend* speaks of 'articles of faith' but the Thirty-nine Articles of the 1571 are 'articles of religion'.

We Westerners think beliefs an important part of religion. We show that today by using the word 'faith' instead of 'religion'; we talk of 'faith schools' or call Hinduism a 'faith'. The word 'faith', today at least, suggests a particular kind of belief, belief which is held tenaciously and without good reason. Beliefs are indeed important to Christians, who formulate them in creeds, but creeds do not exist outside Christianity, and what we call 'beliefs' play little part in the conscious thinking of non-European civilisations. Our distinction between beliefs and desires corresponds to the grammatical differences in reported speech – I believe that you *are* seated, desire that you *should be* – which do not exist in many non-European languages.

Our concept of a belief, I have argued in 'Is the Concept of the Mind Parochial?', is a legacy from the philosophers of ancient Greece. We have inherited from them the idea that being rational is a matter of having reasons for your behaviour, and a reason is something that can be formulated in words as a belief. We are reluctant to say that only educated Westerners are rational, so we attribute to sane adults in all societies, including the most primitive, beliefs that would rationalise the customs they follow. Émile Durkheim bases his definition of religion on this assumption. He says in *Elementary Forms of the Religious Life* (p. 36):

> Religious phenomena are naturally arranged in two fundamental categories: beliefs and rites. The first are states of opinion, and consist in representations; the second are determined modes of action. . . . The rites can be defined . . . only by the special nature of their objects. . . . It is in the beliefs that the special nature of this object is expressed. It is possible to define the rite only after we have defined the belief.

It is unrealistic to suppose that these 'beliefs' are always consciously held. A scholar would be puzzled to say what religious beliefs were generally held by the Classical Greeks or Romans, and spokesmen for what we count as non-Christian religions, including Judaism, often deny that what we call 'beliefs' play an important role in them. The general beliefs that rationalise people's customs are held by them not as solitary individuals but as social beings, and whether they are held consciously and formulated depends on the history of their society.

Christian beliefs divide into two varieties. There are doctrinal or dogmatic beliefs like the belief that the universe depends on the Jewish God, and that Jesus returned to life from death. What makes these beliefs religious is not that they lack justification – many beliefs are unjustified without being religious. Nor are they religious because they concern non-physical entities: pure mathematics is about non-physical things, but the belief that every even number above two is the sum of two primes is not religious. They are religious because the rites and practices for which they provide a rationale are paradigmatically religious. In themselves, however, they are theoretical and aspire to objective truth.

Second, Christian principles of conduct are counted as beliefs. That is because they can be formulated in sentences the surface grammar of which is indicative, sentences like 'Abortion is wrong' and 'Generosity to the poor is good'. Some philosophers hold that these sentences are more like counsels and commands than statements which are true or false. Certainly, orders and prohibitions and advice for or against a course of action cannot be true or false; it does not follow, however, that they cannot be right or wrong and, in general, we think customs and practical principles actually are right or wrong, good or bad. To mark the difference, however, between doctrinal beliefs and practical principles or convictions, people today often call the latter not 'beliefs' but 'values'. The word is confusing, because they are not the sort of values provided by professional valuers, but the thought is that those who say that something is good think it valuable, and those who say something is bad value avoiding it or preventing it. Christians regard beliefs of both kinds, dogmatic and practical or moral, as essential to Christianity. Not necessarily, however, quite the same beliefs. Different Christian denominations have slightly different beliefs. That is why they are sometimes called different 'religions'.

Christian beliefs of both kinds are indeed essential to Christian culture, and Christian culture is our paradigm for a religious culture; but, if not every culture is religious, what is distinctive of Christian beliefs apart from their being held by followers of Jesus of Nazareth?

Crane in *The Meaning of Belief* starts by saying that 'religious belief' (p. 35) or the 'religious world-view' (p. x), besides being essentially social, essentially involves a 'sense of the transcendent'. The Judaeo-Christian God is transcendent in that he is not part of the spatio-temporal world of which he is the source. This idea of transcendence, however, is no more universal than the modern idea of the supernatural, which depends on a modern idea of what is natural. Crane's idea of transcendence seems limited to Jews, Christians and Muslims. To obtain a definition of religion which will justify his claim on p. 2 that 80 per cent of the world's inhabitants are religious believers, he has to invoke Durkheim's conception of the sacred and the profane (pp. 106-17). In *Elementary Forms of the Religious Life*, we read:

> The first criterium [sic] of religious beliefs ... is that they always suppose a bipartite division of the whole universe, known and knowable, into two classes, which embrace all that exists but which mutually exclude each other [p. 40].

> [The distinction] is very particular: *it is absolute*. In all the history of human thought there exists no other example of two categories so profoundly differentiated or so radically opposed to one another [p. 38].

Durkheim takes his idea of the profane from the prohibitions (sometimes called 'taboos') which are the means of regulating many primitive societies that have no positive rules or rule-enforcement. They do not, however, establish a permanent division of all that exists. Prohibitions of foods are often restricted to seasons, and others can be lifted if there is good reason, as Herman Melville found in Taipivai. Durkheim was a prisoner to the idea that to say what a word means you must specify something common to all the things to which it applies.

What we consider the religious beliefs and practices of Christians are those which were taken from the Jews. The first followers of Christ were Jews who came to form a sub-society within the larger Jewish society. At the time of Christ, the Jews did not have a sovereign state of their own; Palestine was part of the Roman Empire and, besides having a Roman governor, it was ruled by client kings. Nevertheless, the Jews had their own internal autonomy; they were ruled, as they had been since the Babylonian captivity, by a hereditary priesthood and they had their own laws, derived from Mosaic law, and their own courts in which those laws were applied. They were themselves a society within larger societies. Christ's disciples formed a sub-society within that. At first, they lived entirely by Jewish law; but to accommodate the increasing numbers of non-Jewish Christians, they relaxed some of its provisions, and, in particular, the rule that males must be circumcised. In Genesis 17:10-14 God states his covenant with Abraham and his successors as follows (I use the Authorised Version translation):

> This is my covenant which ye shall keep. Between me and you and thy seed after thee: every man child among you shall be circumcised. And ye shall circumcise the flesh of your foreskin; and it shall be a token of the covenant betwixt me and you. And he that is eight days old shall be circumcised among you, every man child in your generations, he that is born in the house, or bought with money of any stranger, which is not of thy seed. He that is born in thy house, and he that is bought with thy money must needs be circumcised; and my covenant shall be in your flesh for an everlasting covenant. And the uncircumcised man child whose flesh of his foreskin is not circumcised, that soul shall be cut off from his people; he hath broken my covenant.

4. What Is Religion?

This covenant, which supposedly antedates the Egyptian captivity and the covenant in Exodus, could hardly be more explicit, so it is not surprising that abrogating the rule produced the tensions with non-Christian Jews recorded in the Acts of the Apostles and the Epistles of Paul. In the end the Christian society, comprising both Jews and non-Jews, was expelled from the larger Jewish society. It then came to be a new sub-society in the larger society of the Roman Empire.

What Russell identified as the paradigms for a dogmatic religious belief, the beliefs that the natural order depends on a person outside it and that there is a life after death, are beliefs about the world taken from the Jews. The Jews alone in the first century believed in a personal transcendent creator, and, although some Jews, we are told by Josephus, did not believe in a life after death, others, the Pharisees, did, and it was from them that Christ's followers were chiefly drawn. The Christians also retained Jewish practical beliefs and rules about life, death and sex. These conflicted with customs sanctioned by law in the Roman Empire as a whole, abortion, infanticide, uxoricide, suicide, divorce and so on; and these Jewish rules today are classed as religious. So, Christianity appeared as a sub-society for life, not essentially confined to one nation or race, existing within a larger society, and holding which had practices and beliefs at variance with those prevalent in the larger society.

Will that do as a definition of a religion? Anything that satisfies it will certainly threaten the smooth running of the larger society. The concept of a threatening sub-society must have existed before the advent of Christianity, and Jews were considered threatening, but as an awkward ethnic minority, a recalcitrant nation within the Empire. Christians were of different ethnicities, so they could not be conceived as a nation, but, when they were persecuted it was as a sub-society with a culture hostile to that of the empire, addicted to secretive unlicensed assemblies. Their hostility to the culture of the empire was shown by their refusal to join in practices by which ordinary citizens showed their attachment to it; the point that these practices were religious was not recognised by officials like Pliny (who wrote to Trajan about them, *Letters*, 10.96-97) because officials did not have the concept of religion. After the Empire became Christian, moreover, the modern notion of a religion disappeared from Europe until Europe was divided by the Reformation on non-ethnic lines. Even since then there has been difficulty in grasping religious differences as independent of ethnic, and people have tried to attribute them to cultural differences between northern and southern or eastern and western races.

Those in the West today who say that they have no religion, mean that they do not attend any Christian church or any mosque or synagogue or comparable building. These buildings belong to sub-societies, and the self-styled non-religious do not feel that they belong to any such sub-society. They do, however, belong to the whole society of which they are citizens, and as social beings they have a culture. They have concepts of day and night, light and dark, the seasons and other things of practical significance, the social roles and the skills that the society recognises, and the plants, animals and weather conditions on which it depends. These concepts appear in 'beliefs', as we should call them, about what is the case that are bound up with their customs and practical 'values'. They share a set of beliefs about the world and its contents, and a set of practices and practical ideas of what is good and bad, right and wrong. Not being the culture of a religious sub-society, theirs may be called, a 'secular' culture. The word, however, has become slippery through the emergence of people who describe themselves as 'secularists', so I shall linger briefly on its history.

It is taken from the Latin word *saeculum*, which perhaps started by signifying a race or breed, but came to mean a human life-span, an epoch or a period of time, in particular a century. In the mediaeval West it was used to distinguish the present temporal order and its affairs from the non-temporal existence of God and those who survive death, what we now call the 'transcendent'. A distinction was made between the 'secular' clergy, who were all male and lived 'in the world', engaged in running dioceses, parishes or schools or in work now appropriated to civil servants, and the 'religious', who included women, and who lived not 'in the world' but in communities governed by special rules and who devoted themselves, supposedly, to the transcendent. The division was between two kinds of church person, not between church people and the laity, and 'secularization' meant release from vows to live by 'religious' rules.

The *Shorter Oxford English Dictionary* dates the word 'secularism' to 1848 and says it means: 'The doctrine that morals should be based only on regard to the well-being of mankind in the present life, to the exclusion of all considerations drawn from belief in God or a future state.' A wide range of further definitions is offered by Andrew Copson in *Secularism*. These show it is now conceived not as an ethical but a political theory about the best relationship between the state and religious bodies. Some people who accept that political theory are also churchgoers, and some who describe themselves as non-religious have no political theory but simply share the culture of the sovereign state in which they live.

Although it is not part of a secular culture to go to a synagogue, church, or mosque, all human beings need social activities, and in Chapter 12 I shall indicate some ways in which people with a secular culture satisfy that need. There is not much difference between religious and secular cultures, which is why the concept of religion, even today, is peculiar to the West. The concept which any society needs is that of a sub-society, the culture of which is at variance with its own.

In every human being there occur tensions between the egoistic, the social and the altruistic parts of human nature. Not everything that is good for us as individuals is permitted by society, nor is everything that is good for those for whom we feel concern. These tensions threaten our unity as rational agents, and it is part of being a mature rational agent to handle them, to bring them under control, and to judge what it is best for us to do, all things considered. Everyone, however, needs a culture in order to function as a rational agent. If you belong to a sub-society with a culture that conflicts with that of the whole, or even, to a lesser extent, that of another sub-society, your unity as a social being is under threat. The good practical judgement we need to prevent conflict between self-interest, social duty and altruistic concern from disrupting our unity as individuals is what Aristotle called *phronêsis* and medieval philosophers *prudentia*. Good political judgement is required in rulers to prevent conflicts between one sub-society and another, or between any sub-society and the state as a whole, from disrupting the unity of the whole state. However, the two kinds of judgement are not quite analogous. It is natural for us to have the three aims in our practical lives, and, though they sometimes conflict, they are not just reconcilable but mutually complementary; human beings need all three. There are rational considerations, then, to help us to bring them into harmony. It is not natural to belong to a multicultural society or to have your unity as a social being torn apart. That is as tragic a predicament as being caught between the demands of society and the needs of a person you love, but even harder to resolve. Ordinary practical judgement is ill equipped to deal with it, and there are no considerations of complementarity to help you. Political judgement (if you have it) has no concern with the fragmentation of an individual's social nature. Besides, our political leaders are of the same species as the rest of us, and in a modern democracy some may themselves belong to a sub-society with a culture different from that of the whole.

Here we see the weakness of the modern ideal of multiculturalism. Rulers are responsible for the unity of their societies and the happiness of the people in them. Both are threatened by a sub-society with a culture that conflicts with the culture of the whole society – either its actual culture or the culture its rulers wish it to adopt. The threat appears when a sub-society becomes conspicuous, and disappears only if either its culture becomes the culture of the whole society or else the sub-society ceases to exist or to be conspicuous. Christians were persecuted when they became a conspicuous sub-society but their culture ended by becoming that of the whole Roman Empire.

The West is now filled with sub-societies. This is a result of easy travel, the internet and globalisation. In Western nation-states there are plenty of people who want to get rid of them. The rulers, instructed by history, shrink from violence. They hope that their own culture will become the culture of all citizens, and talk, on the one hand, of pluralism, on the other, of 'liberal values' or, in the United Kingdom, of 'British values'.

In *Philosophy as a Humanistic Discipline* (2007), Bernard Williams enquires how far a multicultural society is a genuine possibility, and how far those advocating it really wish their own culture to be that of everyone. He observes (p. 131): 'There must, on any showing, be limits to the extent to which the liberal state can be disengaged on matters of ethical disagreement. There are some questions, such as that of abortion, on which the state will fail to be neutral whatever it does.' Other matters like euthanasia, sex and the education of children are in the same state. Perhaps, however, people will cease to care: 'The convictions that people previously deeply held, on matters of religion or sexual behaviour or the significance of cultural experience [may] dwindle into private tastes.' Perhaps (p. 133) the best hope for toleration may lie in 'modernity itself, ... and in its principal creation, international commercial society. Despite unnerving outbreaks of fanaticism in many different directions, it is still possible to think that the structure of this international order will encourage scepticism about religious and other claims to exclusivity.'

Does he mean that, since we all wear the same clothes, drive the same cars, fly in the same aeroplanes, and use the same electronic devices, we may settle for a unified culture of consumerism, whatever that may be? His actual conclusion (p.134) is inconclusive:

> It may be that liberal societies can preserve, in an atmosphere of toleration, a variety of strong convictions on important matters. Only the future can show whether that is so. ... Perhaps toleration will prove to have been an interim value, serving a period between a past when no one had heard of it and a future in which no one will need it.

4. What Is Religion?

A past, one might say, like before anyone had heard of Christianity, and a future like when it had become the religion of the Roman Empire. Williams does not use this example, but it is hard to doubt that he himself would like to see a society, to borrow a phrase from him, 'asymmetrically skewed in the liberal direction'.

That completes what I have to say about society and religion, generally. I want to pass to Christianity and consider how our nature as social beings bears on its beliefs. However, since, as I said, we are told that religion is a matter of faith, and since Christians not only accept this but regard faith not as a weakness but as a virtue, I shall first consider what the Christian virtue of faith is.

5
THE DIVINE VIRTUE OF FAITH

Faith sounds to modern ears like something wild and anarchic: a leap into the dark, either daring and adventurous or rash and stupid. It can give us the strength to be heroes, or hurl us blindfolded into folly and disaster. To some, it is contrary to reason; it is believing ten impossible things before breakfast. To others, it takes over where reason breaks down; reason is a pitiful thing, timid and logic-chopping, and, if we wish to get anywhere, we must leave it behind and take faith's leap. Faith in another human being, in a lover or a leader, goes beyond what reason can prove; so does faith in a system or a cause; and so, above all, does faith in God. To atheists it seems, as Paul puts it, 'madness, but to those who are saved, the power of God' (1 Corinthians 1:18).

Christian theologians have tended to resist the idea that religious faith is opposed to human reason; rather, they claim, it supplements it. 'Grace,' says Aquinas at the beginning of his *Summa Theologiae* (1a, Q. 1, Art. 8, Ad. 2), 'does not do away with nature but perfects it.' Human beings naturally seek knowledge about God, the source of the natural order, but they cannot attain either the deductive certainty of mathematical knowledge or the empirical certainty of natural science. They need belief in what God has revealed. This is a kind of belief on hearsay which we call 'faith' and which Aquinas describes as a 'supernatural participation in God's goodness' (2a 2ae, Q. 2, Art. 3).

5. The Divine Virtue of Faith

From the time of the earliest church councils, Christians have formulated creeds, lists of things they believe or should believe. These are called 'articles' of faith. People sometimes object to creeds on the ground that they cause divisions and have been used to control people and justify religious persecution. Aquinas argued that faith must be capable of such formulation. His argument was not that rational thought generally depends upon language, but rather that *truth* depends upon it, that what cannot be put into words cannot make any claim to truth. He adds (2a 2ae, Q. 1, Arts 2, 6-9) that the word 'article' is used to express the idea that Christian beliefs are related to one another like the limbs that make up an articulated living body; the Christian faith is an organic whole, not a mere aggregate of beliefs. That is understandable if religious beliefs generally are held by people not as solitary individuals but as members of societies and as part of a culture; different societies have different conceptions of God or gods.

The notion of faith (*fides, pistis*) covers three slightly different things. It covers a kind of belief, such as the belief that God exists or that a statement is true, and it is faith of this kind that is formulated in creeds. It also covers a kind of trust: you can have faith *in* God or *in* your friend. Thirdly, it embraces a kind of constancy: you can be faithful *to* a person or *to* a system, keep faith *with* those who rely on you. In his great praise of faith in Romans chapters three to five, it is the second of these things that Paul has in mind. Abraham was justified by putting his trust (*episteuse*) in God (Romans 4:3) and our salvation comes through 'trust of Jesus Christ' (*pistis Iêsou Khristou*, Romans 3:22-26) – not the trust Christ had in God, but the trust we have in Christ. Abraham believed that God would fulfil the promise that he should have numerous descendants, and we too must believe that Christ's death has the power to redeem us from sin and death (Romans 4:17-21), but in both cases the emphasis is on the steadfast confidence of the believer rather than the content of the belief. The same conception of faith seems to underlie Hebrews chapter eleven. Here too Abraham is given as the exemplar of a man with faith. The third conception of faith is perhaps what inspires Christian martyrs: they die to keep faith with Christ.

Early Christian emphasis on belief comes from Classical Greece; in Western Europe it appears in the twelfth century when programmes were introduced for religious instruction of the laity. These programmes included teaching people simple prayers, the Our Father and the Hail Mary, a simple creed, the Apostle's Creed, various customs, embodied in the Ten Commandments, and practical lists, the Seven Deadly Sins, the Seven Corporal Works of Mercy, the Seven Virtues, and, as the centuries went by, Spiritual Works of Mercy, Beatitudes, Gifts of the Holy Ghost and so on. Religious instruction received a huge new impetus in the fifteenth century from the invention of printing. Caxton, for example, appended a long 'exposition' of the Mass to his translation of *The Golden Legend*. The abundance of catechetical works in England before the Reformation is documented by Eamon Duffy in *The Stripping of the Altars* (1992). Simple catechisms continued to be used for religious instruction until quite recently. The Seven Virtues that were listed were divided into two groups, the 'cardinal' virtues of temperance, prudence, justice and courage (taken from Wisdom 8:7) and the 'divine' 'godly' or 'theological' virtues of faith hope and charity. I quote from a brief 'penny' catechism printed in Newcastle in 1790:

> Q: How many divine virtues are there?
> A: Three; faith, hope and charity.
> Q: Why are they called 'divine' or 'godly'?
> A: Because they relate to God.
> Q: As how?
> A: Faith is believing in God; hope is trusting in God; and charity is loving God above all things, and our neighbours as ourselves for God's sake.

This catechism, it will be seen, assigns belief in God and trust in God to two different virtues, though, as Joseph Ratzinger (Pope Benedict XVI) points out in *Spe Salvi* (s.2), citing Hebrews 10:22-3, 1 Peter 3:15 and Ephesians 2:12, in several Biblical passages 'the words "faith" and "hope" seem interchangeable'. But is either of them really a virtue? What conception of virtue is being used here?

When the catechism lists the 'godly' virtues, the word 'virtue' is used as the Greeks used *aretê* to signify any kind of excellence or useful quality. Aristotle distinguished intellectual and practical excellence. The theoretical sciences, including logic and mathematics, and also technical knowledge of how to bring about desired effects, he classed as forms of intellectual excellence. Practical excellence was the ability to judge rightly what it is best to do in the situation in which you find yourself. Since how we see situations is affected by our emotions our practical judgement is affected by our emotions. Practical excellence, therefore, includes dispositions to see things and to react to them emotionally in ways that facilitate good judgement. Faith does not fall neatly into either category, but, in a way, straddles both. Theoretical and technical knowledge concern the natural order and are acquired naturally. Our natural intellectual powers do not give us any apprehension of the supernatural happiness after death at which Christians are taught to aim, but faith takes the place of scientific knowledge in assuring them that it is a real possibility. 'By faith,' says Aquinas (*ST*, 1a 2ae, Q. 62, Art. 4) 'the intellect apprehends what it hopes for and loves.' And, while faith does not help us to arrive at correct practical judgements in the same way as a good disposition with regard to such emotions as fear, anger or sexual desire, I shall suggest that it does affect the way in which we view situations.

Aquinas seems initially (*ST*, 1a 2ae, Q. 62, Art. 2) to restrict faith to teachings based on revelation. He is followed in this by some later apologists. They say that we can assure ourselves by using human intelligence that the natural order depends upon a personal source who is not part of it, and also that this personal God has revealed certain things first to the Jewish nation, and then, through Jesus of Nazareth, to the world at large. We have rational grounds for thinking that Jesus was sent by God and that the Gospels contain his teaching. Faith is restricted to believing things about God and life after death that are stated in the Bible and taught by the Church. R.A. Knox in *The Belief of Catholics* (pp. 46-47), took this line:

> Is it really so difficult to see that a revealed religion demands, from its very nature, a place for private judgment and a place for authority? A place for private judgment, in determining that the revelation itself comes from God, in discovering the Medium through which the revelation comes to us and the rule of faith by which we are enabled to determine what is, and what is not, revealed. A place for authority to step in, when these preliminary investigations are over, and say 'Now, be careful, for you are out of your depth here ... from this point onwards you must ask, not to be convinced but to be taught'.

Aquinas goes on, however, to allow that many people need faith to believe things that can be proved by natural reason, and it is widely supposed today that we need faith to believe that the Judaeo-Christian god exists, and even more faith to believe that Jesus Christ was the Son of God and therefore a trustworthy teacher about things we cannot know by natural intelligence. Certainly, the existence of God and the divine sonship of Christ are presented as articles of faith in Christian creeds.

The sentences 'God exists' and 'Jesus Christ was the son of God' or, more challenging, 'Jesus Christ was both God and man' look as if they state things which some people believe, but the truth of which might be questioned and therefore requires proof. They look like 'Black swans exist' and 'The Duke's wife is both a mother and a head of state.' In fact, however, they are not straightforward statements, and not only is it not obviously clear whether or not they *are* true, it is not obviously clear what it is to *think* them true. The early Christian Fathers, as Jonathan Barnes argued in his paper 'Belief Is Up to Us', were inclined to imagine that believing that God created the universe is simply a matter of being prepared to *say* he did. However, I may assent to a declaration without believing it true or even understanding it, if the consequences of dissent are frightening. Only if we can understand what it is to think that God exists or that Christ was the son of God, can we understand in what way people need faith to believe these things and in what way they are accessible to ordinary reason.

I start with 'God exists'. To think that black swans exist is to think that some swans are black, to think that leprosy exists is to think that some people have it. God is not, like a swan, a natural substance with a particular colour (though Zeus notoriously took the form of a swan); nor is God, like leprosy, a bodily condition. We in the West take our idea of God chiefly from the Bible, and there we read, on the one hand, that God created Heaven and Earth and, on the other, that God was worshipped by the Jews. Many passages in the Old Testament contrasts the god of the Jews with the gods of other nations and the passages in which it does that give us a concept of a god as whatever it is that a society worships. The Old Testament Jews seem to waver between saying that the gods worshipped by other nations did not exist at all and saying that they were weak and feeble compared with the god they themselves worshipped. Some passages identify the gods of other nations with human artefacts, statues, which exist but, being inanimate, are powerless. Other passages seem to suggest that other nations believe that there are powerful unseen beings who can protect them or take offence at what they do and harm them, but that these beliefs are false: Yahweh is the only such agent. The Greeks and Romans had words, *theos* and *deus*, which they use to signify an unseen potential protector or punisher of a nation; we translate these words by 'god' and sometimes take this as the concept which underlies our own use of 'god'. Anthropologists expect every nation not enlightened by us to have gods of this kind and, when atheists question whether God exists, they sometimes mean to question whether anything satisfies this concept, whether there is any non-physical protector and punisher of nations and individuals.

In point of fact (as the author of Wisdom 13:1-7 recognised) the Greeks and Romans sometimes used their words to express a slightly different concept, that of something in some way superior to human beings. The

5. The Divine Virtue of Faith

Sun, the Moon and the stars, seeming to be everlasting and impervious to any human action, are spoken of by Aristotle as divine; and fire, which seems to have a life of its own and has such power to harm and benefit us, could also be recognised as a god. The whole natural order seems superior to human beings, and in Stoicism could be identified with god. If we use this mundane concept of a god, the question is not whether the whole natural order or any part of it exists but whether it is really superior to human beings. An atheistic humanist might say not, though to claim that human beings are superior to the whole natural order from which they arise sounds arrogant. The contrary position, that the natural order is superior to human beings, is best described neither as humanism nor as atheism but as pantheism.

If, instead of going by Bible passages which contrast the god of the Jews with other gods, we go by its claims that God created the whole natural order and everything in it, the question whether God exists becomes the question whether the natural order is created by some being who is not part of it nor even the whole of it. I say 'nor even the whole of it' because some people who deny that God exists nevertheless think that the natural order somehow creates itself or is the source of its own existence. The belief of Christians, and also Muslims and many Jews today, is that the whole natural order has a source that is both somehow separate from it and personal.

The question 'Has the whole natural order such a source?' is not like questions about what there is within it. What exists within it can be established by observation and experiment. If we want to know whether giant sloths exist in the cold rainforests of the Andes, we can go and look. If we want to know whether there are particles that carry the gravitational force, we can build expensive particle colliders. Whether the whole spatio-temporal universe has a source outside it, even an impersonal source, cannot be settled either by travel or in the laboratory. I consider in the next chapter what sort of rational grounds there might be for holding any opinion on the subject. Here, however, my question is not what would make it reasonable to think that God exists but what it *is* to think this.

What is it to think that any person exists? It is the kind of thinking that, in Chapter 3, I call 'altruism'. Although we loosely identify persons with human beings, and although human beings are biological organisms, consisting of heads, bodies, limbs and so forth, which in turn consist of cells, we think of human beings as persons in thinking of them as living beings that are sentient and move and act on purpose. This is for our thought of them to have a certain form.

Often in our dealings with people we do not think of them as persons. If I ask the man next to me the time, I may expect to be told it in the same way as I expect to be told it if I call a telephone number that connects me to a speaking clock. I do not think the clock believes that it is, say, 10.23, and, if I say that the man next to me believes it is 10.23, I may mean no more than that he says it is. I may no more attribute to him a belief than I do to a book in which something is written. I may not think that the man I ask wants to be helpful, any more than I think the speaking clock does. We can predict and, in a way, understand each other's movements without considering whether or not they are intentional. However, imagine the following scenario. I know you have to catch a train at 10.30. The station clock says '10.23'. I see you running frantically for the platform. I shout to you, 'No need to run. That clock is wrong. It's only five past ten.' Then I think your movement is intentional, that you are running for the *reason* that it is 10.23 and that you *believe* it is 10.23.

What is it for me to think you are sentient? If I hit you with a cudgel, I may expect you to emit a cry, as when I hit a gong, with it I expect it to make a sound; but whereas I do not think the gong feels pain, I think you do. I think you are aware of the impact as something unpleasant, something to be avoided. What is it to think that? I must either regret hitting you, if I did so unintentionally, or rejoice at it, either as an end in itself or as a means of influencing your behaviour, of getting you to do something you don't want to do, or of preventing you from doing something you do want to do. To think of you as sentient I must engage with you as your friend or enemy. The thought is not merely idle or technical, like thinking of some substance as malleable or friable. Tolstoy brings this out in *War and Peace* (3.1.15) where he describes Nicholas Rostov's wounding of a French dragoon.

An experiment was devised, I was told when I was at Trinity College Dublin by members of the Psychology Department, in which psychology students were instructed to administer, as they believed, electric shocks to volunteers. In fact, the apparatus did not administer shocks and the volunteers were actors who pretended to be in pain. The experiment showed that, believing the volunteers to be in pain, the students wanted to stop using the apparatus, but went on despite their reluctance because people find it hard not to do what they are told. The belief that a human being is a person may be inactive for most of the time. If the psychology students had passed the volunteers in the street, they would have supposed in a way that they were persons, but the belief became active only when the experiment was in progress, the volunteers grimaced and screamed, and the students wanted to stop.

5. The Divine Virtue of Faith

To believe that a person exists, we must attribute aims to that person and act either to further them or to frustrate them. To believe that the natural order has a personal source is to think at least that its source has a purpose and is aware of what happens within it. The creator cannot be supposed to have limbs or consist of cells; anything like that would belong to the natural order. Nor can the creator need the universe as we need warmth and nourishment. Nor can the universe have been created out of a sense of duty. Duties are attached to people in societies, and societies are part of the natural order. The only possibility is that the universe is created and exists for the benefit of the living creatures within it. A personal creator must be conceived on the model of a human altruist.

Someone who does not believe that the universe exists for a purpose may nevertheless attribute purpose to living things within it, and may want them to thrive for their own sakes. Atheism does not entail general indifference to the well-being of living things; it merely excludes loving them for God's sake. Belief in God, however, does exclude total indifference to the well-being of living creatures. The position known as Deism is that the natural order needs a source outside it, but we know nothing about this source, its aims or its knowledge of what goes on. This position has no practical implications. It is idle; if professing it is not like the utterance of a speaking clock, it is a piece of theoretical academic cosmology or just a conversation-filler. Belief that the natural order has a personal source, however, entails some concern for all living things as such, and therefore has implications for the believer's social life. Someone who never has that concern may profess belief in God, and do so sincerely, but we can be mistaken about what we believe. We can look into our minds, so to speak, and read what we are accustomed to *say*, but we cannot be sure that we mean it until something occurs to put our supposed belief to the test. Belief in God is put to the test if it is likely to cost us our lives, our liberty or our jobs; but it can also be tested whenever we are conscious of the needs, feelings, perceptions and efforts of other living things.

In the account of creation in Genesis 1:26-8 God tells human beings they are to rule all living creatures. Although some Christians may have interpreted this as a licence to treat non-human species as they please and even, as Mary Midgley complained in *Science as Salvation*, to dominate and reshape nature for human convenience, the sense of the passage is clearly that the delegated ruling should, like God's own, be for the benefit of all the subjects. In particular, Christian belief in God is incompatible with indifference to the fate of generations after our own.

Not only does it entail disinterested concern for all living things; it entails concern for them for God's sake as well as for their own. It is therefore inseparable from charity, as defined in the old catechism. It requires feeling as well as intelligence, and a kind of feeling that is beyond what is natural for us simply as intelligent persons. Our natural sympathies are finite; they are pretty well limited to the people, animals and plants with which we have dealings. Even if the universe is finite (as perhaps anything physical must be), it is very much larger than the sphere in which a single human being can act, and we can feel for every living thing everywhere, if at all, only through God.

The belief that Christ was the Son of God is different in character from believing that God exists; it is more apt to bring Christians into conflict with a non-Christian society, and it is harder to say what it consists in.

No Christian believes that Jesus of Nazareth stood to God in the causal relationship in which Isaac stood to Abraham or Heracles to Zeus, the model that seems to lie behind the passages in the Koran which criticise this belief. To say that Christians believe he was the Son of God is to sum up a variety of beliefs, attitudes and practices which may vary slightly from one Christian or group of Christians to another. Two main strands can be identified.

Christ is spoken of as being himself God by Thomas in John 20:28 and by Paul in Romans 9:5. The doctrine of his divinity was developed only over several centuries. The creeds do not offer any neat formulation. If the doctrine is true, however, it implies that his life had enormous historical importance, overshadowing anything in human history or natural cosmology. In Jesus the source of the natural order became a part of it. The life of Jesus is an historical fact. An historical fact can have a central place in a culture and widely ramified consequences for it. The life of Mohammed and the exodus of the Jews from Egypt are examples.

Belief in a personal God commits the believer to a general regard for creation, but that in itself is unlikely to conflict with the culture of any human society. The historical interventions, however, accepted by Jews, Christians and Muslims have involved detailed revelations of how the creator wants us to act, and these commit the believer to recognising a source of law superior to human legislators and custodians of local customs. That recognition has made Jewish, Christian and Muslim sub-societies a greater threat to the larger societies in which they exist than other ethnic or religious minorities.

Christians also believe that God entered the created world in the person of Jesus in order to save us – as the Nicene creed puts it, 'for our salvation' (*sôtêria*). Belief in Christ's divinity is interwoven with belief in

5. The Divine Virtue of Faith

him as a saviour. A saviour from what, and how? The New Testament uses two words, *sôtêria*, which also means 'safety', especially from death, and *lutrôsis*, which means 'release', especially release of prisoners by paying ransom. Different Christians have had slightly different ideas of salvation. For some it is being freed from sin – and that in itself may be conceived in various ways. We could take the view that Christ's offering of himself on the Cross was a reparation to God for all the actions against his rules and wishes done by human beings, past and future. The second of the Thirty-nine Articles calls it 'a sacrifice, not only for original guilt [the sin of Adam] but also for all actual sins of men'. Paul in Romans 8:22 speaks of freedom from 'the slavery of perishing (or being destroyed)' (*phthora*). If we are mortal in the sense that we shall all die, and if dying is for us the end, then Christians can say that Christ saves us from extinction at death. Many Christians, however, believe that it is *natural* for human beings to have a life after death. If that is correct, Christ cannot, strictly speaking, save us from the finality of death, since death is not final anyhow; but he may save us from Hell, from unending misery after death.

I consider ways of understanding what salvation is in Chapter 7. However, from whatever we are saved, the Christian belief that Christ saved us by offering his life on the Cross is not just an historical belief like the belief that Darwin saved us from reading the Genesis account of creation as science, or that Wilberforce delivered African people from slavery. Peter addressing the Jewish hierarchy after the healing of the lame man, in Acts 4:10-12, says:

> It is in the name of Jesus Christ the Nazarene, whom you crucified, and whom God raised from the dead, that this man now stands in your presence healed. This is the stone that was despised by you, the builders, but has become the keystone. And salvation [*sôteria*] is in none other. There is no other name under Heaven given to men in which we are to be saved.

Peter means that it is only through now invoking Christ that we can be saved. In John chapter six Christ says it is only through our now eating his flesh and drinking his blood, that we can have eternal life. In John chapter ten he describes himself as the gate of the sheepfold through which people must always enter to have salvation and life in abundance. In John chapter fifteen he takes the image of the vine, traditionally used to represent the Jewish people, and says that he himself is the vine from which we as branches are constantly to draw life. Paul's letters, in passages I shall cite below, speak of eternal life as life that is somehow in Christ.

That being so, however salvation is understood and however these texts are interpreted, anyone who believes that Christ was the Son of God will call on him for help in danger or deep distress and for guidance when faced with a serious practical choice. Not only that. Belief that the personal source of the natural order, with complete control over our destiny, is accessible through the historical Christ is hardly consistent with giving no thought to him in ordinary daily life, or with indifference to Christian practices.

Including evangelisation: believers will want their friends to be saved too, and their children to be educated as practising Christians. This too shows that belief in Christ's divinity is inseparable from charity and it too may lead to conflict between Christians and larger societies in which they live. To hold to faith in Christ in the face of human cruelty or natural disaster may require a fortitude that transcends what is natural. Mere historical judgement that Christ really said and did the things reported in the Gospels is unlikely to be enough.

'Faith', 'hope' and 'charity' are words that belong to the vocabulary of English, but they are not understood in exactly the same way even by all English speakers. Overlooking such divergences in linguistic usage may have hardened divisions between Catholics and Protestants in the sixteenth century. Besides recognising the elusiveness of the meanings people attach to psychological words, we should recognise that the mental phenomena to which speakers refer are not really discrete from one another in the same way as bodily parts. Mental life is something continuous, without internal boundaries. Our notions of intellect and will or desire are schemata received from ancient Greece that we impose on human life for the purpose of understanding and influencing it; and the notions of faith, hope and charity are further schemata fitted on by theologians as life rises above what is natural. All human behaviour has, we might say, both a cognitive and an appetitive aspect: it expresses knowledge, belief, awareness of the agent's surroundings, and also character, desire, aversion. All action that depends upon God's gratuitous assistance, on what theologians call God's 'grace', has the same two aspects. It is steadfast and persevering, it seeks the good of others, and it is rational and conscious, an exercise of thought. Although Christians consider faith, hope and charity as all being gifts of God, not qualities we can acquire naturally, they need not suppose that they are three separate gifts, like socks, gloves and a woolly muffler. Insofar as Christian life is steadfast and persevering, it is an exercise of hope; insofar as it seeks the good of others, it is an exercise of charity; and insofar as it is rational and conscious, it is an exercise of faith.

6
NATURAL SCIENCE AND CREATION

That God created Heaven and Earth is a belief shared by Jews, Christians and Muslims. In the nineteenth century the idea gained ground (especially among people who had had Christianity thrust down their throats when young) that it is a piece of primitive natural science that modern science has discredited. If that is right, any practical principles based on belief in God are irrational, and should have no place in a society's culture. Believers reply that there is no conflict between their belief and science. To pronounce on this issue, we must not only grasp the character of the Christian belief but also recognise how the notion of science has developed.

Today we contrast what is natural with what is supernatural. Before the advent of Christianity there was no conception of the supernatural. The ancient Greeks considered their gods just as much part of nature as human beings, animals, plants, the heavenly bodies and substances like water and gold. Aristotle could speak of theology as a branch of zoology like ichthyology (*De Anima*, 1, 402.b7) – indeed as comprising astronomy (*Metaphysics*, E, 1026.a15-32, *Nicomachean Ethics*, 6, 1141.b1-2). The Olympian gods were immortal, but Homer had a natural explanation of that: they had a special diet of nectar and ambrosia (*Iliad*, 5.342), and in any case they were no more immortal than the stars. Magic was not thought supernatural. Like Evans-Pritchard's Azande (*Witchcraft, Oracles and Magic among the Azande* [1937], pp. 81-83), the Greeks thought it perfectly natural, though rare and lending itself to faking. If they contrasted nature with anything, it was with art and skill. Trees are natural, houses artificial; and, as I said in Chapter 2, the Greeks contrasted nature, as what is the same everywhere, with custom, which is different in different societies.

The fourth-century philosophers Plato and Aristotle established our modern conception of an academic discipline, and set up institutions for tertiary education, the Academy and the Lyceum, from which all subsequent universities are descended. They distinguished the study of nature in the narrow sense, nature as contrasted with technology, from mathematics, which, like logic, is an art, from the discipline we call 'philosophy' and from political theory. Earlier thinkers had used the notion of nature but had not tried to analyse it. Aristotle offers an analysis in his *Physics*, books one and two. Nature, he says, is whatever it is *within* things that accounts for their changing, and he claims that this notion covers two different things, that there are two different kinds of internal source of change. The components of a thing and the material from which it arises, what Aristotle calls its 'matter' [*hulê*], account for the changes it undergoes when acted upon by other things; they also account for how it moves when nothing else is acting upon it, they account, that is, for what we call 'attractive' and 'repulsive' force. Insofar, however, as a thing moves, or as changes occur in it, for the purpose of benefiting the thing itself, its behaviour has a different kind of internal source. What is benefited is not the thing's matter but what its matter constitutes. This, see pp. 102-3 below, is what Aristotle calls its 'form'. Changes brought about in a thing by a craftsman do not fall into this category, because they are caused by the craftsman's action upon the thing, and they benefit not the thing but the craftsman. Intentional movements, however, including the craftsman's, do have this second kind of internal source. Aristotle's concept of nature, then, covers everything we consider natural, everything natural rather than supernatural; but it embraces both what is natural rather than artificial and also human artifice or skill.

Aristotle's ordering of academic disciplines has survived fairly well to this day, and physics, chemistry and biology are pursued along with mathematics, philosophy and other disciplines. By 'natural science', however, we have come to understand, primarily, the 'hard' sciences, physics, chemistry and biology and, secondly, any science specialty within those three like astronomy, neurology and zoology.

That is because we have come to identify natural science with the study of the first of Aristotle's sources of change. The distinction between the two kinds of explanatory factor is derived from the distinction between

6. Natural Science and Creation

two kinds of explanation which go back beyond philosophy to the earliest imaginable rational life. People have always had the idea of bringing about a change in something by acting upon it. You can make a piece of flint into a knife by chipping bits off, a lump of clay into a pot by pressing it with your hands and baking it, grapes into wine by crushing them, wool into clothes by carding and weaving it. In this way of thinking we distinguish a causal agent, the craftsman, causal action over time, periods of chipping, pressing, crushing, weaving, and a desired effect reached *in* a period or *at the end of* a period: a knife, a pot, wine, clothes or the coming into being of these things. The causal action necessitates the effect, or rather *is the necessitating of it by the agent*. People have also, however, always thought that human beings and many animals do things, or refrain from doing things, for reasons and purposes. They have distinguished purposive behaviour, which can be explained in this way, terms of benefit and beneficiary, from movements and changes that can be accounted for by Aristotle's first kind of internal source, a thing's matter.

Explanation in terms of matter, of course, is characteristic of the 'hard' sciences, and is the basis of our present conception of natural science. Natural science as we now conceive it begins with noticing that natural objects that are not craftsmen also act causally upon things and thereby cause effects. People struck by effects such as the growth and ripening of fruit and the melting of ice into water ask what agent caused these effects and by what action. At a later stage they may notice movements or changes which are not obviously caused by agents acting causally, and try to explain them. They may think there are unseen causal agents acting on them, or, alternatively, that the things which move or change are alive like themselves and animals familiar to them, and that their behaviour needs to be explained in terms of purpose. Still later they may recognise that some movements and some resistance to causal action can be explained only by certain forces or tendencies internal to the things in question.

Material objects resist being pulled apart, and also resist being compressed together. If they didn't resist compression, the whole could be crushed into an infinitesimal volume; if they didn't resist being pulled apart, everything would dissolve into infinitesimal grains of dust. Ancient atomists postulated little moving bodies which could not be compressed or pulled apart by any force whatever, and which had shapes that made them engage together like pieces of jigsaw. This merely transferred the problems from material objects that are accessible to the senses to material bodies that are not. What stops the atoms from being divided or compressed? Rom Harré in *The Principles of Scientific Thinking* reminds us that in 1763 R.J. Boscovich pointed out in *A Theory of Natural Philosophy* that, if the little bodies are absolutely incompressible, motion cannot be transmitted from one to another by impact. European philosophers thought they could because they were familiar with the game billiards. In billiards the balls transmit motion to one another, and to the philosophical observer it appears that the balls are incompressible; the observer imagines they are perfectly hard. In fact, they are elastic, and (as Harré goes on to argue) on any view it is necessary to suppose two fundamental natural forces, an attractive force that resists pulling apart, and a repulsive force that resists pushing together. These fundamental forces act in bodies continuously, independently of any causal action upon the bodies, and explain what is otherwise mysterious, the motion of bodies large or small. Attractive force brings things together until it is balanced by repulsive force, repulsive force drives them apart until it is balanced by attractive force. Mathematics enables us to quantify motion and calculate the directions in which it takes place, but motion and change themselves must be explained not by the mathematical properties of bodies or particles but by these forces. All explanations in terms of these fundamental forces or in terms of causal action upon bodies may be classified as physical and as causal. Conversely, a physical or causal explanation must be of this kind, and physical science is limited to it. We think of biology as a kind of natural science, and many biologists hope that eventually all biological phenomena will prove to be explainable physically.

It should, perhaps, be noticed that natural science has always been under pressure from philosophy. A string of philosophers from the fifth century BC to the twentieth century of our own era argued that the world open to empirical investigation is an illusion: a discouraging message to empirical investigators. More serious, the fact that mathematics, like logic, is deductive, and mathematical claims can be proved true or false deductively has led philosophers to hope that physical science might ultimately be reduced to mathematics. Plato flirts with this idea in the *Timaeus*, endowing his fundamental particles only with shape. They are tetrahedra, hexahedra and so on, just, apparently, of empty space (*khôra*). Descartes in his *Discourse on the Method of Correctly Conducting One's Reason and Seeking Truth in the Sciences* (Part 2) confesses: 'Those long chains of very simple and easy reasonings which geometers are accustomed to use to arrive at their most difficult demonstrations had led me to imagine that all the things which can fall under the knowledge of men are interconnected in the same fashion.'

6. Natural Science and Creation

Non-philosophers may be less optimistic, though in economic and political quandaries we are all urged to take seriously only considerations that can be quantified and therefore subjected to mathematical treatment. There is no notion, however, in mathematics, of force, and philosophers since the seventeenth century have held that the whole notion of causing is empty and should be replaced by that of regular temporal succession. Hume in *A Treatise of Human Nature* (1.3.14) defines a cause as: 'An object precedent and contiguous to another, where all the objects resembling the former are placed in a like relation of priority and contiguity to those objects resembling the latter.'

Given however, that we conceive science as an enquiry into causes and take our conception of causation from artistry, the question whether the doctrine of creation is primitive natural science becomes the question whether it causal. Is it the belief that God is the source of the natural order as a causal agent?

The Bible begins with the words, 'In the beginning God *made* [in the Septuagint, *epoiêsen*] Heaven and Earth', and early Christian writers do speak of God as the divine Demiurge or Craftsman. The word is used by Plato in the *Timaeus*, and the idea of God as a craftsman appears in the Old Testament, in, for instance, Job 38: 1-10; Proverbs 8: 24-30. Nevertheless there are strong objections to conceiving God's relation to the natural order on the model of a craftsman's to a work of art or, in general, to regarding God as a causal agent.

Causal explanation applies within the natural order. In the natural order nothing arises out of nothing. What comes into being naturally does so, at the end of a period of causal action, out of what is already there. Anything so explained is within the natural order. The whole natural order, in which things come into being out of other things and are changed, cannot itself be brought into being by causal action.

Early theologians asked not whether God stood to the natural order as a causal agent but whether the universe had always existed. The Greeks were inclined to think it had never *come* into existence but had always been there. It had existed, apparently, for a very long time; there was no empirical indication that it had existed only for a finite time; and they did not at first distinguish between a very long time and an infinite stretch of time. Aristotle (in *Physics*, 3, chapters 3-7) was the first person to analyse the concept of infinity. He said that an infinite series is one that cannot be 'gone through', and he argued plausibly that there cannot be something infinitely large or an infinite number of things actually existing at any time; but he also held that the universe had no beginning, which seems to imply that an infinite number of successive events has actually been gone through.

Christian, Muslim and medieval Jewish thinkers understood the Bible to declare that the universe had a beginning. They also understood Aristotle to deny this. It seems to have been a rule of the academic game in pre-Enlightenment days to try, so far as possible, to reconcile authorities who appeared to contradict each other. In this case, a simple solution was to hand. You could say that so far as human reason went, the universe might just as well have had no beginning as it could have existed only for a finite time; that it has in fact existed only for a finite time is for Jews, Christians and Muslims an article of faith.

This was the solution adopted at the end of the twelfth century by Maimonides. In his *Guide for the Perplexed* – the Perplexed (according to the Preface) being those whose studies in philosophy had brought them into conflict with theology – Maimonides argues (2.15) that Aristotle never supposed he was offering a rigorous proof that the universe has always existed; he was offering merely persuasive arguments. Maimonides denies that these arguments are refuted by the Islamic philosophers known as the Mutakallimun. He accepts the *Genesis* account on the authority of prophecy, and he also holds that there are arguments for a beginning of the universe which, without being decisive, are more persuasive than the arguments of Aristotle. Aquinas in the thirteenth century takes a very similar line. His short essay *On the Eternity of the Universe* begins: 'Granted that according to the Catholic faith the universe has not existed from all eternity but had a beginning for its duration, the question arises whether it could always have existed.' He argues that there is no way of proving that it couldn't. In the *Summa contra Gentiles* (1.15) he writes almost as if to argue that the universe must have had a beginning were unsporting, like shooting a sitting bird: 'The most efficacious way of proving that God exists is from the supposition that the universe is eternal. On this supposition the existence of God is not so manifest, whereas if the universe and motion had a beginning it is plain that some cause is required.'

Not all writers were equally eirenic. In the sixth century John Philoponus in Alexandria argued that Aristotle is simply inconsistent. His arguments were developed by the Muslim thinkers Maimonides criticises, notably, Al-Kindi (ca 801-873) and Al-Ghazali (1058-1111). Aquinas' contemporary Bonaventure in his *Commentary on the Sentences* of Peter the Lombard (1250-52, d. 1, p. 1, a. 1, q. 2) offers six arguments to prove that the universe must have had a beginning. There was, then, among faithful believers a genuine difference of opinion: some thought it could be proved deductively (not empirically) that the universe had a beginning, others than it could not. Richard Sorabji in *Time, Creation and the Continuum* supports Maimonides and Aquinas.

6. Natural Science and Creation

The arguments are technical in character and turn on what logicians call a difference of 'scope'. One side concedes, to put it crudely, that no finite number of years is the greatest for which the universe might have existed: whatever finite number you mention, the universe might (logically) have existed for more years than that. This side, however, denies that the universe might (logically) have existed for an *infinite* number of years; it couldn't have existed for a number of years greater than *every* finite number. The other side asserts that this is possible. Neither side was aware of the empirical considerations now used to argue that the universe actually started with a bang about thirteen billion years ago.

Although orthodox belief that God created the universe does not require adherence to either side, a couple of logical points may be worth making. First, it does not follow, if the universe has existed only for a finite time, that there was a time before it existed. There could have been time before the universe existed only if there could be time without change, time in which thing happens. Some philosophers say there could be, and there certainly could be if, as Newton said in his Scholium to the definitions in *Mathematical Principles of Natural Philosophy*, 'Absolute, true and mathematical time, of itself and from its own nature, flows equably without relation to anything external.'

If, however, (as I argued in *The Analytic Ambition*, Chapter 6) time is simply the actual going on of change, then (as Augustine observed, though not for this reason, in *Confessions*, 11.13), whether the universe has existed for a finite or an infinite time, it has existed for all the time there has been. There could not be a time before there was a universe, and hence we cannot say that *before* there was a universe the universe did not exist. (Nor is it correct to say that God existed before there was a universe.)

Second, it does not follow, if the universe has existed only for a finite time, that there was an instant at which it began. By an 'instant' here I mean something durationless, a temporal analogue of an unextended point in space. In an actual finite length like a yard of string for every point at which it might be divided there is a point nearer to the end; there is no first or last point in the length. Similarly, for every instant in a finite period of motion there is an earlier instant in the period; there is no first instant at which a body is in motion.

The belief of Jews, Christians and Muslims that God created the universe does not entail that the universe had a beginning; nor, if it did have a beginning, does it entail that there was a time before it existed, nor even that there was first instant in its existence.

Besides the very general word 'make' (*poiein, facere*), which was applied, as our word 'poetry' attests, to literary composition as well as to handicrafts, Christian theologians used words we translate in English by 'create': Greek *ktizein*, Latin *condere* and *creare*. *Ktizein* and *condere* are words also used for the founding of cities. Creation is sometimes defined as making something out of nothing. Aquinas accepts this form of words (*ST*, 1a, Q. 45, Art. 1); but no theologian says that there is something which is nothing, but upon which God acted and out of which God made the universe as a potter makes a pot out of clay. The claim that God created the universe is to be understood rather as a denial that there is or was anything out of which he made it. That is a denial, by implication, that he is the source of it as a causal agent acting upon something already there.

Genesis represents light as existing, the earth as producing plants, the sea fish and the land animals, in obedience to God's orders. It certainly does not suggest that this was a form of causal action, that God brought the universe into existence by making certain sounds. To think that today, we should have to suppose that there was already a natural order in which making those sounds would result in a Big Bang. Nor does Genesis suggest that light heard the order, while not yet in existence, and obeyed it in the way an intelligent being might obey an order to come into a room. The imperative mood is used to express what you want, and to express it as something good. The suggestion of Genesis is that God wanted things to happen, that he thought they would be good, and that they happened because he wanted them to happen; and Genesis tells us explicitly that God saw they *were* good. That is the kind of explanation correlated with Aristotle's second kind of internal source of change, which we give of intentional action and inaction. An intentional movement is made for a purpose; it is made because the person who makes it wants to make it; it is not a consequence of the person's wanting to make it but a fulfilment of the person's want; not an effect of a desire but a carrying out of a desire. Insofar as Genesis provides a model for understanding God's relation to the universe, it is that of our own relation to our intentional acting and refraining from action. Our legs go on moving when we walk, because we so desire, our hands move when we write or sew because we so desire, and natural processes generally go on because God so desires.

Spinoza tried to reduce this kind of explanation to causal. When we say a builder assembled materials because he wanted a shelter, we give his desire for a shelter as the cause of his building activity (*Ethics*, 4, Preface) Subsequent philosophers have mostly followed him: Donald Davidson, for example, taking desires as 'reasons', argues in 'Actions, Reasons and

Causes' that reasons are causes. The uses of the English conjunction 'because' in explanations like 'He went to the lake because he thought there were big trout in it' and 'He went to the lake because he wanted to catch a big trout' make it easy to assimilate both desires and beliefs to causes. However, they are hardly causal agents; if they are forms of causal action, what is acting upon what? Descartes suggested they are actions by the human soul on a little gland in the brain. When Princess Elizabeth of Bohemia (a niece of England's King Charles I) wrote asking him how something 'unextended and immaterial' like a mind could act on something material, even something as small and easily moved as a pineal gland, he replied that it was in the way he once mistakenly imagined gravitational attraction works; and, when that did not satisfy her, he advised her to stop using her intellect and engage in ordinary life and conversation. The correspondence can be read in *Descartes: Philosophical Writings* (pp. 274-80).

The problem disappears if we adopt Hume's definition of a cause (*A Treatise of Human Nature* 1. 3. 14), since it is indeed a regularity in nature that certain sensations which we see by introspection and classify as desires are attended by certain bodily movements. However, we must then give up the notion of causal necessitation, and Aristotle was right about causation in *Posterior Analytics* 2, chapter 12, when he said that causes and effects must be contemporaneous. Action for a period of time can necessitate an effect within the period or at the end of it, but nothing after it. Philosophers under the influence of Hume have claimed that earlier periods of movement or action can cause later. J.L. Mackie in *The Cement of the Universe* (p. 156) says: 'The earlier phase of a self-maintaining process [such as the spinning of a top] surely brings about, or helps to bring about, the later phase. If the concept of cause and effect does not yet cover them, it should: we can recognise immanent as well as transeunt causation.' Wishful thinking. A period of spinning might bring about a change of shape in the spinning object, but how could it *bring about* another later period of spinning?

To explain someone's action by a desire is to explain it as the carrying out of a desire, and the relation of a desire to its carrying out is not causal, rather, the carrying out of a desire is its fulfilment. The claim in Genesis is that God is responsible for the natural order as we are responsible for our actions. The universe exists, and natural processes generally go on, because that is what God thinks best.

Two questions arise about this way of understanding the doctrine of creation. First, is it satisfactory as an interpretation – is it intelligible, I mean, and does it give believers the doctrine what they want? Secondly, how are we to decide if it is true? A third question, of course, is whether it is true, but, if my answer to the second is correct, this third question is not one for the philosopher of religion.

As to the first question, some believers might say that what they mean by 'creation' is the bringing into existence of the original materials out of which everything else is produced. If, as they believe, the universe had a beginning, then material must have come into being which did not arise out of anything that was there already, and surely to say that God created the universe is to say that he brought this primal material into being? Such believers still want to understand creation as causing. Bringing into existence is a causal process. I think, however, that underlying their protest is the idea that existing is a kind of precondition of doing or being anything. It is conceived as a kind of activity in which things engage 'like breathing only quieter' (as the philosopher J.L. Austin is reputed to have said), or a kind of inactive state like sleep. Questions about existence, generally, and about coming into existence belong to metaphysics, and it may help us to avoid confusion about creation to digress briefly into metaphysics.

Anything that is or might be found in the world around us can be thought of and spoken of in two ways, as something possible and as something actual. Swimming is something real. We can think of it as something actual if we say that there is a lot of swimming in the river this afternoon: many people swimming for long periods. We can also think of it as something possible: it is a possible form of movement and there are possible forms of swimming, breast stroke, crawl etc. The word 'snake' signifies something that does or might exist. Cicero speaks in *De Officiis* of a house that has actual snakes in all the bedrooms. We can say that a snake is a possible animal, an animal there can be, and that an adder, a python, a cobra, are possible snakes or kinds of snake. Animals, movements, and qualities are things that can be thought of as possible or as actual; but possibility and actuality themselves are not. There is a real way of thinking which is thinking of things as existing in actuality and, when we think of fundamental particles as interacting, we think of them as actually existing, but existing itself is not something that does or might exist. If God is truly responsible for all the basic physical interactions that take place in the universe, he is responsible for the actual existence of the universe and existence is not something further with which he has to endow it.

As we can think of things as possible and as actual, so we can explain them as possible and actual. A journey from London to York may be thought of as a two-hundred-mile journey or as a five-hour journey. A two-hundred-mile journey is a possible journey, one that can be made. A five-hour journey is an actual journey, a making of a journey from one place to another, and the five hours are hours of being in motion between the two places. Causal explanation applies to movements considered as possibilities. A movement or any other kind of event can be caused or prevented if it is considered as a possibility, but not if it is considered as an actuality. I can cause my car to move two hundred miles by pressing on the accelerator for five hours. I cannot cause it to be moving. My action on the accelerator is not causing it to be for those five hours in motion; at best it is for five hours preventing it from stopping or coming to rest. If, as I said earlier, time is the going on of change, there can be no causal explanation of a stretch of time. My pressing for five hours on the accelerator, however, can be explained as a carrying out of a desire, and, in general, a period of time, if it can be explained at all, can be explained in terms of a reason or purpose. This is a fact about thought and language, not about the real things, the people, cars, planets and so forth about which we think in these ways.

Given that we are responsible for our own purposive movements, can a theist hold that God is responsible in this way for the movements of things like stars and molecules, in the way in which we are responsible for our own intentional movements? These are the movements of our bodies, our limbs. If God is responsible in this way for physical movements generally, will it not follow that the universe is God's body? Isn't that pantheism? Surely the Judaeo-Christian God is outside the universe.

God is not present in the natural order as a part, but not outside it either. The 'penny' catechism asks: 'Where is God?' and gives the answer: 'Everywhere.' Similarly, if the question were asked: 'Where in your body are you?' the correct answer would be: 'Everywhere' – not, as some people might wish to say, 'In my brain'. I am in every part of my body that is alive with my life, though perhaps especially in those parts which are obedient to my wishes. I am more in my hands than my brain or my hair, and you are more likely to say, '*You* touched me', if my hand touches you, than if my hair does. However, I am not in my hand as a part of it, as blood is in it as a part, still less as something contained by it as a ripe plum might be.

The difference between our relation to our bodies and God's relation to the universe lies in the purposes for which we want our movements to go on and the purposes for which God wants physical processes generally to go on. I go to the shop to buy food I need as a living organism. If we were to say that natural processes go on to supply needs the universe has as a kind of organism, we should be giving a pantheistic answer, equating

God with the universe. The Judaeo-Christian answer, however, is not pantheistic. It is that physical processes go on in order that living things may come into being and flourish; and that God wants this not because he needs meat and vegetables, nor even because he needs a society in which he can practise the virtues of kindness and compassion. God wants it simply for the benefit of the living creatures that arise.

Belief in a personal creator does not require a theory of how creation is done, but only a theory of what it is for. Grasping the purpose of the whole physical world is not a different kind of understanding from grasping the purpose of a single artefact or action, but it involves taking a leap, and one that is initially blind.

When we think that some human movement is a carrying out of a person's will, we can imagine the source of that movement: it is someone like us, a person with limited capacities and acquired know-how. It is otherwise with a personal source for the whole course of nature. I am interpreting the doctrine of creation as the doctrine that every physical process throughout the universe that is now going on goes on, and every physical process that ever went on in the past went on, because that was and is God's desire. It is, I think, impossible to imagine a being that could be aware of every physical process in the universe in the way in which we are aware of our intentional movements. Our consciousness of our intentional movements is the result of having learnt how to cause effects we desire, something that takes place within the natural order. A creator could not *learn* what physical action will cause or prevent what; a creator would have to decide that. Furthermore, our knowledge of what is happening in the world independently of us comes to us through the senses. In a created world nothing happens independently of the creator; all the creator's knowledge is similar to our knowledge of what we are doing. According to my interpretation of the doctrine of creation, creation is a mystery to us partly because we cannot imagine a being with only that sort of knowledge.

It may be added that this applies to the creator's knowledge of what other purposive agents think and want. Our knowledge of this is derived from our perceptions of what they do, but philosophers often suppose we know what goes on in our own minds by some kind of direct intuition, and theologians may be inclined to think that God knows this by some similar though perhaps more accurate intuition. On my interpretation, God could have certain knowledge of what creatures think and want, not by some kind of intuition of their states of mind, but by knowledge of the physical processes involved in their purposive response to what they believe to be case. The strength with which we act is physical, our limbs are physical, and, if the universe is created, the creator is in them, and they continue to exist because that is the creator's desire. When we act intentionally, our limbs move as we desire, but they could not move as we desire if it were not the creator's desire that the physical processes in our muscles and nerves should go on. We may act against the creator's wishes, but in that case the creator must still want the physical processes to go on in order that there may be creatures with free will. This presence of God in intelligent creatures, and this interrelation between their responsibility for what they do and God's, is hard to grasp when put in abstract terms and impossible to imagine.

I have argued that belief in a personal God involves concern for all living creatures for God's sake. It is difficult to feel concern for them for the sake of so mysterious a being. Even if we find great beauty in the works of nature and revere them for that beauty, it is difficult to see it as a kind of reflection of so unimaginable a being. These difficulties can be mitigated, I think, by belief in Christ. The creeds attribute creation chiefly to God the Father. John 1:2-3, however, identifying Christ with the 'Word' or utterance of God, says, 'All things came into being through him, and nothing that came into being did so apart from him.' Similarly, Colossians 1:16: 'All things were created through and for him [*di' autoũ kai eis autón*].' It may become easier to see natural beauty as a reflection of a creator who can take on human nature. The suffering Christ can provide an 'image' (*eikôn*), however unexpected, 'of the unseen God' (Colossians 1.15).

To sum up this part of the discussion, there is no more to the actual temporal existence of the universe than the going on of natural processes, so whatever is responsible for the latter exhausts responsibility for the former. If there is *some* purpose for which natural processes go on, then it follows there is a personal creator – of what sort, whether pantheistic or Judaeo-Christian, depends on the purpose. If there is *no* purpose for which they go on, then the universe has no creator; it exists, it has existed for a finite time and its existence is inexplicable.

This brings us to the question: how can we decide whether there is a purpose or not?

I start with a negative point: it is no use asking scientists. That is because purpose falls outside the scope of science. Science is similar to skill. We can ask a cook, 'What must I do to what in order to produce white sauce?' but not, 'What must I do to what in order to produce white sauce on purpose?' There is nothing additional I have to do for my melting the butter, adding the flour etc., to be for the purpose of making white sauce. Philosophers in the past, Descartes, Locke and others, have imagined there *is* something additional: I must perform a 'volition', a non-physical act of will which turns my physical action on the butter into purposive action. 'What is an action?' asks Mill (*A System of Logic*, 1.1.3), and (working with Hume's definition of a cause) replies, 'Not one thing, but a series of two things; the state of mind called a volition, followed by an effect.' But these volitions are chimerical. A chimera is a biologically impossible mixture of different animals: a lion, a goat and a snake. Philosophers conceive their acts of will as just like pushing or heating except that they are non-physical. Such a concept is a logically impossible mixture of different ways of understanding, by causes and by purposes. What is causal is physical and vice versa.

Hence, while it is a question for the cook, whether some given action (say melting margarine) will suffice for making white sauce, it is not a culinary question whether some white sauce was made intentionally or inadvertently. Similarly, we can ask a scientist by what natural processes a rainbow is produced, or an organism of some particular species. No additional process has to take place for these processes to go on for a purpose, and hence it is not a scientific question whether they go on for a purpose or not. If they go on for no purpose, science tells us by what mindless interactions planets and plants and animals arise; if they go on because God so wishes, it tells us how God intentionally brings planets and plants and animals into being; but which of the two it is telling us, science cannot say. To put it another way, just as there is nothing special I must do for my white sauce to be made intentionally, so there is nothing special a creator has to do for natural processes to be a carrying out of his will. If God created the universe, then 'How did he do it?' is either not a genuine question at all, or precisely the question ordinary science answers. In the Middle Ages, and even quite recently, most people working in natural science were not atheists but committed believers; often working alone; perhaps it attracted them partly because they thought they were seeing how God made the world.

What is called 'intelligent design' theory does not deal with creation or with the source of the natural order, but only with the emergence of life within it. William A. Dembski, one of its leading proponents, states emphatically (*The Design Revolution*, p. 38): 'Creation is always about the source of being in the world. Intelligent design is about arrangements of pre-existing materials that point to a designing intelligence.' As the theory is highly controversial, however, its supporters and opponents exchanging charges of bigotry bordering upon intellectual dishonesty, it may be worthwhile to point out that the part played by the Intelligent Designer in it is still strictly causal. Neither Dembski nor Michael J. Behe, whose book *Darwin's Black Box* effectively introduced the theory, recognises any kind of explanation other than causal. 'When trying to explain anything,' says Dembski, 'we employ three broad modes of explanation, *necessity*, *chance* and *design*' (p. 87). Behe argues (p. 193) that the fundamental forces of nature together with natural selection cannot account for the species of animal and plant we see around us; they cannot account for wholes consisting of parts that perform complementary functions; and infers that these living organisms were 'designed by an intelligent agent', design, here, being understood as 'the purposeful arrangement of parts'. These writers offer no analysis of intelligence or purpose, but their model for an intelligent agent is a human craftsman or musician; God might 'interact with the universe' as a musician plays an instrument. They concede, though they dislike the phrase, that their Designer is a 'God of the gaps', and that the gap is causal: nature does not possess 'the causal powers necessary to produce living forms' (Dembski, p.146). How a non-material designer can act upon matter, of course, Behe and Dembski can no more tell us than Descartes could tell Elizabeth of Bohemia how a non-material mind can act upon the pineal gland. Dembski suggests (pp. 154-55) that the Designer might avoid violating conservation laws by taking advantage of indeterminacy at the quantum level, but 'the precise activity of a designing intelligence' at the points at which design is introduced 'will require further investigation *and may not be answerable*' (p. 179, my italics, cf. p. 157).

So much on whether the doctrine of creation can be either proved or refuted by scientific investigation. If natural science cannot settle the question whether it is true, how should we tackle it?

A model sometimes used is the *objet trouvé*. Archaeologists dig up things which might have been produced on purpose, and decide that some are indeed artefacts even though the supposed artificers are long dead and have left no records. They reach their decision by asking, 'Could these things arise without human intervention?' and 'How well adapted are they to human wants and needs?' Can we argue in the same way that the universe is created by God: pointing out that natural processes do enable living organisms to arise and thrive, and calculating that that this would be highly unlikely without divine intervention? Richard Swinburne took this line in *The Existence of God* (Chapter 8, especially pp. 144-45, and Chapter 14). Earlier versions of what is sometimes called the argument *ex gubernatione rerum* argue that the existence of any natural laws at all are evidence of design; see, Cicero, *De Natura Deorum* (2.95-104) and Aquinas, *Summa Theologiae* (1a, Q. 2, Art. 3). That the particular natural laws we have do favour life is argued by Paul Davies in *The Goldilocks Enigma: Why Is the Universe Just Right for Life?*.

There is an important difference between the archaeologist's dilemma and the question of the origin of the universe. Archaeologists have to choose between attributing what they find to human skill and attributing it to ordinary natural processes. The issue over creation is whether the natural processes themselves go on because God wants them to. It is not whether God interferes with them or harnesses them as craftsmen and gardeners harness and interfere with natural processes. We think it improbable that, say, a black-figured ceramic vase should come into being without human intervention because we have some grasp of the natural laws governing clay and pigmentation; but we cannot estimate the probability that the laws of physics should foster the emergence of life because we do not know the laws governing laws of physics. Indeed, it makes no sense to speak of such laws. The notion of physical probability can be applied only against an assumption of an existing natural order. Also, we know what skills human craftsmen have and the sort of tools they use; this gives us a basis for judging whether what we find in the excavated tomb was made on purpose. There can be no such knowledge applicable to judging whether what goes on generally in accordance with the laws of nature goes on for purpose. The notion of an ability, analogous to human skill, to shape the laws of nature, confuses creating with making.

Intelligent design theorists do not claim that the laws of nature are produced by intelligent design; rather, their Designer supplements the inadequacy of natural forces to produce life. Employing only causal notions, they think that showing something is not the work of natural causal agents is showing it was designed or intended by an intelligent agent. The distinction between the two is unimportant to archaeologists. They want to know whether the causal action that produced things they dig up was the action of human craftsmen such as potters and smiths, or the action of wind, rain and falling rocks. They reason: 'We don't know how this object was produced, but, since it has functional adaptation, it was probably the work of a potter manipulating clay.' They do not reason: 'This was clearly produced by a potter, and, since it has functional adaptation, the potter was probably acting intentionally.' They assume that craftsmen act intentionally, and refer anyone who questions this to philosophers. What the theist needs to show is not that the production of animals and plants was the work of a superhuman craftsman, but precisely that it was intentional. The arguments of intelligent design theorists, if successful, can show only that the complexity and functional adaptation of animals and plants must have been produced by causal agents other than those currently recognised by scientists. That is the price they pay for claiming to be scientific.

6. Natural Science and Creation

Better models, I suggest, than archaeology provides for considering whether the universe is created by God, are uncertainties about the intentions of ordinary human agents. Different kinds of statement need to be supported by different kinds of reason. Statements like 'There is no highest prime number' can be proved true only by deductive reasoning, and not, for instance, by observation or experiment. Science simply takes mathematical statements for granted. Statements like 'Water contains oxygen' or 'That man's death was caused by a stab' *can* be proved true by experiment and observation. Statements about purpose like 'Macbeth stabbed Duncan on purpose' cannot be established either by mathematical or by scientific methods. On the other hand, they are not questions about our feelings like 'Is Mozart's music pleasanter than Beethoven's?' or 'Which is more offensive, nudity or blasphemy?' They are questions of fact and we certainly think that they can be proved, since proving them is one of the chief aims of advocates in courts of law. In courts of law it is usually assumed that anything you do is done intentionally, and the burden of proof is on you to show that the action is *not* intentional – that it was done in ignorance, or by accident, or because of some physical abnormality, or something like that. That assumption is not available to the theist, since God is not a causal agent within the universe like Macbeth. In ordinary life however we sometimes wonder with *what* intention something is done. Do you consort with me because you enjoy my company, or just out of politeness or pity? If we are lovers, can I be sure you have told me the truth about your intentions, or is your purpose to see someone else without my knowing? The way in which we try to read the behaviour of those we love is comparable to the way in which, when we wonder the the universe is created by God, we view natural processes generally when we wonder if the universe is created by God. Believing it created is like trusting your beloved; thinking it is not, is like thinking you are not loved.

We ourselves are products of the natural order, and we may start by asking whether the universe is a good one to be in. Natural beauty would be evidence of this. Do we see it in clouds, in the stars, in lakes and rivers? And what of other living creatures? Only if we have some regard for them and wish them to flourish, can we usefully consider whether natural processes are well adapted to their flourishing. Are they likeable, or are most of them hateful or disgusting? That may seem a subjective question, but the best botanists and zoologists seem to care for the organisms they study. In a famous passage (*On the Parts of Animals*, 1.644b31-645a30) Aristotle speaks of the delight in studying even the smallest and simplest forms of life. J.-H. Fabre writes with real affection about the wasps and spiders in his wilderness (*Fabre's Book of Insects* [1936]), and Bernard Gooch about the adders in his garden: 'A warm hand is the key to an adder's heart' (*The Quiet World of Nature*, p. 176). People who profess themselves atheists or agnostic may nevertheless work to keep up populations of threatened species like ospreys and sperm whales, not for any benefit to themselves, not even the aesthetic pleasure of seeing the ospreys swoop and the whales spout. However, as I said in Chapter 5, belief in God has practical implications, and someone who does not care at all whether or not living things generally flourish and are happy will find it hard or impossible to believe that the world exists because God wants living creatures to thrive. That belief is inseparable from desire either that God's wish should be fulfilled or that it should be frustrated.

What intentions a person has is a question of fact, but our interpretations of people's behaviour are influenced by feelings. Anger, fear, gloom, elation, and sensations of pain and pleasure can make us misread people's behaviour. That is one of the arguments for trial by jury, since the feelings of the jurors, we hope, are either disengaged or cancel each other out. If we wish to reach the truth about other people, just as if we wish to have good judgement about the best way to act, we must cultivate good dispositions to react emotionally. This is not just a matter of reining in emotions like anger, fear and sexual desire, but of schooling oneself to attend to some things and ignore others. Lovers will be less prone to unreasonable suspicions if they form the habit of noticing each other's kind acts, and if they try to act affectionately and considerately themselves. It will be hard to form a reasonable judgement about the universe if you are an abject prey to the emotions that move you as an individual and as a member of society, and never notice how it is with others or act altruistically.

Emotional balance and habits of selective attention go together with each other and with general practical principles. A cynical or purely self-interested system of morality inclines us to overestimate the evil in other people and to see the world as godless. When the Melians mentioned God in their plea to the Athenians for mercy, the Athenians, according to Thucydides (*History of the Peloponnesian War*, 5.105), replied in words I quote again in Chapter 11: 'We do not fear the disfavour of Heaven, for we judge right and we do nothing beyond what men believe of the gods and wish for themselves. Of the gods we think, and of men we know, that by every necessity of nature they rule where they can.' It is a very short step from this attitude to not believing in the gods at all.

6. Natural Science and Creation

A final consideration. Pascal said that, if we wish to take out insurance against trouble after death by becoming believers, we can come to believe by going to church and using holy water. This strategy may seem grossly self-manipulative, but a good deal of traditional religious worship – the annual cycle of feasts, the Rogations, the Psalms and so forth – is either based on the changing seasons or relates in other ways to the order of nature. People who do not take part in any of this will find it harder to judge that the natural order has a purpose.

We are unwilling to accept that a question can be one of fact, yet hard to settle decisively. That inclines us to say that, since it cannot be proved either that the universe is created by God or that it is not, the question is one not of fact but of feeling. However, when we think of proof, we have in mind deductive proofs of theorems in mathematics and the successes of science since the seventeenth century. Hypnotised by these disciplines we forget that most people spend most of their time thinking not about transfinite numbers or quantum mechanics but about human behaviour. The intentions and purposes of people around us are matters of fact, and judgements about them have their own standards of rationality, which our legal system tries to formulate and enforce. So has religious belief. The universe, we might say, is on trial, and we all make up the jury. In an English trial by jury, the verdict is given by the jury, not the judge, and, although the judge may have a firm opinion upon the prisoner's guilt or innocence, a judge is limited to giving the jury directions about rationality: telling them what they should and should not take into consideration, and warning them against being unduly influenced by emotion. The question whether the universe is created by God is a question for a jury, and the philosophical standpoint is that of judge, not juror.

That the natural order is created by a personal God is one of the two theoretical doctrines fundamental to Christianity. The other is that Jesus of Nazareth was the Son of God and the saviour of mankind. I said in Chapter 5 that it is less clear what this second doctrine amounts to and what it is to believe it. In the next chapter I shall consider salvation and theological approaches to it – what is called 'soteriology'.

7
Atomism and Holism in Soteriology

The doctrine that Jesus of Nazareth was the Son of God developed over several centuries. By the end of the fourth century it was agreed that he came 'out of the being' (*ex ousias*) of the Creator 'before all ages' (*pro pantôn tôn aiônôn*), that the natural order came into being through him, and that for us human beings and for our salvation, he became incarnate from the Virgin Mary and human (*sarkôtheis, enanthrôpêsas*) – in short that the son of Mary was God incarnate. No Christians, as I said in Chapter 5, understood this as a piece of genealogy like the doctrine that Dionysus was the son of Zeus and Semele. From its first statement in John 1:10-14 the becoming incarnate is coupled with the purpose of benefiting human beings. While all Christians, however, agree that it has this purpose, there are two different ways of understanding it, one holistic and the other atomistic. Probably most Christians today take an atomistic view; but the first Christians were Jews and probably inherited a more holistic view, which, I shall argue, has advantages if it is true that we are essentially social beings.

Atomists are people who hold that explanation should proceed from the small to the large, that the properties and behaviour of wholes are determined by those of the parts of which they consist or into which they can be divided. In itself this is a purely philosophical idea, belonging to metaphysics or the theory of knowledge. It may be applied in various fields. Physics deals with bodies interacting in space and time, and physical atomists hold that all the behaviour of every such object can be explained by the laws governing the behaviour of the entities – atoms, quarks or whatnot – of which, ultimately, it consists. The social sciences deal with human societies, and a social atomist holds, in the words of Mill quoted earlier (*A System of Logic*), that, 'men in a state of society are still men; their actions and passions are obedient to the laws of individual human nature. . . . The effect produced, in social phenomena, by any complex set of circumstances amounts precisely to the sum of the effects of the circumstances taken singly.'

Logic deals with things that are true or false – usually called 'propositions'. Logical atomists hold that there are simple propositions, each of which is true or false of itself, independently of any other, and that, if there is any proposition that is true or false but not simple, its truth or falsehood is determined by the truth or falsehood of simple propositions of which it is a construct. Russell not only accepted logical atomism but, in his *Principles of Mathematics* (s. 447), applied atomism to metaphysics by taking an atomistic view of time and change. He advocated regarding time as a continuous series of instants, temporal items of no duration analogous to extensionless points in space; and he declared that 'motion consists *merely* [his italics] in the occupation of different places at different times'. My flying non-stop from London to New York consists in the presence of a humanoid figure at infinitely many intervening points at successive instants, each presence being logically independent of every other. This way of viewing change, of course, leaves no room for the notions of a causal agent and causal action. The successive instantaneous states of affairs form a continuous sequence but are not causally related.

Christian theology deals with a being that is not part of nature but the source of it. That may seem to commit theologians to atomism, since they say that the natural order has a single and indivisible source. They sometimes represent the Trinity as a society united by love, but developing this idea atomistically leads straight to tritheism. There are at least two further ways, however, in which theologians can be atomistic. First, they can accept Mill's social atomism. They can say that the behaviour of men in society is determined by the laws of individual human nature, and that God's relationship with mankind is the sum of his relationships with individual men. Second, they can accept Russell's atomistic view of time. They can regard history, including the history of salvation, as an aggregate of logically independent episodes. They can treat the Incarnation, the Last Supper, the Crucifixion, the Resurrection, the Ascension, and Pentecost as successive episodes, each making its own contribution to salvation, and salvation as the sum of these contributions. No doubt the later events could not have occurred without the earlier; Christ could not have risen from the dead if he had not died, or died, if he had not been conceived. We can however try to treat each episode as complete and intelligible independently of its sequel, as we think of ordinary events in our own lives like travelling by air from Athens to London, from London to New York, and from New York to Los Angeles.

In Chapter 2 I criticised the idea that the behaviour of men in society can be explained in terms of the laws of individual human nature. I argued that human intelligence depends upon language, and language upon society: the concepts we use in understanding mathematical proofs, the causes of natural phenomena and the reasons for people's actions seem to presuppose an ability to put things into words. A human child cannot develop distinctively human capacities except among people who have customs, recognised ways of doing things, which are not universal throughout the species but vary from society to society. In Chapter 3 I argued further that we have living in society, conforming to social customs and benefiting other individuals as ends in themselves. These desires can be discerned even in species we think less intelligent than our own. We pursue our own interests and we espouse the interests of others in the framework of our customs. Not only do those customs shape our ideals; without the support of our fellows and shared belief about how it is good to act we should lack motivation: Neither in unselfishness nor in selfishness can we go it alone.

One consequence is that if God is to have any communication with human beings he must deal with a society. The same is true even of a human anthropologist. If you discover an unknown society, to communicate with its members you must not only learn their customs, including their linguistic customs or language, you must also convey to them some of your own custom-shaped ways of thinking. In the natural order species arise only over long periods of time. The human species exists in diverse societies with customs that have developed over time. For God to communicate with human beings a species must arise not only with the organs necessary for speech, but with a society in it that has suitable customs and concepts.

The Old Testament can be read as describing this: God takes a vine from Egypt and domesticates it. Psalm 80:8-9 tells us this; Isaiah 5:1-2 develops the idea; Ezekiel also uses the images of cultivation and a vine, (17:3-10, 22-24 and 19:10-14). In the last four books of the Pentateuch God gives a nation laws and customs. The Jews by the age of Augustus were not only monotheists, they had a theocratic state, ruled by priests, and their moral ideals and their customs with regard to slaves, women and the poor compared well with those of gentile societies. It is hard to imagine a Greek or Roman either teaching what Christ taught or finding in Athens or Rome many followers like Peter and Paul except among the resident Jews. Christians like to think that God may reveal things to us as individuals, and accept that some individuals have had mystical experiences, but a whole culture can be revealed only to a society, and such deeply mysterious doctrines as the Trinity and the Incarnation can be revealed only to a society with a culture ready for them.

The Jews did not form the only society that existed in Antiquity. Besides the Greeks and the Romans, there were the Persians, the Chinese and other civilised societies, compared with which we might think the Jews feeble and insignificant. It might also seem arbitrary for God to single out one nation from many for special favour. However, perhaps the weakness of the Jews was an advantage. A larger and more powerful society might not have wanted a Messiah, and the message of such a person might more easily have been smothered in political and economic concerns. The Jewish diaspora constituted a ready-made means of propagating an apolitical divine society. If God singled out the Jews and gave them a moral code in order to prepare a society for a divine incarnation, that choice would be consistent with giving other societies customs that would contribute to a globalised society in due course. It is easy to see Greek poetry and philosophy and the *Pax Romana* as such contributions; contributions from societies further east have still, perhaps, to be made or recognised in the West.

A second consequence is that we cannot separate our need for God from our nature as social beings. We are plainly imperfect and have difficulty in behaving well. Theologians, however, have been inclined to see our imperfections as part of our inheritance as individual organisms, coming to us from our parents like skin pigmentation, height or mental capacity. The *Catechism of the Catholic Church* (a document issued in 1992 under Pope John Paul II with much the same authority and the same intentions as the *Syllabus of Errors* issued in 1864 under Pius IX) says our sinful nature is 'transmitted by propagation' from our first parents (paras 404, 419). That is inconsistent with what we know of genetics. Sinfulness is supposed to have been a characteristic acquired by our first parents and acquired characteristics cannot be transmitted by propagation. The doctrine of original sin is also inconsistent with evolutionary biology, according to which species evolve out of early species by some continuous process, so that a species does not have first members. Every human being is the child of human parents, but we are directly descended from creatures of a different species, with whom we could not interbreed. Not only does evolutionary theory rule out first parents, it makes it incredible that our remoter ancestors should have had the intellectual and moral perfection attributed to them by theologians like Aquinas (*ST*, 1a, Qs 94-95) have attributed to them. If our species started with two human adults without ancestors and without any pre-existing human society, they must, as Aquinas says, have had knowledge of everything human beings can be taught and every ordinary human virtue, otherwise they could not have survived and brought up a family. Genesis chapter three, however, represents Adam and Eve as dependent like animals upon nature to provide food and shelter, devoid of moral responsibility and extremely limited in knowledge of good and evil; the best they could do was to see that such knowledge was good. Far from falling, they had a long way to rise. I agree with Fitzpatrick that the chapter depicts the next step in God's programme after the creation of animals: the passage of our species to moral maturity.

Heredity by blood-descent is the wrong direction in which to look for an explanation of our moral imperfection. Our bodies, which really are the work of our genes, are, when healthy, perfectly fitted for good behaviour. However (as a number of theologians, since 1992, dissatisfied with Augustine's understanding of original sin have been pointing out) societies have cruel or unjust institutions like slavery, infanticide, killing of the old and sick and subordination of women, they have bad ideals such as military aggrandisement, power over others, limitless wealth, sexual conquest, high social status and celebrity, which lead to defective judgements in practical situations, and they tolerate poverty, unhappiness and brutality in a way that dulls conscience and sympathy. Bad aims and practices are transmitted not through propagation but through society; they are as unavoidable, however, and as severe a handicap as original sin is traditionally held to be.

We are not responsible for the practices and beliefs prevailing in the societies in which we are brought up, any more than for the deeds of our first parents, if first parents we have. Hence Christians are inclined to say that God judges us by how well we have lived up to the standards we have adopted. The decree *Lumen Gentium* of Vatican II says (s. 16):

> Those who, through no fault of their own, do not know the Gospel of Christ or his Church, but who nevertheless seek God with a sincere heart, and, moved by grace, try in their actions to do his will as they know it through the dictates of their conscience – those too may achieve eternal salvation.

7. Atomism and Holism in Soteriology

Our consciences, however, are largely shaped by our society, and the extent to which we can adopt principles different from those prevalent within it is limited. If a conscientious life according to our society's lights is sufficient for eternal salvation, what need was there for an incarnation?

Some theologians have believed that the human race itself is fundamentally corrupt, and a theological atomist might think that its salvation, if it can be saved at all, is the sum of the salvations of every member. This view of salvation does not fit well with the New Testament. The Jews of the first century, including Christ's own followers (Luke 24:21; Acts 1:6), looked forward to salvation as a society by political means: by getting rid of the Romans and a restoration of genuine Jewish kingship. The Idumaean Herods were kings, but hardly Jews; they were not the Davidic dynasty, and the Jews preferred rule by an hereditary priestly oligarchy. It is against the background of this hope that Christ's life is related by the Evangelists. In Matthew 1:21 Joseph is told that Mary's son is to be called Jesus ('Saviour') because 'he will save his people from their wrong-doings'. In Luke 1:32 Mary is told that her son is to have 'the throne of his father David'. With the idea of political independence may have gone some dream of world domination. In *The Religion of Jesus the Jew* (p. 123), Geza Vermes says: 'The recognition of the God of Israel by the Gentiles was expected to be accompanied by simultaneous submission to the Jews, and worship in the Temple of Jerusalem.' Vermes quotes Isaiah 49:23 and might have added Psalm 72:9-10 and Isaiah 54:2-3 and 60:1-12. Christ's temptation in the desert culminates with his rejection of world domination but his preaching starts with the message, 'The Kingdom of the Heavens is near' (Matthew 4:8-17), while in Luke 4:16-21 he begins his address at Nazareth with a quotation from Isaiah chapter 61, which is a prophecy addressed to the Jewish people about restoring ruined cities and making famous the race God has blessed.

Much of Christ's teaching (for example, Matthew chapter thirteen) concerns the 'Kingdom of Heaven' which can be nothing but a society. He accepts from Peter (Matthew 16:16-17) the title of Messiah, which refers to a society, and from Pilate (John 18:33-7) that of King. That it is a society that has been saved, not an aggregate of individuals, is taken for granted by Paul. Salvation is a fulfilment of the promises to Abraham (Galatians 3:16-18). Paul's letters are addressed either to communities, or, if to individuals (Timothy, Titus, Philemon), to them as people working in communities. There is no suggestion in them that anyone is saved as an isolated individual; on the contrary, people are saved not just as members of communities but, in some way, 'in Christ' (Galatians 2:20 and 3:28; Ephesians 2:6 and 4:12-13; Romans 12:5; 1 Corinthians 12:12.)

Just as the Old Testament may be read as showing how God brought into being a society with which he could communicate, so the New Testament may be read as showing, not how God set aside this carefully prepared society in order to communicate with individuals, but how he developed from it a supernatural society with himself, a society in which we are transformed not just as individuals but as social beings.

Jeremiah 31:29-34 may be thought to tell against such a reading:

> Look, the days are coming, Yahweh declares, when I shall make a new covenant with the House of Israel (and the House of Judah), but not like the covenant I made with their ancestors the day I took them by the hand to bring them out of Egypt. . . . No, this is the covenant I shall make with the House of Israel when those days have come, Yahweh declares. Within them I will plant my law, writing it on their hearts. Then I shall be their God and they will be my people. There will be no further need for everyone to teach neighbour or brother, saying 'Learn to know Yahweh!' No, they will all know me.

This is quoted twice in Hebrews (8:8-12 and 10:16-17) but the stress there is not on the content of the New Covenant but on its novelty (and the implied senility of the Old). My quotation from Jeremiah is taken from the 1985 edition of *The New Jerusalem Bible*, which comments: 'In vv. 31-34 Jr reaches its highest peak of spirituality. . . . The covenant is 'new' in three respects: 1. God's spontaneous forgiveness of sin; . . . 2. Individual responsibility and retribution; . . . 3. Interiorisation of religion.'

The commentators seem to suggest that in the New Testament salvation becomes an interior, not a public affair, something between each individual in his heart and God. I do not think such an interpretation fits with the whole chapter, which is addressed to the *Houses* of Israel and Judah, and concludes with an assurance that the whole race of Israel will last as long as the natural order.

This brings me to the second form of theological atomism I mentioned, treating salvation, to borrow words from Aristotle (*The Metaphysics*, N, 1090.b20), 'as episodic, like a bad tragedy'. The Incarnation is God's becoming incarnate in a single human being at the instant when the Virgin Mary conceived. The act that, in the words of the *Catechism of the Catholic Church* (para. 613), 'accomplishes the definitive redemption of man' is the offering of a single victim, Jesus, by a single priest, himself. The institution of the Eucharist is logically independent of it. It occurred before that act, and the discourse in John chapter 6 which seems to foreshadow the institution of the Eucharist, is set before it is clear that Christ will be condemned to death. The Resurrection is the resurrection of a single individual, though it will be followed, we hope, by the resurrections of many others. And (I quote again from the *Catechism of the Catholic Church*, s. 659) Christ's Ascension is the ascent of a single individual, 'the irreversible entry of his humanity into divine glory.'

To obtain a different view we may start with Christ's offering himself as a sacrificial victim. This was not a solitary act of suicide; he did not position himself on an altar and cut his own throat. Arrested by the official Jewish police, he had, according to the Gospels, a full trial before the Jewish supreme court and was found guilty. He then had a further trial before the Roman authorities and was executed by Roman soldiers. His own contribution to his death was that he went willingly. Israel being at that time hierarchical, the judges who condemned Christ were also the High Priests, and, although the charge on which he was found guilty was blasphemy, John 11:47-53 tells us that Caiaphas, speaking as High Priest, said that it was best for one man to die on behalf of the nation, since otherwise the Romans would destroy it. Christ's execution was therefore a sacrifice by the High Priest of the chosen Jewish nation, and a sacrifice, John himself says (11:52), 'not for that nation alone but to bring together into one the scattered children of God'. The Roman official who sentenced Christ was the actual governor of the province and the representative of the most comprehensive and civilised non-Jewish society the world had ever seen; and we are told that he condemned Christ not because he believed him guilty of insurrection, but because he judged that there was no other way of preventing a riot in which many other people would have been killed. For Pilate too, therefore, Christ's death was a kind of sacrifice. It could be said that, so far as was possible at the time, Christ was offered as a sacrifice not by himself alone but by the whole human race or its best representatives.

Neither Pilate nor Caiaphas acted in full knowledge. We have the advantage over them there, and Catholics at Mass participate consciously in the offering. The priest invites them to pray 'that my sacrifice and yours' should be acceptable to God, and, when they have done so, he describes it as one 'which I offer for them or which they offer'.

A sacrifice is not just the killing of a living thing or the destruction of a valuable object; it is an offering to a god, and it is successful only if the god receives it. The gods of Greece did not always accept what was offered, and there is a suggestion in Genesis chapter four that God accepted Abel's slaughtered animal but not Cain's vegetarian produce. The priest at Mass prays that the sacrifice should be taken up to the altar in Heaven, and at the same time that those who receive the body and blood of Christ should be 'filled with heavenly blessing and grace', 'gathered together by the Holy Spirit into one', 'one body and one spirit in Christ'. We think of being sacrificed as unpleasant for the person offered; but to be accepted by God is good for the person accepted. This was recognised by some non-monotheistic societies. In the Marquesas before the arrival of the Europeans only people of high status were thought to have a life after death. After the death of a chief, however, persons of low status (who might be kidnapped from a different tribe) were sometimes sacrificed to attend on the chief in the afterlife, and would thus share his immortality. William Golding in *The Scorpion God* makes fun of similar thinking among the ancient Egyptians. The celebrant's prayer at Mass is not only that the slain Christ should be accepted as a sacrifice by the Father; it is that we, having been made one in him, may be accepted as an offering with him. A traditional prayer attributed to Ambrose of Milan speaks of Christ as both victim and priest, *sacrificium et sacerdos*, and the congregation aspires to be the same.

On this view the Eucharistic rite is neither a repetition nor just an image of the redemptive sacrifice, but (by virtue of representing it) an extension of it; the sacrifice will not cease before the last Mass has been said.

Viewing the Crucifixion in this non-atomistic way may enrich our view of the Ascension and the Resurrection. The Eucharistic offering is taken up by God, 'carried' (*perferri*) up to Heaven, but it is only at the Ascension that Christ is 'taken up' (*aneilêphtheis*) into Heaven, so the sacrifice cannot be understood separately from that. If the Ascension is linked in this way with the act on Calvary, both may be linked with the Resurrection, since that is surely the beginning of God's reception of the victim. Since only the risen Christ was taken up at the Ascension, perhaps just as the offering is still being extended by additional worshippers, so it will not be completed until the last worshipper has made the ascent.

Christ's death, resurrection and ascent are here understood not as discrete incidents but as a whole, and one that is not complete with Christ's own Ascension, but still continues. Although we participate in this whole of our own free will, we do so as members of a society following liturgical rules. I have not, however, yet drawn on the idea that Christ's purpose was primarily to save a society rather than the individuals in it, and before looking at his life in the light of that idea, I must flesh it out and meet some difficulties in it.

If Christ wished to save a society, that can only have been the Jewish nation: there were no other existing societies available as candidates. But, it may be objected, if that was his aim, he failed. The Jews did not

7. Atomism and Holism in Soteriology

obtain political independence, far from it, and, although as a result of the teaching of Jesus and Mohammed, a great many non-Jews have indeed come to accept the Jewish God, it is not clear that this has greatly benefited the Jewish people. This objection, of course, is simplistic. Christ made it clear that he did not mean to restore the kingdom of Israel as a kingdom 'of this world'. What else, however, would constitute salvation for the Jewish nation? They already had a good set of laws. The laws might be fine-tuned and brought up to date. The Sermon on the Mount suggests some refinements. Christians pay lip-service to these, but it is not clear that they form a society which is a continuation of the first century Jewish society of which they were a part, and, with all their divisions, they are less of a unity than the Jews were then or are today.

An answer to the question 'In what did Christ take the salvation of the Jews to consist?' is to be found in the New Testament, but it is so surprising that it is hard to accept. Christ took the image of the vine, which was familiar as an image of the Jewish people, and applied it to himself. *He*, he said, was the vine, and other people were his branches, living in him with his life. Paul says the same. He speaks of himself and his correspondents as people living in Christ, with Christ's life, living, moving and having their being in him. The simplest interpretation of this is that the Jews are to be saved by being made into a single organism. In the Old Testament an ordinary human society, the wild vine or olive, is elevated into a divinely domesticated but still natural society. Christ transforms this domesticated society into a supernatural living organism, an organism living with God-given life.

It may be objected that Christ and his followers, whether before or after his death, though they may have formed a society, were not the Jewish people, and still less were they a living organism. As to the first point, they were Jews and certainly thought of themselves as part of the Jewish people, even after admitting Gentiles and waiving the requirement of circumcision. Salvation, Paul says, does not miss out the Jews, but comes to them first, and only afterwards to the Greeks or Gentiles (Romans 1:16). The first people to join Christ's followers in Jerusalem must have been Jews (Acts 2:4) and included a large number of priests (Acts 6:7); what proportion of the Jewish communities in cities like Corinth, Alexandria, Rome and Vienne accepted the teaching of Christ's followers we have no means of knowing.

Less intractable than how much continuity there was between the Jewish nation and the early Christian communities is the question whether Christians formed a living organism. They certainly did not form a natural living organism, and we may therefore be inclined to take it as metaphor to say Christians make up the body of Christ, or stand to him as the rest of a human body to the head. Such metaphors are often used of natural human societies. Talk of sharing in divine life may also be taken as metaphorical. If we had lived in the Castle at Eisenstadt, eating with the family, and listening to the music of Haydn, we might have said that we shared in the life of the Esterhazys, though we should not have formed a single organism with the princes, and it is in this figurative sense, we might say, that, if we get to Heaven, we shall share in God's life; for, of course, we cannot hope actually to become Gods. The fullness of divinity was in Christ (Colossians 2:10), but, despite 2 Peter 1:4 (a letter of doubtful authenticity), the rest of us cannot share in the divine nature, the *theia phusis*, in that literal way. The *Catechism of the Catholic Church* (paras 1997, 2000) says: '*Grace is a participation in the life of God* [the editors' italics]. It introduces us into the intimacy of Trinitarian life.' However, grace is defined as 'an habitual gift, a stable and supernatural gift that perfects the soul itself to enable it to live with God'. A kind of clothing, perhaps, that enables us to sit at the same table as the Trinity and listen to the music of the angels. Before we conclude, however, that we are members of Christ's body or live with his life only in this 'spiritual' sense, let us try considering whether the Incarnation can be understood as God's becoming incarnate in a society.

We may note, for a start, that incarnation in a society need not be inconsistent with incarnation in an individual. On the contrary, it is hard to make sense of the idea of becoming incarnate in a society except through becoming incarnate in at least one member of it. Incarnation is a matter of taking flesh. A human society, since it is not a material object at all, has no flesh apart from that of its members. The question is whether the Incarnation should be seen, not as something completed at the instant at which Mary conceived, but as something that started then.

Next, while we are taught that Christ was 'very God', *deum verum de deo vero*, it is not theologically accurate to say that *God* became incarnate in Mary's womb. It was the Second Person of the Trinity who became incarnate. The three Persons of the Trinity do not share in divinity in the way the three Triumvirs Anthony, Octavian and Lepidus shared in humanity. The Triumvirs were three men, but the Persons are not three Gods, each with the same nature. Rather there is a divine nature peculiar to each, these natures being in some way inseparable and complementary.

I touch here, of course, on the most baffling of Christian doctrines. Christians can take models from the natural order to help them to conceive the Trinity, but they deceive themselves if they imagine that any such analogue shows God as he is. Simple models that have been proposed are a flame passing from one torch to another, and the petals of a shamrock. Augustine looked for models in human psychology: a lover, a beloved and love, a mind, its knowledge and its love, or the three mental faculties of memory, understanding and will. In Chapter 8 of *The Physical, the Natural and the Supernatural*, I advocated using as a model the three elements in human beings that I distinguish here in Chapter 3. If, as Genesis tells us, we are made in the image of God, and if, as the 'penny' catechism used to say, our likeness to God is not in our bodies but in our souls, my suggestion is that we resemble God in being at once living individuals, social beings and altruists. The Persons of the Trinity can be matched with these parts of us. Thought of as unique, as the one solitary source of all, God is the Father; considered as one who speaks and who desires to associate with others, God is the Son, also called the Word or Speech (*logos*); considered as acting for the benefit of others, and as breathing life into them, God is the Spirit or Breath (*pneuma*). In us the solitary individual, the social being and the altruist are not three persons but one. That is because we act causally. As causal agents we are physical bodies, and the diverse rational agents have a single body; we are united by our bodies. The Judaeo-Christian God is not a physical body, however; his action is not causal; so while he is unique, the single source of all, he acts in three persons, as a being unique and self-sufficient, as an altruist who desires the good of others, and as a being who desires society.

In us conflicts can arise between what is good for us as individuals, what is good for us as social beings, and what is good for those for whom we care. There can be no such conflicts for God, since, as a solitary being, he needs nothing, and the living beings he acts to benefit are those he creates and those with whom he desires to associate. God cannot have society with inanimate creatures, or act to benefit them; but the natural order, so far as natural science can reconstruct it, is one in which living beings arise out of inanimate, and intelligent social beings out of living beings that are merely sentient. God's creative activity is extended in time; indeed, if time is the going on of natural change, it creates time or is time itself. However, we need not regard the activity atomistically, as complete at each instant, an infinite succession of creations. We can regard it holistically, as a single divine act, which so far as we temporal beings are concerned is not complete yet.

Against this way of understanding the Trinity, it might be objected that the Second Person is regularly spoken of as the Son of God, and the notion of a son seems quite different from that of a social being. The notion of a son is indeed partly biological, but the idea that God has a son in the biological sense is as alien to Jewish as to Muslim thought. In every society, however, the biological relationship is thought to carry rights and duties, even if different societies attach slightly different duties and rights to it. The notion of sonship is social as well as biological. When in the Gospels Christ speaks of himself as God's son, he is using the social notion; he speaks of himself as doing what God tells him. Moreover, the title 'Son of God' seems to be first applied not to an individual but to a society, the Jewish nation as a whole (Exodus 4:22), the society in which Christians believe the Second Person became incarnate.

There are at least two further ways in which Christians (prompted by John's Gospel) can think of Christ as God's Son. First, they believe themselves adopted as children of God. If it is through union with Christ that we are adopted, Christ himself must have that relation of sonship. Second, the Old Testament personifies the words God addresses to Abraham as a messenger (Genesis 22:11-18; cf. Genesis 16:7-12; 2 Samuel 14:17) and the beginning of John's Gospel treats God's speech (*logos*) as a person. The comparison may seem grossly indelicate, but speech issues from a speaker somewhat as semen from a begetter.

We as social beings are products of society and subject to it. God is not a product of society, but he creates beings with a social nature and, as a creative social being, he speaks with societies and gives them laws and customs that raise them towards his own level.

Ezekiel chapter seventeen uses horticultural images in a different way from the authors of Psalm 80 and Isaiah chapter five. It speaks of a cutting from a cedar that is planted and grows into a cedar tree which bears fruit and in which winged creatures come and rest, or perhaps grows not into a cedar but a fruitful vine. A cedar does not naturally bear fruit, let alone grow into a vine, so the chapter as it stands is puzzling, even if we interpret it to refer to Israel's experiences with Babylon and Egypt. Christ, however, may have had it in mind when he compares the Kingdom of Heaven to a mustard-seed, which is the smallest of seeds but grows into the largest of domesticated shrubs (*lakhanôn*), in the branches of which birds come to dwell (Matthew 13:31-32). Similarly, in Romans 11:16-24 Paul speaks of olive-grafting and compares the entry of non-Jews into Christianity to the grafting of wild olives onto the domesticated Jewish stock.

No doubt the Incarnation was a 'unique and altogether singular event' in human history (*Catechism of the Catholic Church*, para. 464). It does not follow that no other human being could ever become divine in a literal way. The scriptural images together illustrate the idea that God as a social being becomes incarnate initially in an inconspicuous member of the Jewish nation but grows into a large supernatural organism which is joined by people of other nations.

7. Atomism and Holism in Soteriology 91

How? How can other people join the organism, and how can they share its life? You can join a society by going through some formal procedure like filling in a form or applying to an official, if such a procedure exists, and you then share its life, as I said in Chapter 2, by living with regard to its rules. Baptism is a procedure for entering Christian society, and there are distinctively Christian moral rules. Moreover, our nature as social beings is shaped by our society. Christians, to adapt the words of Jeremiah, teach their neighbours and brothers to love Yahweh, and this might be compared to the way in which a vine's branches communicate its life to one another: the tip of a branch receives sap and life from the parts nearer the root.

This still, however, leaves it a figure of speech to say that Christians form a single organism. Christ himself in John 6:53-57 speaks in a cruder and literal way:

> If you do not eat the flesh of the son of man and drink his blood you do not have life in yourselves. Anyone who chews [*trogon*] my flesh and drinks my blood has eternal life, and I will raise him up on the last day. For my flesh is true bread and my blood is true drink. Anyone who chews my flesh and drinks my blood remains in me, and I in that person. As the living Father sent me, and I live through the Father, that person, too, who chews me will live through me.

We are told that his hearers disputed among themselves and asked, 'How can he give us his flesh to eat?' Catholic theologians take Christ to be referring here to the Eucharist, and all theologians might agree that individuals receiving Communion are given a helping of sanctifying grace: or, since 'grace' (*gratia, kharis*) can be used as a term of aesthetic praise, that their souls become more beautiful. That, however, is no answer to the question of how Christ gives us his flesh to eat. The traditional Catholic interpretation, which goes back at least to Aquinas, is that, when we consume the consecrated bread and wine, we eat the living flesh and drink the living blood of Christ in the literal way in which we eat the living flesh of a raw oyster, and might eat the living flesh and drink the living blood of a small living bird we had plucked. Christ is compared to the pelican, which is supposed to nourish its young with its own blood. That is a striking simile, but does not provide a model for sharing his life, since we do not share the lives of animals or plants we consume alive. In 'The Real Presence' I advocated a different interpretation. The consecrated offerings, when we receive them, are digested; they turn into living flesh and blood. My suggestion was that this flesh and blood is not just ours, living with our life, but Christ's, living with his life. If that is part, at least, of what is involved in Christ's presence in the Eucharist, then we quite literally become parts of a single organism, living in him with the life he has from the Father.

What is that life? That is a question which bears on the Christian belief in life after death, and I shall consider in Chapter 9. For the present, however, I am concerned with the Incarnation. If we put together Christ's words in John chapter six and in John chapter fifteen, the institution of the Eucharist will appear not separate from the Incarnation but a stage of it and as a means of extending it to people other than Christ himself.

Christians expect to receive Communion many times in their lives. Is each reception, then, a separate incarnation? We need not take such an atomistic view; instead we may say that incarnation, or 'divinisation' as it is sometimes called, is a gradual process. The botanical model of grafting, or the physiological model of a donated organ or a reattached limb that had been severed, helps us to conceive this. It takes time for the organ to grow into the body, for the graft to become part of the tree. If we do not try to match the episodes too atomistically, we might compare baptism to implanting a graft, and the Eucharist to the flow of sap. I suggest, at least, that as the Second Person becomes incarnate over time in an increasing number of individuals, so he becomes increasingly incarnate in a single individual over time: time in which the individual's aims and desires become closer to God's.

Would it be too temerarious to extend a certain graduality to Christ himself? When Mary agreed to conceive a national saviour who would be called the Son of God (Luke 1:31-38), what lived in her womb lived with divine life. However, it did not, when first conceived, have a brain, a nervous system or even flesh. A human being has at conception the potentiality (through nourishment from its mother) to develop these parts, not the parts themselves. Similarly, a newborn baby has only the potentiality to develop intelligent aims that are in harmony with God's; it cannot actually have any such aims. Life, human and, in Christ's case, divine, is present, but the body, the whole human being, has still some way to go. If we wish to think of God's incarnation in Christ as the beginning of an incarnation in a society, we might think of it as continuing into his maturity and throughout his mission. It is first fully manifest, at least, in his glorified body after the Resurrection. The glorified body, it seems from the Gospel accounts of the women at the tomb, the meeting on the road to Emmaus, and the meeting at the lake, was no longer fixed in the features of a single recognisable individual.

7. Atomism and Holism in Soteriology

Earlier I criticised the atomistic idea that salvation was complete at the instant at which a single priest, Christ, offered a single victim, himself, for everyone. I said that at Mass the whole congregation makes the offering and is included in the victim. If that is right, the Crucifixion in a way looks forward to future Eucharistic meals, as at the Last Supper Christ looks forward to the Crucifixion. Could incorporation into Christ, however, be understood independently of the Crucifixion?

In John chapter six Christ says that eating his flesh and drinking his blood is necessary for eternal life, without mentioning any sacrifice. As his hearers recognised, however, surely that required his death. The idea that sharing in a person's life can be accomplished through a meal might be intelligible in many societies. Nevertheless, the Hawaiians, for example, who wanted to acquire some of Captain Cook's powers by eating him, had to kill him first. Christ does not, in John chapter six, prophecy his crucifixion, and neither the Jewish nor the Roman authorities were under any necessity to bring it about. It was slightly paranoid to think that if Christ continued teaching the Romans would destroy Jerusalem, and, although the decision of Pilate to execute him could be defended on grounds of act utilitarianism, if we go by Cicero's *De Officiis*, 3, '*fiat justitia et ruant coeli*' was nearer to Roman orthodoxy.

The Crucifixion may be thought necessary for the Eucharist for two reasons. First, the meal to be shared required not only a death but an offering to God and an acceptance by him. Second, the life to be shared was a human life fully imbued with divinity, raised to a divine level. The peaceful life of a theologian or moral philosopher who dies in his sleep is hardly that. A divinised human life must be one able to endure the worst sufferings that can befall a sentient and intelligent organism; it must be capable of total self-sacrifice – a life a human being must lose to find.

I have argued for saying that God's purpose for us is as creatures with a social nature. Any reading of God's purposes must be conjectural; but that being remembered, we are free to speculate. The Old Testament presents God's relations with a society, the Jewish people or the descendants of Abraham, and uses two main models. One, which I have not discussed, is that of a Bridegroom, a person cherishing the whole society as a bridegroom cherishes a single woman. The other is that of a Gardener, who domesticates a wild plant. Both models require the society to be viewed as an individual organism. Both models appear in the New Testament, and there is symbolic significance in the fact that, when the Perfected Man first appears after his Resurrection, he is taken, according to John 20:14-15, for the Gardener (*kêpouros*). My suggestion is that the New Testament shows the cherished society transformed into a living organism that is supernatural, living with God's creative life. God effects this transformation by becoming incarnate in the society. A society cannot be made into a natural organism. If we try to give it the unity of an individual, then (as Aristotle observed, *The Politics*, 2, 1261a10-22) we destroy it. However, God enables members of a society to become parts of a supernatural organism by choosing freely to be incorporated into Christ. On this view the Incarnation and our Salvation are not discrete successive events but merge into one another in a continuous creative process that starts with time itself and is still going on.

8
THE CHRISTIAN SOUL

In contrast to Christian monotheism, which is shared, perhaps, only by Jews and Muslims; the idea that there is some sort of life after death is diffused through nearly all societies and cultures. We used to be told by anthropologists that it was ubiquitous, though according to Josephus, as well as the New Testament, it was rejected by some first-century Jews. Nevertheless, different societies have had different conceptions of post-mortem existence and the nature of the beings that enjoy it. Some societies talk about ghosts, revenants or phantoms. A ghost is a residue of a dead human being. In Homer's world there were ghosts. Hermes in the *Odyssey* (24.1-14) shepherds with a golden rod the residues of the dead Suitors, and they fly off to the land of dreams shrieking like bats. Homer calls them 'souls', but Homer does not distinguish soul and body in living human beings. The revenants of Darius and Clytemnestra brought onto the stage by Aeschylus are called *eidola*, insubstantial likenesses like the one fabricated by Apollo in the *Iliad* (5.449). Christianity does not rule out ghosts, but Christian belief in life after death is chiefly connected with the notion of a soul (*psukhê, anima, âme*) as distinct from a body. Human beings, it is said, have both. The human body is mortal and can be destroyed, whereas the human soul is immortal and indestructible.

Although superficially Christians are agreed about this, these words 'soul', *âme* and the rest provide an illustration of how the meaning of psychological terms is not fixed in the same way as the meaning of words for things to which we can point like horses, water and swimming. Different societies have different conceptions of the human soul, and so do different Christians. The ancient Greeks contrasted soul, *psukhê*, with mind, *nous*; every living thing, they said, had soul, but only intelligent beings had mind. The Romans used the word anima and *mens* or *animus* in a similar way. Our society has the words 'mind' and 'soul', but ties the notion of soul to immortality. Anyone who can think has a mind, but only those who believe there is something in them that is immortal claim to have souls. In the Septuagint version of Genesis 2:7 man is said to have come into being as a living *psukhê* (*eis psukhên zôsan*), where *psukhên* seems to mean 'animal'. The evangelists put the word *psukhê* into Christ's mouth in several places, but in most of them it means simply life, and in Luke 12:18-20, where Christ speaks of a rich man addressing his *psukhê* and telling it to eat, drink and enjoy itself, it perhaps stands for his animal life personified. Paul in his letters contrasts soul, *psukhê*, with spirit, *pneuma*, and assigns animal or bodily desires to the former and spiritual motivations to the latter.

What Christians believe about death depends on how they conceive the survivor. In fact, two quite different conceptions of the soul and its relation to the body have been held by orthodox Christians. In this chapter I try to explain how they differ; and in the chapter that follows I discuss the beliefs about post-mortem existence which go with these conceptions.

The Jews of the Hebrew Old Testament, were like Homer. They viewed a human being as a unity. They did not distinguish psychological states or activities from physical, nor did they form a conception of a non-bodily inhabitant of a body. Ezekiel 37:6 describes a vision in which God says to a heap of dry bones: 'I will make breath enter you, put sinews into you, cause flesh to grow on you and cover you with skin.' Ezekiel may have been thinking primarily of the revival of the Jewish nation, but the Maccabees probably imagined the resurrection of virtuous individuals like this, and Christian belief in an afterlife is continuous with that of the Maccabees. The creeds express it as a belief in 'the resurrection of the body'. Christ had a bodily resurrection and many Christians have probably hoped that God will revive our bones or ashes, reassembling the material particles of our bodies.

Reflection brings to light difficulties in that scenario. What if the particles have at different times formed the bodies of several different people? What about the interval between my dying in the odour of sanctity and the revival of my bones? Do I not exist at all in that interval? If I don't, how can the person who lives after my bones have been revived be identical with me and not just a look-alike? Isn't spatio-temporal continuity necessary for identity? These problems would not occur to a simple believer, and anyone with enough faith to be confident that Christ has saved us might trust Christ to get round them. However, theologians are not simple and some of them are shaky believers. One purpose for which the Church developed a theory of the soul was to defend belief in an afterlife against philosophical criticisms.

Most of the first Jewish followers of Christ probably had Greek as a second language, if not as their first, and many of them were probably acquainted with Greek thought. They would have had relatives in Egypt and other countries bordering the Mediterranean including Italy and southern France. The latest books of the Old Testament, Wisdom especially, show some knowledge Greek philosophy. Philo, whose life overlapped Christ's, was evidently well read in it, and so, no doubt, were many educated Jews in Egypt and Greece itself. For Jews and Christians, the philosophy of Plato had considerable attraction. Justin Martyr, the first surviving Christian philosopher, was steeped in Plato's thought. Augustine speaks of his debt to Plato in *Confessions*, 7.9 and 20. Besides, as I said, creating the concept of the human mind, Plato took it that an ordinary human being has both a soul and a body. By a human body he meant, as we often do, the whole of which head, torso and limbs are parts. By a soul, *psukhê*, he meant that, whatever it may turn out to be, by the presence of which a person thinks and acts intentionally. In one of his best-known dialogues, the *Phaedo*, he enquires what this is and how it is related to the body; and he offers two possible analogues for the relationship.

One is that the body stands to the soul as a lyre stands to the attunement of its strings, the way they are tuned or tightened onto its frame. It is because of this attunement that the lyre, when the musician acts upon it, produces music. If we use this model, we give a physicalist account of human beings. We say that it is solely by virtue of the physical structure of the human body and its parts that, when our sense-organs are stimulated, we have thoughts and feelings and act in the way we call 'intentional'. No Christian who understood what it implied would be happy to say that.

The other analogy Plato offers is that the soul stands to the body as a weaver stands to his clothes. The weaver lives in his clothes, repairs them when they wear out, and may even have made them out of wool or similar materials. If we use this model, we will say that our souls dwell within our bodies and sustain them by eating and drinking, but they alone are the entities that think and feel and actually do the things we do intentionally. Plato himself argues in favour of this model and against the first. It has the effect of identifying us with our souls, and Socrates does that explicitly at the end of the *Phaedo* (115b-c). 'How shall we bury you?' a friend asks. 'However you like,' Socrates replies with a laugh, 'if you can catch me and I don't escape you.' Philosophically minded Christians recognised a potential ally in Plato and tended to follow him in conceiving a human being as a combination of two different things, one living in the other. Comparatively few Christians are philosophically minded, but most Christians are probably unconscious Platonists about soul and body. In Sonnet 146 Shakespeare says:

> Poor soul, the centre of my sinful earth. . . .
> Why dost thou pine within, and suffer dearth,
> Painting thy outward walls so costly gay?
> Why so large cost, having so short a lease,
> Dost thou upon thy fading mansion spend?

Plato's conception of the soul certainly gives Christians an easy way of understanding life after death. At the beginning of the *Phaedo* (645c), Socrates says: 'Isn't this what it is to have died, for the body, released from the soul, to have come to be separate, and for the soul, released from the body, to exist separately all by itself?'

It appears to fit well with two other Christian beliefs. One is that we have free will and are morally responsible for our actions. John Stuart Mill analysed the concept of a human action as the concept of a physical event in the body caused by a non-bodily event, a volition or act of will (*A System of Logic*, 3.5). We may think that this analysis is obviously right; so, if there are free human actions, there must be non-bodily acts of will. These must be acts by a non-physical agent, a spiritual soul. Mill prefers to use the word 'mind', which, he says, is not difficult to define: 'mind is the mysterious something which feels and thinks'. However, he adds, 'On the inmost nature of the thinking principle, as well as on the inmost nature of matter, we are, and with our faculties must always remain, entirely in the dark.' Christians hope to provide a light.

Although the idea that we need souls to act freely is initially appealing, it runs into difficulties. First, as Elizabeth of Bohemia asked Descartes: how can the soul, unextended and non-material, move the body? If we say that the soul does not have to move the body, that the body merely moves as the soul wants it to move, why introduce souls at all? Why not say that our bodies move as we human beings want them to? In any case, merely saying that it is the soul that acts does not ensure our

8. The Christian Soul

freedom. Since the soul, we are supposing, is non-material, its actions cannot be determined by physical action upon it; but either they are then determined by something else, or else they must be completely random and as luck would have it. What we need for moral responsibility is not a non-material agent but a non-causal mode of determination. We need, in fact, a kind of non-causal, rational explanation, which explains action not as rendered inevitable by anything whether physical or non-physical, but precisely as freely chosen.

These difficulties are not offset by any ethical advantage. Christians who condemn homicide, enslaving people, abortion, mercy-killing and experiments with human embryos, often give it as a reason that all human beings have souls, and souls, moreover, made in the image of God. Genesis 1:26-27 says that God created not only men but women too in his own image, and the 'penny' catechism tells us our likeness to God is chiefly in our souls. Part of the purpose in mentioning this when discussing acts like killing and enslaving is to distinguish human beings from animals. It is all right to kill animals for food, to force them to work for us and to put them down when decrepit; why shouldn't we treat human beings in the same way? Because human beings have souls made in God's image and animals have not.

This is a poor line of argument. If death is not the end, killing people or forcing them to work during their life on earth is surely not so bad. They will have pie in the sky when they die. Christian beliefs about the soul have actually retarded condemnation of slavery and capital punishment. Besides, the conclusion of a piece of reasoning ought not to be more certain than the premises. Many people loudly proclaim we should treat others with respect and denounce murder and slavery while not accepting that we have souls made in the image of God. That premise is less certain than that murder and slavery are evil, and Christians can argue against abortion and euthanasia without using it. A Platonic conception of the soul may still seem necessary to defend the doctrine of life after death.

A Platonic conception of the soul was endorsed by two pre-Reformation General Councils. In 1215 the Fourth Lateran Council declared that God 'created all things, visible and invisible, spiritual and corporeal; by his omnipotent power at the beginning of time he created out of nothing both kinds of creature, spiritual and temporal, that is, angelic and mundane; and then human beings, as a kind of product of matter and spirit' (Denzinger-Schönmetzer [DS], 800). The Fifth Lateran Council three hundred years later was even more explicit, and declared that each person's thinking soul (*anima intellectiva*) is immortal and 'infused' (*infunditur*), that is to say *poured*, or in some other way inserted, into the person's body (DS, 1440). Plato thought that souls were not only immortal but had always existed and migrated from one body to another. Although a belief in the transmigration of souls has been accepted in many societies, Christians have never had any time for it and Pope Pius XII in his encyclical *Humani Generis* (1950) stated that souls are 'immediately created' by God. In the fourth century Vincentius Victor held this view that the soul is immediately created by God, and Augustine developed his theory that they come about by parental propagation in opposition to it. Augustine could not see how, if souls were immediately created by God, we could inherit a nature flawed by Adam's disobedience. The *Catechism of the Catholic Church*, however, brushes that problem aside and states both that souls are not produced by parents (para. 366) and that original sin is 'transmitted by propagation' (para. 404).

The awkwardness about original sin is not the only difficulty for Christians in Plato's dualistic account. It requires soul-body interaction; and Christians, in contrast to Socrates, have traditionally cared deeply about how they are buried and held that we should treat our bodies with respect. Although saying that we are really just our souls sounds an edifying line to take, in practice people who have taken it have often inferred that what their bodies do has no consequences for their true selves, and therefore shrugged off some very bad behaviour. Besides, if I am really my soul, and my soul can exist apart from my body, why am I imprisoned in one? Plato himself suggested I might have misbehaved in a previous existence. It might also be suggested that souls need bodily stimuli to trigger their thinking. Nevertheless, some reflective Christians have been led to seek a unitary conception of human beings, and a model for the soul, which is neither physicalist, like Plato's attunement, nor dualistic, like his weaver. They have thought that the right sort of account can be found in Aristotle.

Aristotle starts from the same place as Plato in taking the soul to be whatever it is in living things that differentiates them from inanimate things. For him, all living things including plants have souls. He however denies that that souls stand to bodies as its attunement stands to a lyre and also that souls generally are separable from bodies. The relationship, he says (*De Anima*, 2, chapter 1), is that of form to matter; a soul is the form of a natural body capable of having life: a body, that is, with the appropriate organic parts. Aquinas adopts this account in his *Summa Theologiae* (1a, Qs 75-76), and in 1312 the Council of Vienne declared: 'The substance of the rational or thinking soul is truly and of

8. The Christian Soul

itself the form of the human body, and anyone who says it is not is to be considered a heretic' (DS, 902). The primary purpose of this council was to please the King of France by condemning the Templars, but the Pope who summoned it was, like Aquinas, a Dominican, and he took the opportunity to condemn also the Franciscan Jean Pierre Olivi. The declaration on the soul was aimed against him and must have been intended to endorse the Aristotelian account as Aquinas understood it. This, then, is the second theory of the soul officially recognised by Western Christians: soul and body are related as form to matter.

Aristotle used 'form' (*eidos* or *morphê*) and 'matter' (*hulê*, literally 'wood') as technical terms. Unfortunately scholars are not agreed about how to interpret his distinction. Most of them would say that for Aristotle the form of, for example, a wooden cylinder such as a rolling pin is its cylindrical shape, the shape given it by the craftsman who made it, and the matter is the wood of which it is composed. Aristotle does sometimes use shape as an example of form. When, however, he says that the soul of a living thing is its form, he does not mean to identify the thing's soul with its shape, but with the properties that are essential to a living thing of that kind. These are its vital capacities, its abilities to feed itself, reproduce, and, depending on its species, to perceive, to move in pursuit and avoidance, and to think. What Aristotle, on this interpretation, identifies as the soul of a living thing is a set of capacities. Thus far, his conception of a soul is similar to Plato's conception of an attunement. The difference is that the attunement of a lyre can be identified with the physical properties of its strings, their tension and relation to the frame – these properties constitute its capacity to produce music; the vital capacities, in contrast, of a living thing cannot (Aristotle argues, *De Anima*, 1, 407b27-408b30) be identified with its physical properties or structure. Aristotle does go on, all scholars agree, to say (*De Anima*, 3, 430a10-25) that the thinking (*dianoêtikon*) part of the soul is separable. Here, however, (the scholars say) he has moved from Plato's attunement model to his weaver model. For an ability cannot exist from a thing that has it, whereas a weaver can exist apart from his clothes.

The upshot of this interpretation is awkward for Christians who want to defend the doctrine of the immortality of the soul by appeal to Aristotle. Aristotle, apparently, has passed without noticing it from one conception of the soul to a completely different one, and, if we stick to his idea that the soul of a living thing is the set of its vital capacities and the 'thinking part' of the human soul is our capacity to think, we cannot suppose that our souls might exist all by themselves unless we suppose a capacity can exist apart from anything that has it.

Aquinas and later Christians smooth over this awkwardness by using the word 'principle'. The soul, says Aquinas, is 'the first principle of life in living things', and the human intellect is the 'principle of intellectual operation' (*ST*, 1a, Q. 75, Art. 1; Q. 76, Art. 1). 'Principle' here is a translation of *principium*, which in turn is a translation of the Greek *arkhê*, which signifies any kind of source, whether it is a kind of attribute like knowledge of how to weave or a kind of subject like a weaver. There is a similar ambiguity with the Greek dative mood-inflexion which can be translated by the English prepositions 'with' or 'by': we see with or by the eye and with or by the sense of sight. Aquinas may not have felt it necessary to disambiguate the term because his problem was not that of a modern Christian. He had no trouble with the idea of a bodiless thinker because he took it, not only that God is such a being, but that God created a great number of beings that have intellectual powers but no bodies, namely angels. (That angels have very small winged bodies was not a pronouncement by any medieval philosopher but a joke by the poet Alexander Pope.) For Aquinas the problem was to show how a thinker capable of existing without a body could be the form of human being. We today are taught that everything that exists consists of subatomic particles, and everything that happens, happens in accordance with the laws of atomic physics. So, Christians today have the problem of explaining how a thinking being could exist that does not consist of subatomic particles.

Although most scholars today think that, if the human soul is an Aristotelian form, it must be a set of capacities, that is not the only interpretation of his form-matter distinction on offer. In *Metaphysics* H, 1043.a29-33, Aristotle asks: 'It is sometimes unclear whether a word signifies the composite substance or the form. For instance, is 'house' a word for the two together [*koinon*], a shelter composed of tiles and stones lying in certain spatial relations, or for the form, a shelter?' Here he speaks of form and matter as components not of a thing but of our conception of a thing, distinguished by words in a definition. We conceive a house as a shelter composed (unlike a tent) of solid materials with a certain physical structure. The physical structure here comes into our idea of the matter of a house while the form is specified in term of its purpose. I offered just now the example of a rolling pin. Aristotle might say that we conceive this as an instrument for rolling out pastry composed of wood in the shape of a cylinder. Here the shape enters into our idea of the matter of the rolling pin, and the form is again conceived in terms of a function. To give an analogous account of a human being, we could say that a human being is a living thing that nourishes itself, perceives, pursues and avoids things and thinks, which is composed of parts (head, trunk and limbs) physically related to one another in a certain way (and the parts themselves are organs composed in a certain way out of flesh, bone and nerves). Here again physical structure enters into our conception of the matter, and the form is conceived as a thing with certain functions. The relation of form to matter is not that of powers or other attributes to what has them, but that of a thing with certain non-physical powers to what constitutes it.

This interpretation is put forward by David Wiggins in his book *Identity and Spatio-Temporal Continuity*. It acquits Aristotle of not knowing what he is doing or requiring abilities to exist apart from anything that has them but it does not show that a thing that thinks can exist without a body. Aquinas argued, following Plato, that anything capable of intellectual operations must be immortal, but his arguments failed to satisfy other medieval thinkers; the Franciscans Scotus and Ockham held that the immortality of the soul cannot be proved and can be accepted only on faith. Aristotle had an argument based on his theory of knowledge. He held that perception depends on some part of the body being sensitive to the objects of perception. Sight, he said, depends on the eye receiving colours without itself becoming coloured material; the retina receives them in the way a screen receives the colours of a coloured photographic slide, not in the way a canvas receives coloured paint. Knowledge of what things are and understanding how they function is expressed in action, and in the action that expresses it, the forms of the things known are, so to speak, reflected in the behaviour of the intelligent agent. Whereas, however, we have to have bodily parts of a physical structure sensitive to colour and sound in order to see and hear, there is no particular kind of part we need for our behaviour to reflect our knowledge.

That may be true. Science fiction, at least, suggests that an alien might have the same knowledge of the world as we, but no part similar to our brains. Nevertheless, it does not follow from the fact that there is no particular material structure necessary for intelligent thought, that there could be an intelligent thinker not constituted by anything material at all. The position is similar to that over altruism. There is no particular structure we need to make the good of another living thing an objective to ourselves, no particular kind of body we need to act altruistically; but without a body we cannot act causally at all.

Someone might reason: thinking is not a physical process, so it is a spiritual process; and, if it is a spiritual process, there must be something spiritual engaged within it. That such reasoning is fallacious can be seen from the following parallel: inflation is not a physical process; so it is a spiritual process; and so there must be something spiritual, the economy or the retail-price index, engaged in it. Still, we easily fall into fallacious reasoning of this sort. Wittgenstein shows this in his *Philosophical Investigations*. We are led to it by describing deliberation and inference as processes, melancholy and elation as states: 'The first step is one that altogether escapes notice. We talk of processes and states and leave their nature undecided. Sometime perhaps we shall know more about them – we think' (*Philosophical Investigations* 1.308-10). Verbs like 'deliberate' and 'deduce' are grammatically similar to verbs for physical processes like 'weave' and 'swim', so we think they signify processes which are like physical processes except that they are invisible and go on in the mind. Our forms of speech lead us to create a shadow-world running parallel to the material world and modelled upon it. 'To have an opinion is a state. A state of what? Of the soul?' (*Philosophical Investigations* 1.573). 'Where our language suggests a body, and there is none, there, we should like to say, is a *spirit*' (*Philosophical Investigations* 1.36).

Moreover, Wittgenstein says in *Blue and Brown Books* (pp. 172 ff.), if, when we are deliberating or contemplating the blue of the sky, we look into ourselves and concentrate on what seems to be going on, we get a strange feeling, and we (or some philosophers) misconstrue this is an experience of a strange thing, a thing that belongs to an inner, non-physical world.

Should we then say that neither the Platonic theory of the soul adopted by the Lateran Councils nor the Aristotelian theory adopted at Vienne will meet the Christian's intellectual needs? The Lateran doctrine gives us something which, if it exists at all, is certainly immortal, but which is insufficiently related to the body; the Vienne doctrine gives us something which certainly exists and is admirably related to the body, but which is ill equipped for survival. Have we reached a dead end?

I think we do best to build on what we have that is certain; that is the Vienne soul; and to take the holistic view of creation I recommended for salvation in Chapter 7.

Some Christians have seen creation as something instantaneous and perfect at the first instant. The six days of Genesis have been thought of as a mere explanatory device: of course, God could and did produce everything we see in no time at all. The first human beings did not evolve from other animal species; all the species of living thing were created separately and just as they are now except for us. We were created morally perfect and immune to natural death. Then, within a matter of hours, our first ancestors committed a sin of disobedience, and their perfect nature was permanently changed biologically and corrupted morally.

They became liable to death and had to work to survive. God's beautiful plan was spoilt. From time to time God made revelations to the Jews, but these produced only limited and temporary ameliorations, and in the end it was necessary for Christ to enter the world to restore us to the state of Adam. At the instant of conception, or perhaps of 'first quickening', an immortal soul is created, and baptism suffices to equip it and the body into which it is infused for eternal happiness with God. This is a picture not of smooth development but of fits and starts.

A different picture is possible. We can believe that God created a world, the physical laws of which make it natural that material bodies should in time arise with the physical make-up necessary, first, for self-replication and self-nourishment, then, for pursuit and avoidance and other vital functions. New species of animal have arisen out of old without any clear breaks; we cannot say that there is any first member of the new species. Although some theologians feel that all the animals that have existed must be divided without remainder into those that have and those that did not have free will, this is a rather dubious application of mathematical concepts to biology. The rational fractions can be divided without remainder into those greater and those less than the square root of two, but it is not like that with living organisms and their vital capacities. They need not fall without remainder even into those with and those without sentience. I am sure that now I sometimes act freely, but there may have been no first time when I did, any more (as Plato suggests in *Theaetetus*, 207b-208b) than there must have been a moment when I first knew how to spell. Instead of saying that there is a single comprehensive capacity for thought, implanted by God in embryos, we may say that the only intelligent capacities we have are the arts and sciences and the good and bad characters we acquire through teaching and practice. Embryos (thanks to their genetic ancestry) develop a bodily structure (that is, a kind of brain) that makes it physically possible to acquire these capacities, but the capacities themselves we acquire as we grow up in families and larger societies. This goes with the view that they belong to us not just as individuals but as social beings.

Continuity may similarly characterise our spiritual development. The Old Testament prophets thought that the Jews, with their God-given set of laws and customs, stood to other nations as domesticated plants and animals to wild ones. Domestication is an extended process, and there is no discontinuity between wild plums or grapes and cultivated ones. Living in a society with good laws and customs civilises the way in which people pursue their interests as individuals. Divinisation through being grafted into Christ may be seen as a further supernatural development of a nature which has already been cultivated in society by good laws. We might expect it to come about in two mutually reinforcing ways: through extending disinterested love of other human beings to disinterested love of God, and through sharing in the life of a society headed by a divine Person.

In Chapter 7 I tried to show how creation and salvation form a single continuous exercise of God's will, present in purely physical processes, individual lives and societies, and culminating in union with God. If Christians develop the Vienne conception of the soul against this background, I think it will help them to fit belief in an afterlife into other beliefs about ourselves and the world, and to integrate religious devotions into the rest of their lives.

9
LIFE AFTER DEATH

In Chapter 5 I quoted Bertrand Russell (*What I Believe*) as saying that the 'dogma of immortality' is part of the 'irreducible minimum of theology'. Here at least he seems to have been at one with the Apostle Paul, who wrote in 1 Corinthians 15:13-19:

> If there is no resurrection of the dead, Christ has not risen; and if Christ has not risen, our proclamation is empty and your faith is empty ... and you are still in your sins, and those who have fallen asleep in Christ are lost. If we have placed our hope only in this life in Christ, we are the most pitiable of all human beings.

Paul was responding to doubts about the resurrection of the dead which may have been a survival of pre-Christian scepticism among the Jews, and which seem to have been expressed in the questions: 'How are the dead raised? What sort of body do they have' (15:35). Paul replies that the risen body is not animal (*psukhikon*) but imperishable and spiritual (*pneumatikon*), different from the perishable body we bury just as a plant differs from its seed when it is sown (15:39-44).

In the world of ancient Greece and Rome there was, not unnaturally, uncertainty about what happens after death. Is death the end? Is there reincarnation? Is there a ghostly remnant of the person? Or does the person enter upon a different kind of existence, and, if so, is its existence pleasant or disagreeable? Paul promised that faithful Christians would have a pleasant life after death. The basis for this was not the philosophical reasoning Plato offered in the *Phaedo*: Plato argued from the forms our thinking takes, something inexplicable in causal terms. The passages in Paul's first letter to the Corinthians chapter fifteen just cited and 1 Peter 1:3 show that Christians based their belief on the actual return from the dead of Christ: after being executed and entombed, he reappeared with a body endowed with heavenly power. No doubt this was a selling point in the first century, and it has probably been a selling point throughout the history of Christianity. It is primarily a life after death, combined with an explanation of the natural order, not a moral code superior to what could be found in the Old Testament or in Greek philosophy, that missionaries have offered the lands where they have preached.

The Corinthian questions, however, are natural and reasonable: How are the dead raised? How is a life after death possible? What sort of body do they have? What sort of existence? To these questions leading Christian thinkers today have hardly as much as Paul to say in answer. Benjamin Disraeli in Book 4, Chapter 1 of *Vivian Grey*, a novel written in 1826, just before Catholic emancipation, says that Catholics were advised by Parliament 'in the old nursery language, to behave like good boys – to open their mouths, and shut their eyes and see what God will send them'. Catholic religious instruction used to run along those lines: the young were told that they should try to get their heads into Heaven, not Heaven into their heads. George D. Smith, in *The Teaching of the Catholic Church*, the 1,332-page book he edited in 1952, deals with Heaven in one paragraph (p. 76):

> Of the reward of the blessed one would be happy to write. But if St Paul, who was rapt to the third Heaven, tells us that 'eye hath not seen nor ear heard what God hath prepared for them that love him,' (1 Corinthians 2:9) then it were folly for the writer to attempt to describe it.

In fact, in this passage Paul seems to be speaking more of what God has done for us in this life than of what he will provide for us after death, since the passage continues: 'But to us God has revealed it through the Spirit; the Spirit searches out all things, even the depths of God.' Similarly, in Ephesians 3:20 God already working in us does more than we ask or conceive. Paul addresses life after death in chapter fifteen of the letter in

9. Life After Death

the passage which I quoted on page 107, and to which I return below. I have not seen any authoritative statement in the last hundred years that goes beyond first Corinthians chapter fifteen, though Edith Saunders in her book *Fanny Penquite* (p. 43) gives a description of Heaven so disconcertingly graphic that it must be ironical:

> The Good sang in unity; pain and sin and all unhallowed moments were forgotten. Fanny would stand near to her good parents and join in a hymn of praise with her voice pitched high. Then she would wander across the heavenly plains, seeing shapely trees and the splendid roses (permanent and brilliant as crystal stones, their thornless stems as smooth as ivory) that grew beneath them. The memory of the wicked earth vanished, its veering winds were forgotten in the still air of Heaven, and the long hours of eternity passed in unchanging pleasure.

So little is heard from Western pulpits today about life after death that one might wonder if Christians are still expected to believe in it. If they do, are they never tempted to ask what it might be like?

They may be able to resist the temptation now, but in the thirteenth century they were not. Aquinas in *Summa Theologiae* (1a, Q. 89) discusses 'the cognition of a soul separated from the body' and considers eight specific questions. The *Supplement* (Qs 69-96) deals with the life of the blessed after their bodily resurrection and raises such issues as their age, sex [*sexus*] and stature. Questions three and four in the first part of the second part of the *Summa Theologiae* identify supreme and definitive post-mortem happiness with contemplation of God. In the Middle Ages there was clearly an enthusiastic demand for paintings of life in Heaven, Purgatory and Hell, and the questions faced in the *Supplement* were bound to be asked by painters. However, the idea that life after death is at least partly contemplative and involves seeing God 'face to face' goes back to the Old Testament and is endorsed by Christ in the Beatitudes (Matthew 5:8). It was perhaps strengthened by Plato. In the Old Testament wisdom is largely practical, a matter of discerning right and wrong. Plato, however, held (or was interpreted as holding) that contemplative thinking, conceived on the model of vision, is superior to practical. In cultures uninfluenced by Greek philosophy people may not value or even conceive contemplative thinking in this way, but it does not follow that those who recognise it as part of their own culture should simply set it aside. We are always limited to doing the best we can with what intellectual heritage we have.

Nor need Christians deny themselves any speculation at all about what is their traditional hope, life with God after death, so long as they remember that it is speculation. Alphonsus Liguori (1697-1787) in his *Preparation for Death* says we can no more conceive life in Heaven than a horse could conceive human happiness. If life in Heaven is some kind of sharing in divine life, it must be far more different from human life than the life of one created species is from the life of another. Unlike horses, however, we have a nature which inclines us to speculate about reality as a whole and our place in it. Even, therefore, if we must become like little children in order to get into Heaven, I do not think this means we are obliged just to 'shut our eyes and see what God will send us'. That looks like a counsel, not, certainly, of despair, but of Hume's Demea in *Dialogues Concerning Natural Religion* (Pt 2): 'It is profaneness to attempt penetrating through these sacred obscurities.'

If Christian teachers today say little about life after death, it may be because they sense that believers are apt to find the idea of such a life unattractive. Ours is an age in which people clamour for the right to pay people to put them painlessly to death: not because they are in a hurry to see God, but because they have had enough of life and think death the end. Offered Heaven, two pictures are apt to come unbidden into the mind. One, suggested perhaps by many hymns, is of an interminable church service in which the blessed, assembled in the presence of God, praise him in unending song, *hymnum gloriae tuae concinunt, sine fine dicentes*. The other is of a vast housing estate in which the blessed are comfortably lodged and able to meet up again with the friends and relations they had on earth. This picture may be inspired by the saying at John 14:2 – 'In my father's house there are many lodgings [*monai*]' – and is sometimes offered to mourners at funerals. It must be admitted, however, that in this life we occasionally feel that a church service has gone on long enough, we know virtuous people out of whose proximity we edge, and we can even be glad when visiting friends or relations say they must leave. We can be uneasy about the prospect of endless time and about our relations with other human beings in Heaven. It is perhaps for this reason that, when in 2001 the British Catholic Theological Association held a conference on 'Paradise: Our Once and Future End', the papers, or at least those published in *New Blackfriars* (January 2002), contained no speculation about post-mortem existence but spoke rather of Heaven as something attainable by the virtuous in this life.

How Christians are to conceive life after death must depend on which they embrace of the two conceptions of soul I discussed in Chapter 8. On the Platonic view expressed by the Lateran Council of 1513, and

9. Life After Death

confirmed by Pius XII's encyclical *Humani Generis*, every human soul is immortal from the moment at which it is created. It is its nature to continue to exist after death, and it is reunited with its resurrected body after the Last Judgement. The blessed would then share in the life of God in Heaven at least in the way in which houseguests share in the life of their host or hosts. They eat and drink at Christ's table (Luke 22:30) and God prepares an endless succession of unimaginably delightful treats for them.

The Platonic conception is open to the philosophical objections I indicated in Chapter 8, and its use by Christian theologians may be criticised on scriptural grounds. It does not give enough weight to passages in which eternal life, and not just eternal happiness, is said to depend on good behaviour and, indeed, on some kind of union with Christ. Furthermore, the texts I cited in Chapter 7 in support of a holistic theology of salvation suggest a different model from that of guests at a large house. This alternative model is of a vine with branches (John 15:1-6). The branches are parts of the vine, and draw their life from the whole vine. In the application of this model the role of the vine is taken by Christ, the Second Person of the Trinity, who is both God and man. Human beings do not grow out of Christ as branches grow out of a vine. Rather they are grafted into Christ as adopted offspring of God. They thereby acquire the immortality of God, or at least of the Second Person of the Trinity, as distinct from the immortality of creatures, something which, according to the Lateran tradition, human souls have on their own before embodiment, and which enables them, if not admitted to God's house, to weep and gnash their teeth in outer darkness or in everlasting fire. On the botanical model they do not become gods – the living branches of a vine are not vines unless separated from it as cuttings – but they do share literally in Christ's life and that life is both human and divine.

Two points in favour of the botanical model for life after death are that it is consistent with the Aristotelian conception of the soul as a person constituted by a human body, and that immortality, at least in Jewish and Greek thinking, is conceived as a divine attribute. In Classical Greece the Homeric gods were thought immortal because they were gods, and the heavenly bodies were thought divine because, apparently, they were immortal. In Genesis chapters two and three, God does not at first forbid the first human beings to eat from the Tree of Life but, after they have eaten from the Tree of Knowledge, he says: 'So, Adam has become like one of us by discerning good and evil; and now, let him never stretch out his hand and take from the tree of life and then live for ever.' These words imply that Adam was not created immune to death. They suggest that we may form an idea of immortality, but we cannot just pick it off a tree. It would be anachronistic, I think, to suppose that the author of this chapter wants to leave it a possibility that, after we have died, we shall naturally live for ever. The earliest Old Testament references to life after death (2 Maccabees 7:9-14, 12:45) represent it not as something natural but as a reward for obeying God's laws. Outside Judaeo-Christian thinking it was thought that a man, as a reward for heroic deeds (for example, Hercules), or through the gift of a goddess who was in love with him (as Calypso and Circe were with Odysseus), might become immortal, but the idea that souls might be naturally immortal and never cease to exist is tied to the beliefs that they have existed before entering the body and migrate from one body to another.

In what follows I argue that, if we wish to defend the traditional Christian belief in a life after death, we can do so without taking a Platonic view of the soul or supposing that we are naturally immortal.

The divine life of Christ is that of the Son of God, the Second Person of the Trinity. If the three Persons are not to be confounded, the life of the Second should be somewhat different from that of the First and that of the Third. In Chapter 8 I used the triune nature of human beings as a model for the Trinity. The Father corresponds to our nature as individuals acting to please ourselves, the Son to the social element in our nature, and the Spirit to the altruistic. If that is right, the divine life of Christ is his life as a divine social being. Being fully human his human life must include life as a human social being. If his divine nature is different from his human, his life as a divine social being must be different from his life as a human social being and I suggest that we share in it in a different way.

You may be said to share in the life of another human being if you share in the life of a human society to which you both belong. For Christians the Church is a human society to which Christ belongs. They imply this when they speak of him as a priest, king and judge, for these are social roles. Human societies have procedures by which people become members. The simplest procedure – the default, one might say – is to be born child of a member. We do not become members of the Church simply by having a Christian parent. We become Christians through being baptised. Entering a society, however, is not the same as living as a member of it. Living as a member is living in accordance with the customs of your society, and that, as I said in Chapter 3, is not just doing what the customs prescribe but thinking them good on the whole. Entering a society need not be a conscious act by the entrant. In the early years of Christianity people received baptism only when they were adults

9. Life After Death

and asked for it. Today the Church has a practice of baptising infants. Baptism is still a matter of choice, but the choice is made by the parents or by other members of the infant's human society. In infancy we cannot make choices or act for reasons at all. We come to live as members of the Church, and to share in Christ's human social life, in acting willingly in accordance with the Church's rules and playing roles within it.

In human societies when children reach an age at which they can understand the customs of the society and act according to them, there is usually a rite of passage in which they accept the customs and enter fully into the society's life. Among Catholics this is split into two rites, making a first Communion and receiving Confirmation; other denominations combine them with one another and with baptism.

Confirmation is perhaps a rite of passage, but receiving the Eucharist, is traditionally considered not just as a rite of passage, but as communion with Christ in closer way than merely by taking part in the life of the Church. In Chapter 8 I quoted Christ's words in John 6:53-57:

> If you do not eat the flesh of the Son of Man and drink his blood, you do not have life in you. He who chews [*trogon*] my flesh and drinks my blood has eternal life and I will raise him up on the last day. For my flesh is genuine food and my blood genuine drink. He who chews my flesh and drinks my blood remains in me and I in him. As the living Father sent me, so I too live through the Father; and he who munches me, he too lives through me.

I suggested that, when what we consume in Communion turns, through the natural process of digestion, into living flesh and blood in our bodies, that flesh and that blood are literally alive with Christ's life in the way that the branches of a vine are literally alive with the life of the whole vine. If that is right, we share in Christ's life in the way in which parts of a single organism share in the life of the organism. Moreover, baptising appears as something analogous to grafting a cutting into the stock of a vine or implanting an organ into a human body. My present suggestion is that the life in which, through the Eucharist, we share, is Christ's divine life, as distinct from his life as a human social being. Baptism gives us a share in his life as a social human being, the Eucharist a share in his life as a divine social being.

Something like this distinction appears in the Pauline letters. Paul sometimes writes of Christ as standing to the Church as one part to others, 'as the ruling part to the rest, the head to the limbs' (Ephesians 5: 22-24), but more often as the whole body to its parts: 'We, who are many, are one body in Christ' (Romans 12:5; similarly, 1 Corinthians 12:12-27; Ephesians 4:12-13, 5:30). It is this latter idea which allows him to speak of members of the church as being in Christ, and say, 'I live, but it is no longer I, but Christ lives in me' (Galatians 2:20).

The mode of sharing is different, and the life shared is different. It is the life of the triune God. That includes creation and imparting creative life to creatures. Although in the Nicene Creed creation is attributed to the Father and vivifying to the Spirit, the Persons of the Trinity are one God insofar as they are a single source of the natural order, and the Council of Florence in 1442 declared that these functions belong to all of them: 'Father, Son and Holy Spirit are not three principles of creation [*principia creaturae*] but one' (DS, 1331).

There is support for this in Christ's prayer for all the faithful (*pisteuontes*) in John 17:21-23:

> As you, Father, are in me and I in you, so may they also be in us; so that the universe [*kosmos*] may believe that you sent me. And I have given them the glory [*doxa*] which you gave me, so that they should be one as we are one: I in them and you in me, so that they may come to completion [*teteilomenoi*] in one; so that the universe may come to know that you sent me, and you loved them as you loved me.

This passage follows the emphatic use of the vine analogy in John 15:1-6 – 'He who remains in me, and I in him, bears fruit in abundance.' The word *doxa* translated here 'glory' means, I think, when applied to God not fame or even brightness but creative activity.

Domestication, which turns wild into edible fruit and grasses into oats and wheat, takes place over many generations. Accepting a graft or implant also takes time, and we may hope that our coming to share in Christ's divine life can increase over a lifetime as we share in the life of fellow Christians, honour the natural order as God's creation and ask God's help for those for whom we care. We may hope, that is, that, insofar as we share in his divine life as a social being, we already share, however imperfectly, in God's creative and animating activity. (I leave open the question whether this participation is limited to practising Christians or can embrace people who 'do God's will' without accepting the doctrine of the Incarnation or even having heard of Christ.)

It is natural to conceive asking God to help someone on the model of asking another human being. If I ask you to help a sick friend, I hope that you will help the friend by yourself; my part is done when I have

9. Life After Death

spoken to you. However, my present suggestion is that, when we pray for somebody to God, we may hope actually to share ourselves in the helping. Perhaps I can illustrate this by something said to me personally by the historian Gervase Mathew. He offered to say Mass for anyone in Classical Antiquity that I named. It is traditional among Catholics to pray that the dead may be relieved of temporal suffering for their sins, and they usually conceive the suffering not only as temporal but as contemporaneous with their prayers. It is hard to see how suffering can be temporal without being physical, and if there is non-physical time, how it can be temporally related to physical and contemporaneous with the prayer. I thought it would be odd to pray now for the Emperor Tiberius. Gervase Mathew said that for the dead time does not matter. I do not know if he had in mind Luke 20: 38 where Christ says that to God 'all men are alive'; but I took him to mean that, though the natural order is temporal, since God's action in sustaining it is the source of time, it is not itself a temporal process, and, therefore, we can pray for God's help to a person at any time in that person's temporal life. We cannot pray to God to change the past, to make what *was* the case *not to have been* the case; but praying for God's help to someone in the past is praying rather to shape the past than to change it. An utterance now is later in time than an event in the first century; but God's awareness of a twenty-first century utterance is not later than God's action in sustaining someone alive in the first. So, while we are alive, we can pray to share in divine activity that had effects then. Accepting this possibility, I think, helps us to make sense of the idea of sharing in Christ's life after death.

We enjoy the natural world through our senses, and it is the loss of that enjoyment – no more to see colours or hear sounds – that makes death hateful to many people: if, however, the blessed share in God's life, they should share in the joy of creating the natural order. In terrestrial life we can enjoy the world only from the outside; the creator must enjoy it from within. There is a hint of this in God's magnificent discourse in Job chapter 38: Where were you when I fixed the foundations of the earth? Who was it that threw down its corner stone when the stars were born? Has the dawn received its orders from you, or the morning star learnt from you its course?

As a human being, Christ certainly had a temporal existence and acted in time, but creation is not a temporal act and, as a Person of the Trinity, Christ's existence must be non-temporal. His choosing of his disciples and his instituting of the Eucharist were acts in time, but the Incarnation itself, his taking of flesh from the virgin Mary, and his communicating of his life through the sacraments cannot be understood as temporal. They depended on temporal action as necessary conditions – Mary assenting two thousand years ago, priests administering and people receiving the sacraments – but they cannot have been effected by that action. Mary's bodily act in assenting did not cause the Second Person to become incarnate, and the communicant's act in receiving the Eucharist does not cause the communicant to receive divine life. It is this complementarity of divine and causal action which constitutes the Incarnation and extends it beyond Jesus of Nazareth to other human beings. Insofar as existence after death is divine, it must be non-temporal – non-temporal rather than of unending duration.

The notion of non-temporal actuality is peculiar to theology. Mathematics deals with natural numbers, which are possible numbers for aggregates of things, and with geometrical shapes, which are possible shapes for things. Actual cubes and spheres are temporal, as are actual countable aggregates. Nevertheless, if we want to make sense of the whole temporal order, we have to postulate the actual existence of a non-temporal source. The existence of such a being is not extended in time, but not instantaneous either. Our conception of an instant, something without duration as a mathematical point is without extension, is still temporal. It is that of the beginning or end of a change, such as the switch (as Colin Strang puts it in 'Plato and the Instant') from being in motion to being at rest.

We can think that a non-temporal being exists, and we can give this being the role in our thinking that we give to human, spatio-temporal persons; we can think that some activity, some period of change, is a carrying out of its desire. However, that is as far as we can go; we can and do think of a non-temporal being in these ways but we can have no conception of it such as we have of living organisms, natural substances, movements, qualities and spatio-temporal things generally. These, as I said in Chapter 6, can be considered either as possibilities or as actualities, and what we reckon as concepts of *what* they are, are our ideas of them as possibilities. We have no idea of God as a possibility in the way we have an idea of an elephant as a possible animal and swimming as a possible movement. In that respect God is like forms of thought themselves. We know *that we actually think* thoughts of such forms as thinking there are or are not things of some kind. Nonetheless, not only have we no idea *how* we think thoughts of these forms, as we may have no idea how we breathe or digest, but we have no idea what it is to have them in the way in which, even without medical knowledge, we can have an idea what it is to breathe and digest if we have some idea of air, lungs, food and stomachs.

The unity of parts of an organism is much closer than that of members of a society, closer even than that of lovers. Passionate lovers, indeed, may desire a more complete and permanent union than that of sexual climax, since that is brief and leaves the lovers each still opaque to the other's mind. Even if we imagine that merging in timeless consummation with the right person would be bliss, it is disturbing to think that the blessed, numbering billions and coming from every background, should all have this intimate union with one another. The housing estate model of Heaven here makes an appeal. Christ, however, did command people to love one another without exceptions, and it may be helpful to consider his role as a judge.

Today we are apt to think of judges as people whose primary task is to punish, to inflict death, flogging, imprisonment, fines. That is because judges are ministers of justice, and our society has come to think that justice is primarily retribution or returning pain for pain, what the Greeks called *antilupêsis*. That is uncivilised. Justice divides, at least according to Aristotle, into distributive and corrective justice. Human distributive justice involves distributing both good things and duties and burdens. For the blessed there should be no burdens, but there could be need to distribute divine life and *doxa* according to how in their terrestrial lives people have made themselves capable of receiving it. Different people come to love different parts of nature, some the sea, some mountains, some particular species of plants or animals. They care for different individuals, embrace different causes. As for corrective justice, though in human societies it sometimes takes a good thing away from one person and gives it to another, in Heaven it might be limited to repairing damage. A Latin hymn to the Holy Spirit attributed to Stephen Langton (Archbishop of Canterbury 1207-28) contains the petitions:

> Wash in us what's dirty,
> Water what is arid,
> Heal in us what's wounded.
>
> Bend in us what's rigid,
> Warm in us what's frigid,
> Straighten what is crooked.

If Christ's role as a corrective judge is seen in these terms, the closeness of the blessed to each other may appear less scary. If revulsion can be overcome, the prospect of understanding persons very different from ourselves and appreciating what they value could be attractive.

As altruists, we already take pleasure in getting to know other people and, when their lives go well, sharing in their happiness. We can do this only from the outside, however, and even our dearest friends remain in part mysterious. I said that, if the dead share God's creative life, they can take a creative joy in the natural world. The created order includes living beings, and, if the blessed join God in creating it, they must know their friends from the inside and perfectly, and must themselves breathe life into them. Furthermore, this happiness must be timeless; not long or short in duration but not instantaneous either.

Aquinas says (*ST*, 1a 2ae, Q. 3, Art. 8) that our 'ultimate and perfect happiness [*beatitudo*] consists in the contemplation [*visio*] of God's essence'. That sounds like a knowledge of the Creator as distinct from creation. The issues here are intricate, but Aquinas does not distinguish God from his activity or his knowledge from what he knows (1a, Q. 14, Art. 2) and, given the simplicity of God (1a, Q.3), I am not sure that what Aquinas calls contemplation of God's essence can in fact be anything different from the sharing in God's activity which I have just tried to describe.

I have not yet spoken of something which is an article of the creed, the resurrection of the body. We first hear if this in 2 Maccabees 7: 9-14 and 12:44, and it is there simply identified with life after death. The Jews of that time (175-134) had a unified conception of human beings, and assumed that a life after death must be that of a psycho-somatic unity. The gospels show Christ having a bodily resurrection, and theologians have reasoned that, since we are beings that depend by nature upon sense organs, movable limbs and a nervous system, perfect life for us after death should be bodily. Hence, Christians have traditionally held that, though at death our bodies perish, at the end of the world we become once more embodied. Two questions arise: what is life like for the blessed before the end of the world, and what is the body like after it?

To the first question it might be replied that God's life does not depend on his having a body, and that Christians believe that we have some share in it already. We depend on our senses for information about the world and on limbs for acting within it. God's creative activity does not depend upon these things, and, if the dead continue to share in it, they should know about what goes on in time in the same way as God. Without bodies, the dead cannot act causally themselves but, if God helps and in some measure animates those of their friends who still can, they might join him in that. The dead cannot intercede with God by speech or gesture, but the traditional practice of praying for their intercession will not be unreasonable if they can actually unite with God – as I have suggested we may hope to do ourselves in our present lives when we pray.

9. Life After Death

I have also suggested that in the course of our lives we become gradually implanted in Christ, and share in his life to a greater or lesser extent. That must depend on our behaviour, and our behaviour depends partly on when and where we live and what people we come to know. It may also depend on how far we do what we do because we think God wants us to do it, how far we act to be the people God wants us to be. In the course of our lives we not only undergo bodily changes; we bring about changes in ourselves as persons. We acquire virtues and vices. Perhaps it does not make sense to talk of sharing in Christ's life to a greater or lesser extent if we mean we become more or less divine; either we have God's life or we do not. However, just as two vines of the same species have the same life, the life of that species, but may differ in size and shape, differ in the wood that has the life, so, in the course of our lives, there may come to be more or less of us to share in the one divine life, and the persons that share in it will differ according to the circumstances of their lives. You and I probably have different friends, different tastes, different charitable projects. These differences are acquired in our lives on earth. At the same time, neurologists tell us, we acquire physical structures in the brain which we did not inherit and without which we could not behave as we do. Perhaps it is not possible for bodily beings like us to acquire new orientations after death. Perhaps the share of the blessed in divine activity is limited initially to fields for which before death they have prepared themselves.

If so, however, it might be extended. If we have had concern for others in this life and are united with them in Christ, we should be able through that union to share concerns they had or have, even if we did not ourselves have them when we were alive. I mean that, if, say, my spouse was a keen gardener while I was not, I might after death be able to share my spouse's delight in gardening; if I prayed for a grandmother who died before I was born, I might come to know friends of hers I never heard of, and, conversely, she, though she never heard of me, might through Christ come to know friends of mine.

The second question was about life after re-embodiment. Paul (1 Corinthians 15:35-49), besides insisting that risen bodies are fundamentally different from our bodies now, heavenly (*epourania*) and not earthly (*epigeia*) and spiritual (*pneumatikon*) not animal (*psukhikon*), takes up the comparison offered in Romans 6:12-23 between Christ and Adam: 'The first man, Adam, came into being as a living animal, the last Adam as a life-giving spirit. What comes first is not the spiritual but the animal, afterwards comes the spiritual. The first man comes from earth and is earthen, the second man comes from Heaven' (1 Corinthians 15:45-47).

These thoughts are consistent with the idea that the bodies of the risen are the risen body of Christ himself, that they live, as Paul puts it in Ephesians 4:13, as parts of 'the perfect man', the *anêr teleios*. This is not inconsistent with the Gospel descriptions of the risen Christ. Apparently sometimes he was not recognised at first by people who knew him (John 20:14-16, 21:4-14; Luke 24:13-32), though sometimes he was recognised immediately (John 20:19-29).

These texts show him cooking, eating, able to be felt and yet not excluded by locked doors. We need a body in order to act causally in the natural world, and the risen Christ acted causally on food and on the senses of those to whom he appeared. However, re-embodiment is supposed to take place at the end of the world. That would be the end of time and therefore the end of causal action. If our ability to share in God's life reflects, in the ways I suggested just now, what we have learned and done on earth, at the end of time our participation in the creative action of God might sufficiently perfect our nature as bodily beings.

It is not clear, indeed, that there will be an end of time. There must have been a beginning of time if (as I think) an infinite stretch of time is impossible, and, if time had no beginning, an infinite stretch of time will have actually elapsed already. There need not be an end of time, however, since for any finite quantity, whether of time or material, there could be a greater. Physicists tell us that space – the three-dimensional space through which it is physically possible to travel – is finite but expanding, and they consider whether there is a physical limit to its expansion. Time is not (despite what some philosophers, as well as H.G. Wells, have said) something through which it is possible to travel. Rather it is the actual going on of change. Physicists sometimes say that after a finite time there will be no more change – the universe will, so to speak, be dead; if that is right, there will be no more time just as there was no time before the Big Bang. So far as logical possibility goes, however, for every physical event there could be a later.

I have argued that the belief that God created the natural order has practical implications. It needs no arguing that the same goes for the belief there is or can be a life after death. If we believe that there is life after the age of fourteen, then, even if we know that some people die earlier, we ourselves before the age of fourteen will prepare ourselves for later life, and parents and guardians of children will try to prepare them. It is the same with belief that there is, or may be, life after death. If you make no preparations, take no precautions, show no unease, then, whatever you may say, you think death is the end. In the past most people have probably been unsure if death is the end; they have thought that there may well be something after it, even if only the only the persistence of a ghostly remnant. Today some people profess to think it certain that death is the end, but it is hard to be sure that they really have this belief when death still seems remote to them unless they consistently act on positive principles that presuppose it: 'Rule where you can'.

While belief in a life after death is not purely theoretical, its practical implications will differ for people with different conceptions of the soul. On the Platonic view life after death is inevitable. Christians who take it have sometimes held that God will somehow ensure that everyone gets to the divine dinner-table. For those with that optimism, it will not much matter what religion you have if any, or even how you behave. Their belief in an after-like may have only minor implications. But many Christians who believe the soul is naturally immortal have held that anyone who, through bad behaviour, is excluded from the divine feast, will have an eternity of acute suffering. How it is possible for anything created to exist in separation from the Creator they do not explain. But if you share that belief, then as Pascal pointed out, the implications are scary.

The view of salvation that I have been advocating, that a life after death is not inevitable but attainable through coming to share in the divine life of Christ, may sound unorthodox. In John 5:28-29, Christ says that the time will come when all the dead will emerge from their tombs, those who did good rising up to life and those who did bad things 'rising up to judgement' (*eis anastasin kriseôs*). That all those who die will be judged is implied also by Daniel 12:2. Nevertheless, it is one thing to say that all will have a post-mortem judgement, another to say that all will have an endless post-mortem existence. In John 3:16, 6:40-58, 10:7-10, 11:25-26 and 14:6, Christ insists that eternal life is available through himself in a way which strongly implies that it is not available otherwise.

Matthew 25:41 contains a vivid description of the Last Judgement, in which the Judge says to those who have failed to perform acts of compassion: 'Go away from me, you accursed, to the eternal [*aiônion*] fire made ready for the devil and his angels.' This is taken as a revelation of eternal punishment for the wicked. The idea of Hell has drawn Christians into sadistic fantasies of infinite divine cruelty. Fire appears in a different role, however, in Matthew 13:30 when it is used to dispose of the weeds that are not taken into the barn, and in John 15:6 when it is used to dispose of branches that have become separated from the true vine and withered. Unlike the fires in which martyrs have perished, it could symbolise a destruction that is final.

Be that as it may, if you think that death is the end unless you become incorporated in Christ, you will probably try to live according to Christ's precepts and show some signs of devotion. Love of their devotions has brought many Christians up against the civil laws. Moreover, belief that life after death depends on Christ must affect a believer's attitude towards multiculturalism. You cannot regard multiculturalism as ideal if you have concern for all members of your society. You may even feel inclined to heed Christ's instruction to go out and teach all nations the good news that there is this way to obtain eternal happiness. That is what carries missionaries to martyrdom.

What, however, if you have come to have a kind of loathing for everything and for the author of everything? Sharing in God's creative activity would be even worse than the interminable church service. Would you strive for extinction? Or would a loathing for the universe and every person and thing in it be incompatible with a belief that it has a personal source? Sombre thoughts, more suitable, perhaps, for a tale of horror and madness than for an essay in Christian theology.

In the last four chapters I have looked at the principal doctrinal beliefs of Christians, and tried to sketch in outline an holistic theology in which faith is not separate from charitable action, and in which we are conceived both as psychosomatic unities and as essentially social beings. Besides doctrinal beliefs Christians have practical beliefs. It is on practical matters, and particularly on issues concerning life, death, procreation and education, that Christianity and other cultures most obviously cause problems to the larger societies within which they are sub-societies. To these issues I now turn.

10
Questions of Life and Death

In the 1934 film of *The Scarlet Pimpernel*, Robespierre says to the Count de Tournay: 'We give you your life.' The Count replies reprovingly: 'God gave me my life.' Less thoughtful people have supposed that we are given life by our parents; and this has been considered a ground for expecting love and obedience from children, and for imposing stiff penalties on parricide. It might be inferred that Life is the greatest good that can possibly be bestowed on anyone. Is it really so good? According to the chorus of Sophocles' *Oedipus Coloneus* (1224-28), 'By far the best thing is not to be born at all, and the second best, to return whence you came as fast as possible.'

Both ways of regarding life are explored in Colonel Fairfax's song in Gilbert and Sullivan's *Yeomen of the Guard*:

> Is life a boon?
> If so, it must befall
> That death whene'er he call
> Must call too soon.
> What kind of plaint have I
> Who perish in July?
> I might have had to die
> Perchance in June!

> Is life a thorn?
> Then count it not a whit!

Man is well done with it;
Soon as he's born
He should all means essay
To put the plague away;
And I, war-worn,
Poor captured fugitive,
My life most gladly give –
I might have had to live
Another morn!

The Count de Tournay was a relic of the *Ancien Régime*. Since the French Revolution people have talked less of gifts and more of rights. Everyone, it is said, has a right to life; that is the most basic of all human rights; and, according to some people, we have, or the law should give us, the right to die, to give back (as J.R.R. Tolkien put it in his appendix to *The Return of the King*) the gift of life. So, the questions arise: Are life and death good or bad? Are they gifts we can be given? Have we a right to them? I propose to consider the last question first because the notion of a right is simpler than those of a gift and a benefit.

Rights are either active rights, rights to do things or to refrain from doing them, or else passive rights, rights to have things done to us or not to have them done to us; and they are held against other people who have corresponding duties to act or refrain. The right to life may sound like a right to do something, but in fact it is passive and negative: it is the right not to be killed. To say it is a *human* right is primarily to say that we all have it by virtue of being human and not just by virtue of belonging to some particular society or having some position in some society; but I think it is usually assumed also that we hold it against all other human beings, whether within the boundaries of our own country or not. We – at least, if we subscribe to the Ten Commandments – have a duty to refrain from killing other people, wherever they come from, as we also have a duty to refrain from inflicting bodily harm and subjecting others to physical constraint; if there are savages who don't recognise a duty to refrain from killing, harming or constraining *us*, then they should. Whether it is really best to regard this restraint as a matter of duty rather than of humanity or some other kind of rationality may be debated; but at least what is meant by 'the right to life' is clear.

The notion of a right to death is much more obscure. Against whom could it be held? Who, if anyone, has a duty *not* to keep us alive, to refrain from impeding the processes that destroy our vital organs? The only possible answer is: 'our doctors'. By '*my* doctors' I mean people who, whether or not they have real skill at healing, are recognised by themselves and by society as having certain duties towards *me* as a patient. Traditionally one of these duties is to try to keep me alive, and in some societies (Italy until recently) doctors have had a legal obligation to refrain from any action that will hasten a patient's death. How could the same people have the obligation both to keep me alive and to refrain from keeping me alive? Perhaps it will be said that a doctor has a duty to keep me alive as long as I wish, and to stop keeping me alive when I wish. Doctors, however, have no duty to treat people who are not their patients, and to claim the right to die from my doctor is not to claim a right to withdraw from the patient-doctor relationship. The idea seems to be that refraining from treating me is a special kind of treatment a doctor might owe me; but how could it be?

The right to death is not a right to commit suicide. Many societies have already ceased treating attempted suicide as a crime, and making it a crime to stop people from killing themselves is not what those claiming a right to die demand. Nor is the right to death simply a right to die. Dying is not like voting in elections or making a will. It is not something we can do only in a society by complying with a procedure laid down by law or custom. Nor is it something positive that we do, independently of society, like walking or drinking. Those are forms of action. We do not have rights to do things we are able as individuals to do unless doing them is restricted by law. Dying is not restricted by law and it is not a form of action at all. It is a breakdown of our vital functions, a ceasing to be able to act in any way whatever. There is some discussion today about which functions must cease for a person to have died – those of the heart or the brain or what – and about the possibility of resuscitation. These discussions arise in connection with removing organs for transplant. In general, heart and brain function together and when they stop functioning you die. Talk of a right to die is as strange as talk of a right to grow old. If someone is threatening to cut me off in my youth, I might say, 'Allow me to grow old', but this is a request not to be killed prematurely. A patient who is dying slowly and in pain or distress might possibly say: 'Doctor, just allow me to die.' Is this, too, a request not to be killed, a plea that their disease should be allowed to take its natural course? That is not how we are sometimes expected to understand it.

What people claim when they claim a right to die is actually to have it legalised to ask others to kill them. It is not illegal to invite a friend to tea. However, it is illegal to ask another person to do something illegal. It is against the law, in particular, to engage a hitman. For it to be legal to ask someone else to kill you, it must be made legal to kill someone who asks you to; so demanding a right to die is demanding that it should be decriminalised to kill people under certain circumstances, especially under the circumstance that they have asked you for this service – or, a not insignificant extension sometimes envisaged, under the circumstance that they would have asked for it, had they been able.

At present the service usually desired is a positive act of killing: administering a lethal injection or something like that. People want a right to request this, not a right to receive it. If it were a right to receive it, it would have to be held against someone with a duty to provide it. Who, however, has a duty to kill? Doctors sometimes kill patients, and seeking their aid is putting your life in pawn, but it cannot be said that killing a patient is part of the duties of a doctor or an aim of medical practice. Aristotle says that a doctor may make a statue, but he does so not as a doctor but as a sculptor. If I ask my doctor to kill me, I want him to use his knowledge of my bodily condition and his expertise in drugs, but I am still asking him to act not as a doctor (nor even as an executioner) but as a hitman. Those who want the law to recognise a right to die do not, I think, as yet want to place a legal obligation on doctors to kill their patients even when the patients ask them to. Rather they want patients to have a legal right to request this service. As the law in England stands at the moment, I do not have the right to ask you to kill anyone whatever, since that is incitement to crime; but I should acquire the right to ask you to kill *me* if it ceased to be illegal to kill people who request this service for themselves. As a sort of partial parallel, we have no right to receive sex (except, perhaps, from our spouses or if we have paid for it), but we have a right to ask for it. If prostitution is legal but pandering not, it is illegal to ask you to sell sex to someone else, but legal to ask you to sell sex to me. Those who speak of a right to die at least want killing people who ask for this service for themselves to be decriminalised. This will not cover all the other cases they have in mind, unwanted babies, handicapped neonates, incontinent dotards and the rest; but it might give people a legal right against someone who has taken money to kill them.

We can have a right to assistance in certain circumstances – joining the AA gives you a right to assistance when your car breaks down on the road – and, instead of killing, people sometimes talk of helping to die. This does not really make sense. It is most natural to talk of helping in connection with purposive activity. You can help me to move a piano or to prevent an attacker from forcing an entrance. Dying is not something like this; it is not causing or preventing anything. We can extend the notion of helping to bodily functions: you can help an asthma-sufferer to breathe or help my heart to pump blood. However, death is the failure and cessation of all bodily functions. You cannot help a person to fail at anything, nor can I help your heart or lungs to fail.

Sometimes campaigners to liberalise the homicide laws speak not just of a right to die, but a right to die with dignity. That is problematic too. I can have a right to shoot over a field, but I cannot have a right to shoot successfully or to hit the birds at which I aim. The Americans say they have a right to pursue happiness but they do not claim a right to achieve it. If we cannot have a right to do something successfully, how can we have a right to do something gracefully or in a dignified way? A right to do something is of itself a right to do it with dignity, and being forced to do it like a buffoon is a restriction of that right. Furthermore, if we cannot have a right to die because dying is not doing something but a failure of bodily functions, *a fortiori* we cannot have a right to die in a dignified way. At best we have a right not to be harassed as our powers fail.

I conclude that talk about a right to die is confused and the result of squeamishness about calling things by their right names. Perhaps it may be felt that, as death draws near, we should avoid language that might be upsetting and cast about for euphemisms; but obscured speech leads to confused thought, and confused thought to bad decisions both in legislation and in practice.

People often quote Clough's couplet from *The Latest Decalogue*: 'Thou shalt not kill; but needst not strive / Officiously to keep alive.' Does this express a Christian view of death?

If we take killing to be causing a person's death, or being causally responsible for someone's death, or being morally responsible for someone's death, killing a person may extend beyond such positive acts as shooting, stabbing and administering lethal injections. An act that prevents the prevention of someone's death gives you a kind of causal responsibility for it. Switching off the electricity that powers a life-support machine is such an act, and might in some circumstances actually amount to murder. Deliberately refraining from doing something necessary to prevent a death, refraining, say, from binding up a wound or administering a remedy or calling a physician, gives you a certain moral responsibility for it.

These are cases in which a Christian may weigh the circumstances. It is one thing if the regimen that prevents death is unlikely ever to restore healthy functioning, another if there is every hope that the patient's treatment will eventually restore health, but the patient's death now would be greatly to your advantage. It is one thing to shrink from the action necessary to save someone else's life when it would bring your own life into peril, another to withhold water from someone dying of thirst in the desert when you have an ample supply. These are matters more naturally decided by the courts than by reference to rules that, of their nature as rules, admit of no exceptions.

I can have various reasons for wishing that someone would kill me. I may be in acute pain; I may fear I am about to be tortured and forced to betray my friends; I may want my heirs to receive insurance money; I may have done something shameful and think that nothing else will save it from being made public. Nevertheless, society needs rules about death, and a Christian may think that Clough's couplet prescribes what is best on the whole. Its prescription is certainly challenged in Western states today.

Let me now return to the question whether life or death is something good or bad. Life, *pace* Colonel Fairfax in *The Yeoman of the Guard*, is on the face of it neither a boon nor a thorn, neither a benefit nor a burden; rather it is a precondition of being benefited or burdened. It is like existence; indeed, for living things life and existence are the same. Non-existent things neither long for existence nor dread it. On a living person you might confer an honour or inflict a penalty, but you can neither confer life nor inflict it on something inanimate. In the story of Pygmalion Aphrodite is said to give life to a statue. She actually does a kindness to Pygmalion, not to the statue. A statue can be damaged or improved but cannot be benefited or harmed. After Aphrodite's intervention, what Pygmalion clasps is not a statue which has come to life, but a living woman who has arisen miraculously out of the statue. To take a more familiar case, when a child is conceived, the parents do not, strictly speaking, give life to an ovum and a spermatozoon. They are already living cells. What grows in the womb is not a pair of gametes endowed with life but a living human embryo into which the gametes have passed away.

Death, in contrast, is not a precondition of being harmed or benefited; far from it. Dying (if we leave aside life after death) is ceasing to exist altogether, so the dead can neither be harmed nor benefited. Life can be prized by those who are already alive, but it is not something that can be given to those who are not yet alive. Death, in contrast, can be given to those who are not yet dead; they can be killed; but it is neither an advantage nor a handicap to those who are already dead. E.C. Bentley in his 1905 *Biography for Beginners* tells us: 'There's a good deal to be said / For being dead.' Not, however, by the dead themselves.

10. Questions of Life and Death

I have been speaking as if life and death were opposites or alternatives, but the noun 'death' covers two different things, dying and being dead. Being dead is a kind of alternative to being alive; dying is an alternative rather to coming to life or being conceived. To put it more formally, living, being alive, is like a *state* of motion: we are alive *for* a stretch of time, for so long as various processes, biological or psychological, are going on. Dying is like *coming* to rest, *switching* from being in motion to being at rest. It is ceasing to be alive, and we die not *for* a time but *after* a time. Christ died, was dead for a time, and, his followers said, returned to life; but 'Christ died *for* a couple of days' and 'Christ died for ever and ever, and so shall we all' are both incorrect ways of speaking.

Because living and dying are like this, dying can be an object of desire or aversion, whereas life cannot. An object of desire or aversion is something we can cause or prevent. We cause someone to die by damaging vital organs and arresting vital processes; we prevent someone from dying by removing impediments to those processes and repairing the organs. However, we cannot cause someone to *be* alive or prevent someone from *being* alive. Being alive and being dead are like being in motion and being at rest. If a body is at rest, we can cause it to *start* moving or prevent it from *starting* to move, and, if it is moving, we can cause it to *stop* moving and *come* to rest, but *being* in motion and *being* at rest are things that can neither be caused not prevented. What is roughly described as a 'desire for life' is not, therefore, a desire to *be* alive (nor, of course, is it a desire to *become* alive, because we must already be alive to have any desires at all) but a desire to *stay* alive, or, more exactly, an aversion to dying; and a desire for death is not a desire to *be* dead but to die.

It is possible to want to die and to kill yourself; but, in general, dying is reckoned an intrinsic evil, an object of aversion for its own sake. I can understand as intentional your doing what is necessary to prevent your dying without attributing to you any further purpose, whereas I cannot understand your acting to end your life without attributing to you some further purpose or some special reason: I suggested escaping disgrace, benefiting your heirs, or preventing a secret from be extracted from you under torture. Hence, death is of itself and for its own sake an object of aversion; life, on the other hand, is not an object of desire of itself, but only inasmuch as ceasing to be alive is of itself an evil.

What about *bringing* into existence or conceiving? Although conception and death can both be objectives, they are objectives of different kinds. We can desire the death of particular individuals, whereas we can desire the conception only of a kind of individual, not of any particular individual of that kind. If Brutus desires the death of Caesar, he knows there is such a person as Caesar, and wants him to die. If Henry VIII, however, desires the conception of a boy, it is not the case that he thinks there is something which is a boy, and desires that boy to be conceived; he just wants-there-to-be-conceived a child of a certain kind, a male one. To be sure, we can also want the death just of an individual of a certain sort. I might go whaling not, like Captain Ahab, with the aim of killing some particular whale, but simply with the desire that there should be something which both is a whale and gets killed by me. Conception as an objective must always be general in this way. A child who has been conceived is, of course, a particular individual, but parents cannot intend to conceive the particular individual they do conceive – my parents cannot have intended to conceive me personally. At most they hoped (perhaps vainly) only to conceive a *sort* of child (affectionate, strong, nice-looking) out of particular gametes.

What intentions, in fact, can parents have? Many children are conceived unintentionally, the parents not intending to conceive a child at all, but just to have intercourse. Often, however, parents have intercourse in the hope of conceiving, or at least being willing to conceive. Why? What benefit do they take a child's coming into existence to be, and to whom? Frequently, I think, they want a benefit to themselves. In the past parents have wanted a helper on the farm, or someone to attend upon them when they grow old and feeble, or at worst have wanted a girl or boy to sell into some kind of slavery. It is also natural to want a companion, someone with whom you can be friends and exchange benefits. Parents might think it good for an existing child that it should acquire a sibling. Might an altruistic parent have the aim of conceiving children for the benefit of the children that come into existence? Coming into existence cannot itself be a benefit to a child that comes into existence. A child must already exist to be benefited. The coming into existence of a child might seem a benefit to an altruist, inasmuch it provides fresh scope for altruistic behaviour. However, is benefiting two people really better than benefiting one? When utilitarians tell us to aim at the greatest happiness of the greatest number, they mean we should maximise the happiness of people who already exist, not the number of people capable of happiness.

Natural processes generally form a system in which living things arise, and I interpreted the doctrine of creation as the doctrine that natural processes go on for the benefit of living things. They went on, scientists tell us, before any living things existed. Before any living things existed, stars and planets cannot have formed for the benefit of living things, but their formation was part of a system in which living things could arise, and it was beneficial in a way to the living things that later arose, because if these processes had not occurred those later living things would not have the benefits they then enjoyed – warmth, nourishment, society. Family life, like the whole natural order, is a system in which living things arise, and it consists of intentional acting and refraining from action by the family members. It includes the actions necessary for producing children. These actions cannot be done for the benefit of the children that do not yet exist. Nonetheless, a child that comes into being may be glad that they were done, rather as we may be glad that planets formed. Moreover, a couple might want to have sex not only for the pleasure involved and the benefit to other existing family members but as part of an ongoing system like the natural order in which new members may arise.

That is perhaps a Christian ideal. Different societies have different conceptions of what family life should consist in. Among Christians the idea that parents give existence to their children may lead to unreasonable demands and even to cruel tyranny. Parental tyranny in Christian families such Samuel Butler describes in *The Way of All Flesh*, is probably responsible for much of the hostility to Christianity that developed in the West in the nineteenth century.

Theologians who accept the traditional doctrine of Hell suggest that that we owe an infinite debt to the Creator. From people in the street the words are sometimes heard: 'I didn't ask to be born.' Superficially they are absurd since, as I said, you cannot ask for anything unless you already exist. However, do we, in fact, owe anything, either to God or to our parents, for our existence? The notion of a debt has its origin in society: we have debts, strictly speaking, only in a society with laws of contract and private property. The more general notion of duty also has its origin in society. Different societies attach different duties to the biological relationship of child to parent, and Hume (*A Treatise of Human Nature*, 3.1.1) is on strong ground when he says that no particular duties can be deduced from it.

Surely at least we owe gratitude? Although we may talk of a duty to be grateful, gratitude and duty are rather different considerations. We can have a duty to thank – omitting to write a letter of thanks may be counted as bad manners. However, the word 'gratitude' is connected with the words 'gratis' and 'grace', it suggests free giving and the virtue of gratitude is a disposition to do more for a benefactor than is required by what duty requires. The 'godly virtue' of charity is a love of God that goes beyond duty. Some Christians have a custom of saying grace at meals, thanking God for the food they receive. Rather than thinking they are under an obligation to do this, they could conceive it as a spontaneous act of charity. Acting out of gratitude to parents should be more than discharging a duty; it is showing concern for them as individuals, a concern, moreover that goes beyond the consideration it is reasonable to have for others generally. Pretty well every society attaches duties to the parent-child relationship, and sees sexual relationships too as creating duties. These biological relationships and the rewards they bring enable people to rise to a kind of rationality that transcends duty as it transcends narrow self-interest: the rationality of selfless devotion to a parent, a child or a lover.

There is not much talk in the West at present of the duties of children to their parents and grandparents. In many countries, England included, the state has largely taken over any duty children might have had to care for elderly relatives who can no longer care for themselves, though as populations age and the numbers of helpless old people multiply, states may increasingly offer euthanasia as an alternative to care. What today, however, is a topic of heated debate is whether women should have the right to terminate pregnancies by abortion. In most Western countries abortion has ceased to be illegal, but many Christians, sometimes supported by Jews and Muslims, resisted its legalisation and still try to impose limits on it.

In Classical Antiquity not only abortion but infanticide was legal and *patria potestas*, the right of a father to kill his children, sometimes lingered beyond infancy. The Christian objection to this and to abortion was that infants and unborn babies are human beings, and killing a human being is wrong unless there is some special reason for thinking it is not – for example, it has usually been held allowable in self-defence. Advocates of abortion have sometimes tried to justify it as self-defence, arguing that an unwanted foetus is an aggressor, but the usual defence is that it is not a human being but part of the mother like a finger, or just living tissue like an area of skin.

In the Middle Ages it was sometimes held that a foetus is not a human being until it receives an immortal soul, and that does not happen until it has the usual human organs including a brain. Until then it is just a potential human being rather as the burden of a tray carrying eggs, butter and flour is a potential cake. The contents of a womb become an actual human being when God inserts a soul. Although some Christians today may favour this idea – Tina Beattie, a Professor of Catholic Studies writing in *The Tablet* of 2 June 2018, suggested that Catholics might consider recovering the medieval distinction between early and late abortion based upon it – Christians mostly hold that from the moment at which an ovum is fertilised by a spermatozoon and splits in two, the two resulting cells form a very young human being. This belief is backed by more medical knowledge than was available in the Middle Ages. The gametes might be said to constitute a potential human being, but the cells into which the fertilised ovum divides constitute something the life and growth of which is determined by the genes inherited from the parents. It will not do to say that it is a living organism of some non-human species. It is eminently human, and no biologist would allow that a member of one species can arise out of a member of another like a prince out of a frog in a fairy story.

The 1984 Warnock Report on Human Fertilisation and Embryology argued that a foetus does not become a human being until a fortnight after conception because until then it may divide into identical twins. I think most people imagine their lives started when their parents had intercourse and brought together semen and ovum, rather than with a non-event, the not dividing of the resulting foetus. That is true even of identical twins; both think their lives began at conception, though they were not separated from each other for some days. The Warnock argument may have been accepted partly because the Committee wanted an argument that would allow the creation of embryos for research, but the concept of a human being is problematic, and those who deny that embryos are human beings do so not just as individuals interested in biology but as social beings. Biologists have fairly clear concepts of a species and species-membership; but, as I said in Chapter 1, the notion of life is not purely biological. It is for philosophers of science to distinguish the notion of life which applies to cells from that which applies to members of a species, and for moral philosophers to tackle questions about human beings which do not arise over unhatched goose-chicks or newborn kittens. If the belief that embryos are actual and not just potential human beings is to be described as religious, and a matter of 'faith', so should be the beliefs that rationalise abortion, that they are just living tissue or complete living organisms of some non-human species.

We form opinions in these matters as social beings. In most societies in the past having a child was considered, other things being equal, something fortunate. I mentioned some of the ways in which it could be advantageous a moment ago. In Europe in the nineteenth century this changed. The industrial revolution, which replaced manpower by machines, was proceeding on capitalist lines. All land suitable for cultivation had been appropriated. Liberals who had read Malthus were convinced that the world was threatened with overpopulation, and that its only hope was for the poor to stop having children. Having a child, at least among the poor, gradually came to be a matter not for pride and congratulation but for reproach and shame. In *On Liberty* (pp. 132-3), John Stuart Mill said: 'The laws which, in many countries on the Continent, forbid marriage unless the parties can show that they have the means of supporting a family do not exceed the legitimate powers of the State . . . they are not objectionable as violations of liberty.'

Such legislation was insufficient. The ancient remedy of infanticide was ruled out by Christianity, efficient contraception was not widely available, using a sheath was aesthetically displeasing and associated with prostitution. Nowadays abortion is legal in most Western countries and contraception is taught in state schools. The young are told to regard having a child as a slightly self-indulgent experiment or adventure, respectable only under certain fairly strict conditions. If a woman feels doubt, abortion is a safe way out.

Our thinking as social beings is influenced by the laws of our society. In many Western countries once a child is born the law gives it a right to life, or sanctions its right to life, but not before. It is easy, therefore, to persuade oneself that an unborn child is not a human being. In the days when it was legal to trade in African slaves their status as human beings was questioned, and, when in Nazi Germany the right to life of handicapped persons and those of non-Aryan ethnicity ceased to be sanctioned, people who had to deal with such persons may have thought of them as less than human. If the ban on uxoricide were lifted women might well be thought imperfectly human in comparison with men.

Caring for newborn children who are severely handicapped both mentally and physically is expensive and time-consuming; so is looking after old people who are incontinent and demented. We wish these troublesome living organisms were not there. Liberalisation of the law to allow involuntary euthanasia of those whose life can be judged 'not worth living' would enable them to be removed. We do not want to think of them as fellow human beings, and it is tempting to say that the old people are no longer persons, and that the monstrous neonates are hardly human persons; tempting to narrow the notion of a person with rights to people who are able to defend themselves or exercise their rights in a conscious way. It could be narrowed further. In an article in *Nordisk tidsskrift for palliativ medisin* 2008, entitled 'A Duty to Die?', Mary Warnock argued that, when keeping us alive costs society more than we can put into it, we have a duty to kill ourselves or ask others to kill us. If state schools taught that this was a duty and the state provided euthanasia centres, it might very well be possible to introduce a law enforcing it.

10. Questions of Life and Death

The use of the word 'person' to distinguish those human beings that should be protected by laws against killing from those that should not is becoming common in Western societies. In Chapter 5 I said that often in our dealings with people, though we know, of course, that they are human beings, we do not think of them as persons. I said we think of them as persons in thinking of them as living beings that are sentient and move and act on purpose. Was I using the word 'person' in the way I say is now becoming common? Very young (or 'early') foetuses are not sentient even in the way we are when we are deeply unconscious and do not act on purpose; severely disabled neonates may be physically unable ever to act rationally; and helpless dotards may have ceased to be physically capable of forming rational purposes and pursuing them. Today, therefore, it might be said that these human beings have not yet become persons, or cannot become persons or have ceased to be persons; they are 'potential' persons or 'ex-persons' or, in Orwell's Newspeak, 'unpersons' of some other sort. They are all, nevertheless, specimens of a sentient, rational species. In Chapter 5 I added that for us to think of human beings as persons is for our thought to have a certain form, the form it has when we act altruistically. We must think of things we may do as good or bad for them, harmful or injurious, and engage with them as friends or enemies. We think of these helpless specimens of our species as persons as I use the word, in thinking of death as good or bad for them. Death is in itself bad for any living organism as such, though there may be situations in which other things are worse; it is hard to think of any situation in which death is not bad for a healthy specimen of a rational species that has not yet developed the organs required, and had the experiences necessary, for forming rational purposes. Some women perhaps think of their unborn children as enemies; but the alternative to thinking of these Newspeak 'unpersons' as persons in the way I used the word 'person' is thinking of them as inanimate objects.

On issues of life and death, Christian culture comes into conflict with that of larger societies in the West today. Abortion, the killing of new-born babies, and euthanasia are widely legalised and carried out by the medical profession, not just by private practitioners. It is contrary to Christian principles to take part or assist in any of these activities. In medical services run by the state, refusal by Christians to do what is contrary to their principles causes trouble, and pressure is put upon them to refer patients to persons who are less scrupulous. That is unreasonable. The moral objections to working yourself as a hitman apply to recommending others for the job. The result may be that Christians have to choose between acting against their principles and leaving the services.

11
SEX AND NATURAL LAW

Every society has developed customs or laws about sex that is necessary for its surviving from one generation to the next. The traditional Christian rules are well-known. Sex should be restricted to marriage and marriage is for life; divorce falls short of the Creator's ideal. Incest, sex with animals and male homosexuality are wrong, so is polygamy. All these rules go back to the Old Testament – on divorce there is Malachi 2:16. The Jews who were the first followers of Christ had more restrictive rules about sex than the surrounding non-Jewish nations, and, far from relaxing them, as they did with the rules about eating, washing and circumcision, they imposed them on non-Jewish converts. In recent years contraception has become readily available and widely accepted both to limit family size and to prevent infection from social diseases, and some Christians, notably Catholics, have added it to the list of forbidden practices.

Many of the Christian rules about sex coincide with rules of other societies. Plato's recommendations in his *Laws* (8, 836b-839b; 9, 929e-930b) come close to them. Many civilised societies have favoured monogamy and frowned on sexual promiscuity. There will always be some sex outside marriage, but adults counsel the young against it and not only because of the risk of disease or because it is obviously irresponsible to bring into the world a child without a known father and with a mother who has no means of nourishing it or educating it. Casual sex may be motivated less by desire for pleasure than by fear of not keeping up with peers or by desire for conquest. Homer's idea of a man and a woman 'thinking alike' in a home is the ideal, and a habit of casual sex can make it harder for a man or woman to achieve it. The Christian rules about sex, though they may not have been formed with this end in conscious view, have an overall tendency to strengthen the monogamous breeding family as a sub-society within larger societies.

This is the smallest society for life. By itself it is too small to meet all our needs as social beings. Nevertheless, it has its customs by which the members live, its little rituals, often its peculiar concepts and style of humour. We need sub-societies within our nation states. Big national festivals and big athletic events are not sufficiently frequent or accessible to satisfy the needs for recreation and display of beings that are essentially social. Industrialisation, which even in the West is still moving people from the country into towns, breaks up rural communities, and though new sub-societies are formed, they lack inherited customs. People keep having to move or retrain, and the societies they form are undermined by the next technological revolution. Until recently people were always interacting with others in their vicinity. Now they are interacting more and more with people who are nowhere near them and also with people who have no real existence at all, speaking with artificial voices or created by computer programmes.

Liberals are traditionally hostile to families. Families are what Rousseau (*The Social Contract*, 2.3) called '*sociétés partielles*', societies intermediate between the individual and the state, and he described banning all such societies as following 'the unique and sublime institution of the great Lycurgus'. Darwin's account in *The Descent of Man* (Vol. 2, pp. 362-63) of primal hordes dominated by tyrannical fathers was cited and expanded by Freud, in *Totem and Taboo* (pp. 124-25, 141-42), and has probably captured and appalled many educated imaginations. Mill, when he says, 'liberty is often granted when it should be withheld,' particularly advocates more control of 'family relations' and continues (*On Liberty*, p. 128):

> The almost despotic power of husbands over wives needs not to be enlarged on here. It is in the case of children that misapplied notions of liberty are a real obstacle to the fulfilment by the State of its duties. One would almost think that a man's children were supposed to be literally, and not metaphorically, a part of himself, so jealous is opinion of the smallest interference of law with his absolute and exclusive control over them; more jealous

than of almost any interference with his own freedom of action; so much less do the generality of mankind value liberty than power.

Mill believed that it was the duty of the state to defend children against their parents, whereas one might naturally suppose that it is the duty of parents to defend their children against the state.

In any case, intentionally or inadvertently, liberal governments favour measures that weaken families. In the United Kingdom the state takes over all their traditional responsibilities. Birth and death normally occur in state-funded hospitals and home births and deaths arouse protest. Families in the past reared children and looked after old members when they became physically or mentally incapable; they can now be relieved of old people altogether, children get deposited at an early age in state-funded playgroups, and home education is allowed only under strict conditions. Most children attend state schools where they are taught what (to borrow words from Mill) 'the predominant power in government' decrees. The introduction of same-sex marriage assimilates marriage to an erotic relationship between two individuals, of which producing new members of society is not an integral part. The liberal attitude towards sex outside marriage has had the consequence, despite the availability of abortion, that more and more children are born outside marriage and are brought up either by a single parent or by a couple of whom only one member is a parent. Where both parents are present, they are both encouraged or sometimes forced by economic necessity to have jobs which take them out of the home. Households like subsistent farms in which the children join in the work of the parents have almost disappeared from the affluent West.

This policy helps the economy: people earn more and spend more. It is expensive to public services because of the psychological damage caused to children and to adults without stable relations, but its advantage to the 'dominant power in government' is that opposition to that power depends upon small groups of people coming together. Educated liberals are familiar with words attributed to Margaret Mead: 'Never doubt that a small group of thoughtful and committed citizens can change the world: it's the only thing that can.' That is how liberalism itself has gained its influence. The traditional Christian family, which is not just a small set of friends but an alliance between families, automatically brings and holds together such groups.

Christians might defend their rules about sex by stressing the need we have, in large mass-societies more than ever, for societies intermediate between the individual and the state, and by comparing Christian monogamy with alternative family arrangements. Catholic authorities today, however, try to show that the whole range of Christian rules about sex is reasonable not on grounds of practical good sense but by appeal to what they call 'natural law'. The *Compendium* of the *Catechism of the Catholic Church* declares (para. 416):

> The natural law which is inscribed by the Creator on the heart of every person consists in a participation in the wisdom and goodness of God. . . . It is universal and immutable and determines the basis of the duties and fundamental rights of the person as well as those of the human community and civil law.

John Finnis in *Natural Law and Natural Rights* (pp. 18, 251) claims that it provides 'principles of practical reasonableness'. In what follows I first say how natural law has been conceived at various times and then how people have understood the relation of law to right and wrong. Readers wishing to verify the details of what I say here about Antiquity and the Middle Ages can find fuller documentation in my essay, 'Natural Law, Aquinas and the Magisterium'.

Over the last two and a half millennia many different theories have been presented as theories of natural law. Natural law theories before the Middle Ages give no support to modern Catholic teaching on sex, and often conflict with it. Finnis' theory is based, he acknowledges, largely on the arguments of Germain Grisez in *Contraception and the Natural Law*. This theory does support Catholic teaching, but the connection with reason is lost.

Our word 'law' (as I said in Chapter 3) covers two different things: the laws of nature, which say what actually happens by physical necessity, and the laws of human societies, which say what people in those societies ought to do. What Grisez and Finnis mean by 'natural law' is law which tells all human beings not what they actually do but what they ought to do: not what is physically necessary, but what is morally necessary. Once that is understood it becomes problematic how such a law can be natural. We cannot either obey or disobey a law which says what happens as a matter of natural necessity. Before we dismiss the concept of natural law as a simple confusion, however, we should see how phrases like 'natural law' have actually been used. Natural law is mentioned in Greek writing of the Classical and Hellenistic periods, in Justinian's sixth-century corpus of Roman Law, in the Canon Law of the twelfth century, in Aquinas' *Summa Theologiae*, and in the jurisprudence that accompanied the rise of the modern nation state, as well as in the Catholic moral theology of the last hundred years.

The ancient Greeks had a word, *nomos*, that covered the written laws and the unwritten customs of societies, but they did not use that word for the laws of physical or biological nature. Those were covered by their word for nature, *phusis*. Perhaps because they had these two words in place of our one, they did not explicitly draw our distinction between descriptive and prescriptive laws. They distinguished between *nomos* and *phusis*, but did so by saying that *phusis* is what is always and everywhere the same, whereas *nomos* is different in different places. That is plain, for instance, in Fragment 44 of Antiphon the Sophist. (The fragment is mistranslated in Kathleen Freeman's *Ancilla to the Pre-Socratic Philosophers*; she makes him speak of 'laws' implanted by nature.) Antiphon distinguishes *nomima*, things which vary from city to city and are imposed by agreement, from *ta phuseôs*, natural things, which are necessary. The majority of things, he says, that are right according to law are inimical to nature; what law prescribes is no more natural than what it forbids. Laws are bonds upon nature. As examples of what is natural, he gives being born, using mouth and nose to breathe, and using hands to eat, things that are the same everywhere.

A.P. d'Entrèves, in his book *Natural Law* (p. 8), quotes Ernest Barker as saying that 'the origin of the idea of natural law' may be traced 'already in the *Antigone* of Sophocles'. The reference is to Antigone's speech at lines 450-60. Asked by Creon whether she knew it had been decreed that her brother should lie unburied, she says:

> It was not Zeus that decreed this to me,
> Nor did that Justice that dwells with the gods below
> Lay such decrees upon human beings.
> I did not judge that your decrees had such strength that you,
> A mortal, might override the unwritten and secure laws of the gods.
> They are not of today or yesterday; they live, I think, for ever,
> And no one knows from where they came.
> I did not intend, through fear of any man,
> To answer for them before the gods.

These are magnificent words; but Antigone has nothing in her mind about nature. What she opposes to Creon's recent decree is the Theban religious custom of burying the dead; and she is not aware, not having read Herodotus, of the very different customs prevailing in other parts of the world.

The idea of natural law might more plausibly be traced back to Heraclitus. He says that, 'All human laws are nourished by one law, the divine law' (Fragment 114), and by 'divine law' he probably means not,

11. Sex and Natural Law

like Hesiod in *Works and Days* (276), a law given by Zeus, but universal natural law. He appears to have been a kind of pantheist. His fragments foreshadow Stoic thinking, but they are oracular, even in the fifth century, before his works became fragmented, they were found obscure, and it is hard to know how far they were influential.

We first find a definite reference to natural law in Thucydides' Melian dialogue. (*History of the Peloponnesian War*, 5.105.2). The Athenian envoys say:

> Of the gods we believe and of men we know for sure that by absolute necessity of nature [*phusis*] they rule where they can; and we, neither having made this law [*nomos*] nor being the first to use it, but taking it as exists and leaving it to abide for ever, make use of it in the knowledge that you and others with the same power would do the same to us.

This may have been a commonplace among liberal thinkers of the fifth century. Callicles in Plato's *Gorgias* (484b, 488b) quotes Pindar to show that it is naturally just and a natural law that the strong should pillage and rule the weak. It is here, I think, that the idea first appears that there is a natural law prescribing human conduct, and, in its first appearance, natural law replaces psychological egoism, the theory that we cannot help being ruthlessly selfish, with ethical egoism, the theory that we ought to be.

Plato not only rejects egoism; he denies that any law whatever can tell all human beings what they ought to do:

> Law can never embrace in a single prescription what is best for everyone and lay down accurately what is most right and just. The differences between men and actions, and the fact that nothing ever, so to speak, remains steady in human affairs, do not permit any skill whatever to declare anything simple in any matter that applies to all people at all times. (*Statesman*, 294a10-b6)

Likewise Aristotle: particular actions 'fall under no set of rules [*parangelia*]; the people acting must themselves look to what the occasion requires, as in medicine' (*Nicomachean Ethics*, 2, 1104a1-10). For both Aristotle and Plato, laws are necessary for society but can prescribe only in outline (*tupôi*) and what is best *on the whole while they are in force*.

Disreputable in Classical times, natural law becomes respectable in the Hellenistic age. Chrysippus said that there is no better approach to good, evil, virtue and happiness than from 'nature that is common' (*hê koinê phusis*, in *The Hellenistic Philosophers*, ed. A.A. Long and D.N. Sedley, 60 A); common, presumably, to everyone and the fundamental principle of Stoic ethics is to live 'in agreement (*homologoumenôs*) with nature, which is to live virtuously since nature leads us to this' (Diogenes Laertius 7 87).

However, 'living in accordance with nature' was expanded to 'living in accordance with experience [*empeiria*] of what happens naturally' (Long and Sedley 63 B). The early Stoics do not seem to have used the phrase 'natural law', but they formulated what was later taken to be the basis of natural law in terms of natural 'impulses' or endeavours, *hormai*. *Hormê* is the word Aristotle uses for the natural tendencies of different materials to move towards or away from the centre of the universe – his equivalent of our fundamental forces of attraction and repulsion. The Stoics say: 'The first impulse of an animal is to self-preservation ... and since reason [*logos*] has been given to rational animals as a more perfect superintendence [*kata teleioteran prostasian*], it becomes natural for them to live according to reason: reason becomes a craftsman [*tekhnitês*] of their impulse' (Long and Sedley 57 A).

They appear, then, to have held that what is right for human beings is for them to use their experience of what happens naturally to guide their impulse towards self-preservation. In sexual ethics the early Stoics were remarkably permissive. Zeno favoured communal wives (Long and Sedley 67 B) and Chrysippus incest (Long and Sedley 67 F), on the ground that animals have no trouble with it.

The character of the Stoic theory of natural law may have been obscured for later thinkers by another strand in Stoic ethics: what Isaiah Berlin in *Two Concepts of Liberty* called, 'The retreat to the inner citadel'. The ideas he attributes to eighteenth-century thinkers all appear in Stoic writings. They are a recurrent theme in Epictetus' *Discourses* (for instance, 2.1-2, 4.1). We should not set our hearts on anything that can be taken from us. External goods like money and social position can be, but not internal goods, not thoughts or qualities of soul, so we should concentrate on them. We should lead simple lives, seeking only those external goods which are absolutely necessary, bread, water, basic clothes and so on. Cicero, summarising Stoic doctrine, says that the truly happy man (the *beatus*) is 'safe, unassailable, walled round and fortified [*tutum, inexpugnabilem, saeptum atque munitum*], so that he has no fears' (Tusculan Disputations 5.40-1). This part of Stoic teaching has little to do with natural law, but it appealed to early Christians, as we can see from the Pauline letters: Romans 6:1-14, 7:14-23, 8:21; 1 Corinthians 7:21-23; and Ephesians 4:17-24.

11. Sex and Natural Law

Natural law, under the name of *ius naturale*, is given prominence at the beginning of Justinian's codification of Roman law. His *Institutes*, Book 1, section 2, divides law into *ius naturale*, *ius gentium* and *ius civile*. *Ius naturale* is defined as:

> What nature teaches all animals. For this law is not proper to the human race but belongs to all animals that are born in the heavens, on earth or in the sea. From this derives the conjunction of male and female, which we call 'marriage' [*matrimonium*], from this the procreation and education of children; for we see that other animals too have experience of this law.

Ius gentium consists of what is common to all societies that have laws and customs, and *ius civile* is law peculiar to a particular society like the ancient Athenians.

This definition of natural law, which was to be taken up by Aquinas, goes back to Ulpian, a prefect of the Praetorian Guards from 222 to 228. Other jurists, however, recognise only a twofold division of law. Gaius, an earlier and more authoritative writer than Ulpian, distinguishes only *ius civile*, laws proper to particular societies, and *ius gentium*, which all societies use and 'which natural reason [*naturalis ratio*] has established among all human beings' (Justinian, Digest 1.1.9). The customs of a society, as I said in Chapter 2, prescribe what seem best on the whole to the society in its circumstances at the time, and, if there are any laws common to all societies, they must prescribe what seems best to all social beings at all times. D'Entrèves says that natural law theory stresses that law is 'an act of intellect' (p. 120), and that was the view at least of Gaius. Similarly, Paulus, a contemporary of Ulpian, distinguishes only 'what is always fair and good, that is, natural law [*ut est ius naturale*]' from 'what is useful to all or most people in a particular society, that is, civil law [*ut est ius civile*]' (Justinian Digest 1.1.11). It looks as if the threefold division, and the recognition of natural law as something distinct from human law and common to all animals, though it has Stoic roots, (Cicero, *De Finibus Bonorum et Malorum*, 3.62-8,) is peculiar to Ulpian.

It is a theme of D'Entreve's study that if we want to see what idea of natural law people at any time had, we should consider what they want it for. The early Stoics lived in a chaotic world in which the city state had collapsed and nothing had yet taken its place. They appealed to natural law because human law, it could be said, had failed them. Chrysippus' famous opening words to his book on law: 'Law is the king of all things, human and divine' (Long and Sedly 67 R) express wishful thinking. The writings of the early Stoics have survived only in fragments, and were known to medieval and modern thinkers chiefly through Cicero and Seneca. These Romans tell us what they took to be the Stoic conception of natural law; but the world to which they belonged was different from that of Zeno and Chrysippus. It was an orderly world basking in the rule of law. Roman jurists used natural law, not as a refuge for the individual from surrounding anarchy, but, says d'Entrèves, to justify applying the laws of a single nation to a worldwide empire embracing many nations with a variety of traditional customs: 'It played a decisive part . . . in elaborating the legal system of an international or rather super-national civilization' (p. 30). They wanted to present the system not as arbitrary but as reasonable and therefore stable. 'Natural laws,' says Justinian (*Institutes*, 1.2), identifying them with the *ius gentium*, 'which are observed equally by all nations, being established by a certain divine providence [*divina quadam providentia constituta*], remain always firm and immutable.' They did not, however, suggest (as Antigone might have suggested if, instead of being an illiterate Bronze Age princess, she had been a graduate of a modern university) that reason could discover a system of law superior 'to positive law, in the sense that, in a case of conflict, the one should overrule the other'. It is significant that, while noting that slavery is 'contrary to natural law', the *Institutes* begins (1.2-3): 'Every law we use pertains either to persons or to actions or to things, and first let us see about persons. . . . The main division [*summa divisio*] of the law of persons is this: that all men are either free or slaves.'

Cicero equates natural law with divine law. Speaking in the person of a Stoic in *De Republica* (3.33), he says: 'There is one common master, so to speak, and master of all, god; he is the deviser, judge and enactor of this law.' This identification is not challenged by Justinian's 'divine providence', but by that time (530-3) the Empire was Christian, and this made a difference to the identification. Though Cicero thought that there were divine laws, he did not attribute them to a transcendent source of the natural order. The gods recognised by the Classical Greeks and Romans were ingredients of the natural order, and did not go in for legislation. Hellenistic philosophers had the notion of an immanent source of the natural order, and it is with this idea that Cicero is working in the passage just quoted. For him we discover the divine law by investigating the laws of nature including those of psychology. Antigone probably just assumed that the duties to blood relations recognised in her city had divine sanction; on her own admission nobody actually knew from where they came. Christians, in contrast, took from Judaism the

11. Sex and Natural Law

idea of a transcendent source of the natural order who has promulgated a code of laws that can be found in the Old Testament. In Book 2 of his *Against Apion*, Flavius Josephus says that the Jews believe the laws given by Moses are of divine institution. Christians, though they dispensed with much of Mosaic law, still held authentic the revelation described in Exodus XX:19-23: divine law is as much of Mosaic law as they retained. This difference did not affect the body of Roman law under Justinian, but it was to have consequences later.

After the *Corpus Iuris Civilis* of the sixth century, natural law makes its next important appearance in the *Corpus Iuris Canonici* of the twelfth. Gratian, the founder of medieval jurisprudence, begins his Decree (c. 1140) in words quoted by Aquinas (*ST*, 1a 2ae, Q. 94, Art. 4):

> The human race is ruled by two things, natural law and custom [*mores*]. The law of nature is what is contained in the [Mosaic] Law and the Gospel, by which each person is commanded to do to others what he wishes to have done to himself, and forbidden to do to others what he wishes not to have done to himself.

D'Entrèves claims that medieval jurists wanted the notion of natural law to establish: 'a system of natural ethics', the 'cornerstone' of which, they thought, 'must be natural law'. He calls this (*Natural Law*, p. 37) a 'new function for the idea of the law of nature' and rightly because, for the Roman jurists, natural ethics, what seems best to everyone, was the basis of natural law, not the other way round. Unfortunately, those laws that are common to all human societies are too few and general to form a complete ethical system. However, if natural law is identified with Mosaic law, it already constitutes a complete ethical system, covering everything in the life of a relatively simple Middle Eastern nation. The price paid for this, though d'Entrèves does not remark on it, is that natural law ceases to be 'an act of intellect'; it is God's will as revealed to Moses.

D'Entrèves says that the new function for the idea of the law of nature 'is nowhere more apparent than in the teaching of St Thomas Aquinas', but Aquinas, it seems to me, bases his moral philosophy more upon the *Nicomachean Ethics* of Aristotle (which had just been translated into Latin for the first time) than on any concept of natural law. He does not use the word *ius*, which has an ambiguity I shall discuss in a moment, but the word *lex*, a word that implicitly suggests a legislator. In the *Summa contra Gentiles*, he does not speak of natural law at all, but only of divine law, *lex divina*. In the *Summa Theologiae* he does speak of a *lex naturalis*, and argues (1a 2ae, Q. 94, Art. 2) that it has more precepts than one.

These, he says, have an order corresponding to three natural inclinations. The first is one common to everything, inanimate objects included: it is to continue in existence. The second is one common to all animals, and here he quotes Ulpian, 'the natural conjunction of male and female, and the education of children'. The third is proper to rational beings: to seek the truth about God and live in society.

Aquinas does not actually formulate any precepts corresponding to these 'inclinations'. He accepts, however, Aristotle's definition of goodness as 'what all things aim at' (*Nicomachean Ethics*, 1, 1094a30). According to this, thinking something good is not judging it to have a property, goodness, but rather having it as a positive objective. A positive objective is something we act to cause or preserve, or something lest we prevent which or destroy which we refrain from acting. Thinking something bad is having it as something we act to prevent or destroy, or something lest we cause which we refrain from acting – having it, we may say, as a negative objective. Good, says Aquinas, is that which is to be done and pursued (*faciendum et persequendum*) and bad that which is to be avoided (*vitandum*). No doubt he thought that, if nature gives us as objectives staying alive, having sexual intercourse and rearing children, learning about God and living in society, nature prescribes that these things are to be done.

What nature? How exactly should we understand his list of natural inclinations? He allows (1a 2ae, Q. 94, Art. 2, Ad. 2), following Plato, that the human soul has several parts, the parts he mentions, the *concupiscibilis* and the *irascibilis*, are Plato's *epithumêtikon* and *thumoeides*. His inclinations, however, correspond not to parts of the soul but to parts of nature as a whole. It might be argued that the first anticipates Spinoza's *conatus*, 'Everything, so far as it can, endeavours to persist in its existence' (*Ethics*, 3.6), and Newton's First Law, that bodies in motion keep moving uniformly and bodies at rest stay put. Ulpian, as d'Entrèves says (*Natural Law*, p. 25), seems to have in mind 'something like the general instinct of animals'. Here, then, we have statements of what actually happens, first, in the whole of nature, then, among sentient beings, or at least those familiar to Ulpian's society; the third 'inclination' can be understood in the same way: rational beings do seek knowledge of the source of the natural order and form societies. Inanimate objects, however, do not endeavour *to continue in existence or in uniform motion*; no precept of natural law can be derived from this first 'inclination'. Many animals do aim (though physicalists would question this) at sexual intercourse and rearing offspring. They do not know, however, that intercourse can result in procreation or think rearing offspring necessary to the survival of their family, flock or herd, and, when Aquinas speaks of parts of the soul (which according to Plato each has its own characteristic forms of desire and aversion), he says that their desires pertain to natural law only 'insofar as they are regulated by reason'. Only if regulated by intelligence and brought back (*reducuntur*) to a reasoned pursuit of objectives, do the desires of these parts correspond to precepts of natural law. Aquinas can hardly mean to erect animal instinct into a system of ethics. Rather his thought is that survival, reproduction, life in society and theological speculation are natural for human beings insofar as they are rationally chosen. Aquinas does not develop Plato's analysis of human nature, as I did earlier, distinguishing self-interest, social life and altruism as rational objectives. He separates reproduction from social life, and he perhaps includes disinterested concern for others in ordinary social life, distinguishing it from the divine virtue of charity which is disinterested love of God. What Aquinas says, however, is consistent with what I proposed in earlier chapters. It is also consistent with the ancient view that no rule can prescribe what is best for everyone in every situation.

What has perhaps given people the idea that Aquinas derives a system of ethics from natural law is that, in the *Summa contra Gentiles* (3.122), he derives a system of *sexual* ethics from the notion of a natural *function*; a system, moreover, that coincides perfectly with the current Catholic teaching. The notion of a function (Aquinas uses the Latin word *finis*, 'end', but the concept is expressed in Greek by *ergon*, 'work') is problematic. Plato, starting from the functions of artefacts, defined a thing's function as 'what it alone or it better than anything else can do' (*Republic*, 1, 352e). Today as L. Wright says in his article 'Functions' we take as the function of an artefact what it was *made for*, and as the function of a natural organ or process, what it was *naturally selected for*. This fits well with Catholic teaching, since it identifies the function of an organ or process with its contribution to the organism's having offspring like itself. The function, then, of semen (which Aquinas calls a 'part' of the human body) and of ejaculation is clearly procreation. Aquinas infers (*ex quo patet quod*) that stimulating or permitting this process to occur in such a way that conception cannot result is the worst of sexual offences, worse even than rape of a virgin still in *patria potestas*. The inference looks invalid. The most that follows is that doing this is silly if you are attempting procreation, and even that is doubtful once *in vitro* fertilisation is possible.

Aquinas tries to bolster his inference by saying that, although procreation is 'superfluous' (*superfluum*) for the conservation of individuals, it is necessary for the propagation of the species; so, although the good of individuals is 'not much impeded' by sex *contra naturam*, it still fights against something naturally good (*repugnant bono naturae*), namely the conservation of the species. Aquinas omits to say *to whom* the conservation of the human species is good. A species is not itself a living thing, and cannot be benefited. In fact, procreation is necessary for the conservation of societies, and benefits individuals as social beings, members of societies. Aquinas, however, does not make this point, and not every individual act *contra naturam* impedes the preservation of the agent's family or larger society; in some circumstances additional procreation may impede it.

In the *Summa Theologiae* (1a 2ae, Q. 93, Art. 6) Aquinas argues that we are subject to eternal law in two ways. Like non-rational creatures, we are subject to the creator's physical laws, the laws that govern acting and being affected causally; when pricked, we bleed. As rational beings, we are also subject 'by way of knowledge', that is, we get to know these laws and act upon our knowledge. The Stoics, I suggested, thought that a wise man would use knowledge of the laws of nature to achieve his objectives as a private individual. If a wise couple want a child, they will apply their knowledge of human biology in choosing for intercourse the fertile period of the woman's cycle; if they don't, but desire sexual pleasure as a contribution to life together, they apply it in using contraceptives.

This is the only way in which we can use knowledge of the laws of nature; but we use knowledge of human prescriptive laws in two ways. We still use it in pursuing our various objectives. Knowing that it is a law of England that motorists drive on the left, I use this knowledge when, stepping onto a road, in order to stay alive, I look first to my right. Motorists also use it in obeying it; and we all use our knowledge of the laws of our society in living according to them. Believing in God involves believing that what happens of natural necessity does so because God wants it to, and this may have led Aquinas to assume that the only right way to use knowledge of the laws of nature is in obeying them. As I said at the start, we cannot either obey or disobey the laws of nature. Nevertheless, once we know the natural function of some organ or process, we can use our knowledge of chemistry and biology to remove or refrain from introducing impediments to the achievement of that organ or process of its natural function and refrain from introducing such impediments. Though that is not obeying any law of nature, Aquinas may have felt it to be the next best thing. In practice it amounts to making the conservation of the human species, and perhaps the evolution of new species, rational objectives for someone with disinterested love of God.

11. Sex and Natural Law

Aquinas lived in the thirteenth century. That was a turning point in Western understanding of the relation of law to right and wrong. The twelfth-century canon lawyers, who reshaped the administration of justice in Western Europe, identified natural law with the law of Moses. At the same time the newly founded universities revived the teaching of logic and Western Europe saw what Alexander Murray in *Reason and Society in the Middle Ages*, called 'the emergence of the arithmetical mentality'. Mathematics, and especially arithmetic, which had languished since the fall of the Western Empire, revived. Proofs in mathematics are deductive. People began to sense that what custom or law prescribes cannot be proved right deductively, and what it forbids cannot be proved wrong deductively. Appeal to Mosaic law, or to divine law, began to appear as an alternative justification.

The seventeenth century saw a flood of literature on *ius naturale*: Suarez wrote *De Legibus*, Grotius, *De Jure Belli ac Pacis*, and Pufendorf *De Jure Naturae et Gentium*; and natural law comes into Hobbes' *Leviathan* and Spinoza's *Theologico-Political Treatise* and *Political Treatise*. The differences between these authors and their predecessors in Antiquity are many and large. Pufendorf rejected the idea that there is a natural law relating to all animals. He and Grotius also rejected Aristotle's teaching, preserved by Aquinas, that there is a formal difference between mathematical reasoning and reasoning about right and wrong. Furthermore, there were two dramatic shifts of balance.

The first is in the relation of law to what is right and wrong. Plato, while allowing that what the gods like coincides with what is right, says that the gods like it because it is right, not the other way around (*Euthyphron*, 10-12). Roman jurists favoured the idea that *ius quod iustum*, that it is because something is in itself just that the law prescribes it. Enlightenment thinkers, in contrast, hold that nothing is right or wrong independently of being enjoined or forbidden by law. 'Good and evil,' says Locke (*An Essay Concerning Human Understanding*, 2.28, 5-8):

> as hath been shown . . . are nothing but pleasure and pain, or that which occasions or procures pleasure or pain to us. Morally good and evil, then, is only the conformity or disagreement of our voluntary acts to some law *whereby good or evil is drawn on us from the will and power of the lawmaker* [my italics].

The lawmaker may be God, who, being our maker, has 'the right' to impose on us what laws he pleases, or 'the commonwealth', or educated public opinion. The doctrine that what makes an action wrong is its being forbidden by a law sanctioned by penalties beyond the natural consequences of the act is defended both by the Protestant thinkers Pufendorf and Hobbes and, Finnis (p. 45) concedes, by the Catholics Suarez and Gabriel Vazquez.

The second shift is in the relation of law to rights. Ancient and medieval authors had no word for rights as distinct from laws; the Latin word *ius* and the Greek *dikê* covered both. Societies recognised specific rights, property rights, parental and matrimonial rights, rights to do or to refrain from doing certain things, but these were sanctioned by laws. Rights are held against specific people, who have corresponding duties that are legally enforced. If I have a right to draw water from your well, you have a duty to let me draw it. We hold the right to life against other human beings (not, of course, against sharks or bacteria) in that they have a duty to refrain from killing us which our society enforces. Enlightenment thinkers make rights prior to laws. 'Right,' says Hobbes (*Leviathan*, 1.14), 'consisteth in liberty to do or forebear,' and:

> the right of nature, which writers commonly call *ius naturale*, is the liberty each man hath to use his own power, as he will himself, for the preservation of his own nature; that is to say, of his own life; and consequently, of doing anything which in his own judgement and reason, he shall conceive to be the aptest means thereunto.

This idea goes back to Suarez (*De Legibus*, 1.2.5) and Grotius, *De Iure Belli ac Pacis*, 1.1.2) and is confirmed, though he is not uncritical of Hobbes, by Pufendorf (*De Iure Naturae et Gentium*, 2.2.3). In equating natural law with natural right, Hobbes brought it back to the natural law of the Athenian envoys of Thucydides' Melian dialogue and Callicles in Plato's *Gorgias*.

It is used, however, in other ways. According to the new conception of law, what a law commands is right because it is prescribed by a lawgiver, and the lawgiver has the 'right', the freedom and power, to prescribe what he pleases. Early writers used this to justify positive laws because they thought the person who prescribes them, God or the head of state, has the power to do so. However, as the light of the Enlightenment brightens, it becomes questionable whether God does lay down these laws, whether, indeed, the God of Moses exists at all. The power of a head of state to legislate as he pleases is challenged, and the new conception of law is then used to justify revolution. Legislation flows from the arbitrary will of the people, so today we recognise as binding only laws laid down by democratically elected legislators. We have also come to think of legislation not as creating rights that ought to exist but as sanctioning natural rights that already exist independently of legal sanction but are discerned by virtuous legislators.

These shifts of balance in jurisprudence can be traced to two innovations elsewhere in philosophy. One, mentioned just now, concerns forms of reasoning. Non-philosophers who have any general idea at all of reasoning about what should be done conceive it precisely as inferring what you ought or ought not to do from what, so far as you can ascertain, is the case. There is no suggestion in Plato or Aristotle that this is not just what practical reasoning, as distinct from reasoning in mathematics, is. Although it was left to Hume in the eighteenth century to say explicitly that an 'ought' cannot validly be inferred from an 'is', such ideas are often operative in people's thinking before they are formulated, and the increasing reliance on law raises in me the suspicion that philosophers were beginning to doubt whether an 'ought' could validly be inferred from an 'is' at least from the seventeenth century when Descartes made mathematical reasoning, which is purely deductive, the paradigm for all rational thought; perhaps even from the thirteenth, when Western Europe rediscovered deductive logic and mathematics.

The second innovation is the development of the concept of the will. Ancient philosophers had no concept of a faculty of will. They recognised something for which Latin authors used the word *voluntas*; but, although this is the word seventeenth-century writers use as the Latin for 'will', it did not originally mean a faculty, but rather what we today mean by 'desire', or by 'will' only in the sense in which we speak of *doing* someone else's will – as in 'Thy will [*thelêma*, Matthew 6:10] be done' – or of doing something *against* one's will. Sentience and intelligence were thought faculties sufficient to account for all human behaviour. Desire and aversion were equated with thinking things (in one way or another) good and bad. All action and inaction could be interpreted in terms of what the agent thought to be the case and judged best in that situation.

This came to seem too simple in two ways. The ancients themselves noticed that we often do what we apparently think wrong and refrain from doing something even when we want to do it. Plato and Aristotle offered ingenious explanations of this appearance which would preserve the simplicity of their psychology. Their explanations, however, traced wrongdoing back to some intellectual failure, to ignorance, stupidity or temporary intellectual blindness, and this seemed to reduce the culpability of wrongdoers and make it hard to justify harsh retributive punishment. Culpability is needed to justify not only private vengeance but a good deal of official penal practice, and harsh divine punishment was part of Christian thinking.

One use for the will was forensic, to establish culpability. The other was philosophical. Philosophy revived in the West contemporaneously with increasing literacy, with demand for naturalistic painting and with skill at executing it. Philosophers came to conceive thoughts on the model of written sentences or pictures by Botticelli or Titian but neither written sentences nor naturalistic pictures can *do* anything. How, then do thoughts, including the thoughts that something is good or bad, get translated into actions that can be rewarded or punished? A new faculty is needed, a divinely given faculty, peculiar to human beings, of free will, which has precisely that function. It is like a kind of switch we turn, that makes our limbs move to enact what is written or depicted.

This faculty, convenient alike for penologists and for philosophers, enables people to do what at the time of doing it they clearly perceive to be bad or wrong. It is free in that whether we turn the switch is not determined either by any causal action upon us or by our judgement of what is good or pleasant. It is this arbitrary choice that becomes the basis for law and morals. The only thing to which nobody can object is acting as you choose; and the free exercise of will in electing legislators establishes law.

Grisez and Finnis have tried to develop a theory of natural law alternative to Enlightenment theory. 'Theoretical reflection,' says Grisez (*Contraception and the Natural Law*, pp. 64-65), reveals an open list of 'natural objects of human inclination', for example, preserving life, mating and raising children, 'developing skills and exercising them in play and fine art' (I suppose he means chess and painting in water colours), seeking truth, consorting with other human beings and obtaining their approval, and establishing 'good relationships with unknown higher powers'. We don't *infer* from our being inclined to these things that we should pursue them, nor, as Plato and Aristotle seem to have thought, is an inclination to them *the same* as thinking them good, but 'practical insight' or 'intelligence' clicks in and '*prescribes*' them as intrinsic goods to be pursued. Since they are 'incommensurable', no one of them should be sacrificed to any other; each, as Mill would say, counts for one and none for more than one (pp. 68-9). Though reason does not prescribe pursuing 'natural objects of human inclination' all the time, it does forbid us ever to 'act directly against' any of them, ever to act to prevent one. These writers do not tell us whom these so called 'goods' benefit or how they are beneficial; like G.E. Moore in *Principia Ethica* (s. 50), they write as though something could be good in itself without being good for anyone or anything.

They claim that this theory is Thomistic, but it differs substantially from that of the *Summa Theologiae* (1a 2ae, Q. 94, Art. 2). Aquinas' three 'inclinations', correspond more or less to the distinction between the laws of physics, the instincts of animals, and the purposes of conscious and intelligent human beings. Grisez's open list of goods and Finnis' catalogue in chapter IV section 2 of precisely eight such items seem to be compiled on no principle; they are just things Grisez and Finnis enjoy. Unlike Aquinas, they confuse an animal's instinct to preserve its own life with an inclination to preserve life wherever it is found (Grisez, *Contraception and the Natural Law*, p. 90; Finnis, p. 86). Moreover, Aquinas does not claim for his natural tendencies what they claim for their 'goods', that each counts for one and none for more than one.

Grisez says that contraception injures 'the unconceived child' (*Contraception and the Natural Law*, p. 94). He may take that idea from the *Summa Theologiae* (2a 2ae, Q. 154, Art. 3) in which Aquinas says fornication is 'against the good of the child that will be born'. If so, he confuses being born with being conceived. Fornication, for Aquinas, is making a woman pregnant *and then abandoning her*, and that, he declares, injures her unborn child. Unborn children exist and can be harmed; unconceived children do not and cannot. Furthermore, Grisez has to step delicately to maintain that, although it is not always good to pursue 'the procreative good', although it can be good to refrain from intercourse because of something (the woman's ovulation) that would make it procreative, and good to have intercourse in spite of something (the infertile period) that would prevent it from being procreative, nonetheless it is always bad to act to prevent procreation.

Whatever we may think of Grisez's footwork here, what d'Entrèves saw in pre-medieval natural law theory theories – 'a plea for reasonableness in action' – is abandoned by him and by Finnis. Both accept Hume's principle that an 'ought' cannot be derived from an 'is'. 'The principles of practical reason,' says Grisez (*Contraception and the Natural Law*, p. 61) are 'fundamental *prescriptions*': 'we are careful not to commit the usual error of inferring from a preferred set of facts to an illicit conclusion that these facts imply obligation' (p. 65; similarly, Finnis, pp. 37, 47). It follows immediately, in Hume's words, that actions 'cannot be reasonable or unreasonable'. They say that their precepts are dictated by reason, but that seems to be just assertion; we are not told why we should act to bring their 'goods' into existence; we are supposed to intuit this and, if our intuitive powers do not extend that far, we must be deficient in practical reason.

Grisez says (p. 64): 'The basic human inclinations, of whose existence and place theoretical reflection thus assures us, become the source of the primary principles of practical reason not by theoretical reflection but by practical insight. The act of practical insight itself cannot be performed discursively or communicated linguistically.' Grisez here admits that his theory is intuitionist; he denies it is a command theory on the ground that prescriptions are not the same as commands, but that seems to be a distinction without a difference. To defend it (in 'The First Principle of Practical Reason', p. 375), he says: 'The imperative contains motive force derived from an antecedent act of will.' Even if there are such acts as acts of will, however, emphasis on the imperative mood (something not all languages have) is arbitrary. 'Procreation is to be pursued' is still not an indicative form of speech.

Finnis' belief that his and Grisez's theory of natural law provides 'principles' of 'practical reasonableness' is confused. For such a principle ought to be one for reasoning from what appears to be the case to what we ought to do, and Finnis agrees with Hume that we cannot do this at all. Aquinas does say, 'The precepts of natural law stand to practical reason as the first principles of demonstrations stand to theoretical reason' (*ST*, 1a 2ae, Q. 94, Art. 2). If, however, there are principles of practical reason analogous to principles of theoretical reasoning, these should take the form, not of 'fundamental prescriptions' from which specific prescriptions about contraception and fornication can be derived deductively, but of rules of inference in deductive logic. They should be rules like *modus ponens*, which says that for any two propositions, if we know that the first implies the second and we also know that the first is true, we can infer that the second is true.

It will be agreed that this is a fundamental principle of deductive reasoning; but can there be any analogous principles of practical reasoning, any rules for deriving counsels from statements of fact? What are sometimes construed as fundamental prescriptions are in fact such rules. I argued in Chapter 3 that 'We ought to obey the rules of our society' is not a prescription from which we can deduce that we ought to take some action or refrain from some action. Rather it defines rationality for social beings. It can be formulated as an explicit rule in the following way: 'If we know that, if something is the case, custom requires us to act in a certain way, and we also know that it actually is the case, then we can judge such action good, and have it as a positive rational objective.'

'Do as you would be done by' provides another example. If we treat it as a fundamental prescription, an Enlightenment thinker may ask 'Why should I?' and no reason can be given. However, suppose we say this: 'If we know that, if a situation exists, certain action by us is necessary to benefit another person, and we also know that that situation exists, we can judge that action good or right and have it as a rational objective.' We have now formulated a principle of practical reasoning, the principle, in fact, that altruism is rational.

The same goes for the principle of egoism, 'Act as will benefit you as an individual organism': that too can be treated as a rule of inference for practical reasoning. That there are several such rules of inference is a consequence of there being several parts to our nature as rational agents; each has its distinct form of rationality. We cannot reduce any one to any other, but nor can any one of them flourish or be completely rational without the others. Unlike the 'goods', however, of Grisez and Finnis, they can be put in order, with altruism at the top and egoism at the bottom.

Three points about these rules. First, if we treat them not as rules of practical inference but as fundamental prescriptions, not only do we lay ourselves open to the charge of substituting intuition for reason, we can also be charged with the fallacy with which the Tortoise charged Achilles in Lewis Carroll's *What the Tortoise Said to Achilles*. Achilles (I slightly simplify what Carroll says) offered an argument in which he used *modus ponens*. The Tortoise asked: 'What if I don't accept *modus ponens*?' Achilles tried to meet the question by making it a further premise that *modus ponens* is true. What he should have said is: 'If you don't accept *modus ponens*, what would count as a reason for accepting anything? You are simply rejecting the concept of theoretical rationality.' Similarly, if a Humean asks, 'Why should I do what benefits me as an individual organism?' We can counter, 'What would you count as a reason for doing anything?' He is simply rejecting the concept of practical rationality as distinct from deductive reasoning.

Second, these rules allow us to pass from a premise starting, 'It is the case that . . .' to a conclusion starting, 'It would be good to . . .' or 'It would be bad to . . .'. They do not permit us to pass to a conclusion beginning: 'It would be best to . . .' or 'It would be best not to . . .'. The conclusions they license are not indicative statements, but nor are they orders or prohibitions settling finally how people should act. They enable us to see behaviour as intentional. When I do something, you may wonder if my action was intentional or inadvertent, even automatic like hiccupping. You can think, 'If so and so was the case, or he thought it was, then he had a reason for doing it and we can understand his action as action for that reason.' A circumstance, however, can be a reason without being an overriding reason. Often, we have reasons both for and against a course of action. If there are crocodiles in a pool, that is a reason for not jumping in, but it might not be an overriding reason if your infant child has just fallen in. When we have reasons for and against a course, these principles of practical reasoning cannot enable us to discern what is *best*; if they could, then, *pace* Plato and Aristotle, there could be laws laying down what is best for everyone on all occasions. In fact, to discern what is best we need what the Greeks called *phronêsis* and medieval writers, *prudentia*.

Third, though these rules of practical inference have their roots in human nature, they do not correspond to the three areas of nature to which Aquinas relates his 'inclinations': physical objects, generally, sentient beings, generally, and rational beings. Some writers today confuse purpose with biological function or evolutionary advantage. They assume that any action that actually helps the agent to survive and reproduce is really self-interested. Mary Midgley has documented this in *Are You an Illusion?* There is no need to attribute such confusion to Aquinas. The rules for practical inference correspond to 'inclinations' of rational beings as such, Aquinas' smallest area.

In Western countries today incest and polygamy are still illegal, but sex outside marriage is no longer thought wrong, nor is male homosexuality, and same-sex couples are allowed to acquire the same legal protection and privileges as breeding couples and may adopt children. Marriage and adoption require official ratification by the state. Male homosexuality is contrary to traditional Christian culture, and most Christians think it a loss to a child not to be brought up in a household where a man and a woman live together. Considerable latitude, also, is allowed to recognised professionals conducting *in vitro* fertilisation. Besides being objectionable to many Christians because it normally entails the killing of some embryos, *in vitro* fertilisation also in some cases conflicts with the Christian belief that it is best for children to be brought up by their biological parents.

On issues of sex and procreation, therefore, as well as on issues of life and death, Christian culture comes into conflict with that of the larger societies, and Christians working in marriage registration, adoption and genetic research may have the same choices as nurses and chemists who object to abortion and euthanasia. In Britain Catholic adoption agencies have had to close, and Christians discriminating in business dealings between heterosexual and same-sex couples have been prosecuted. In

1673 the English Parliament passed a law that no one could hold any office, civil or military, paid by the state, who would not declare: 'I do believe that there is not any transubstantiation in the sacrament of the Lord's Supper.' This excluded Catholics from such offices for 150 years. Parliament today, or at least after leaving the European Union, could legislate that no one may have employment funded by the state who will not declare 'I do believe that there is nothing wrong in anything permitted by British law.'

12
EDUCATION AND MULTICULTURALISM

What is the purpose of education? If you ask that today in a gathering of unsuspecting people you will be taken to mean: 'At what should schools and universities aim?' Answers might be: 'To impart the skills, starting with literacy and numeracy, and the factual information about the world, sufficient to enable children to survive and be independent', or, 'Yes, to do that, and also to impart values, principles of good behaviour', or 'Yes, and in addition, to broaden the mind.' The question will be understood in this way because we take two things for granted. The first is that education is primarily a matter for schools and universities. It divides into primary, secondary and tertiary education, primary and secondary education being provided in schools and tertiary in universities or equivalent institutions. Secondly, we expect schools and universities to be provided by the state.

These are assumptions of advanced mass-societies, but in small primitive societies there is no state and there are no schools, let alone universities. Education is provided by all members of the society, starting with the parents. Schools and universities are in fact means of education peculiar to Europe. Even in the advanced empires of the East which had literacy, law-enforcement, taxation and civil servants, schools as we know them and universities did not exist until they were imported from Europe. In the West until recently they were not provided by the state. Nevertheless education exists in every society down to the smallest. It is as necessary as customs concerning birth, sex and death if the society is to survive for more than one generation. For education is, in essence, simply the process by which customs, including those relating to birth, sex and death, are transmitted from one generation to the next. That is its function, whatever the conscious aims of those engaged in it.

If education is the transmission of the customs of a society and the concepts associated with them from one generation to the next, it seems to follow that state education is incompatible with a multicultural society. A multicultural society is one embracing a plurality of sub-societies, each with its own concepts and customs, and each, therefore needing to do its own educating. This is not recognised by Western liberal societies like Britain, where multiculturalism, or 'pluralism', or the word 'difference' is sometimes used, is presented as itself a 'value'. Education, we are told, ought to implant it, and only state education can.

Liberals perhaps see themselves as having a role like that of a farmer on whose farm there are animals of different species, hens, ducks, sheep, cows, pigs, dogs; these species have their own forms of life but on a farm they live peacefully together. Plato in his *Statesman* considers this as a model for good government and argues against it. A farmer manages his animals by coercion – he uses dogs and sticks – whereas human beings want not to be coerced but persuaded. A human farmer can manage a mixed farm because human beings are superior to animals of every species. What would happen if an animal attempted that task is depicted in Orwell's *Animal Farm*. Making a success of a multicultural state would require rulers blessed with a culture superior to all the constituent sub-cultures. Rulers, Plato says, would have to be more godlike ('*theioteroi*', *Statesman*, 271e) than their subjects, as we are more godlike than hens and sheep. Moreover (272b-e), if the rulers really were superhuman, people would be infantilised, as they would have been in the Golden Age of Cronos – the Greek mythical equivalent of the time in the Garden of Eden before Adam and Eve acquired moral responsibility and had to provide for themselves.

Members of a sub-society (whether one of Jews, Christians, Muslims or what you will), who wish to preserve the integrity of their culture and are conscious that it is different from that of their fellow citizens, must also wish their fellow citizens to respect the difference. People who do not belong to any such sub-society may wish to see varied colourful forms of dress in the streets - as they can be seen in the cartoons of Tintin's creator Hergé and in early Hollywood movies set in cities of the *Arabian Nights*. These differences, however, which once marked differences of culture, are disappearing from modern civilised life through globalisation. All over the world people wear similar clothes and follow similar fashions. What serious liberals want is not diversity of cultures or sub-societies but diversity among individuals.

I said in Chapter 11 that legalising same-sex marriage weakens the family as a sub-society by assimilating marriage to a sexual relation between individuals. Liberals who favour it also question the idea of a natural diversity between men and women. In the past that idea has resulted in men and women forming sub-societies of a sort. That is today regarded as a defect in primitive societies and one that civilisation has overcome; but, even in civilised societies, people who feel that being a man or a woman is part of their identity will look for support and sympathy from other men or women. Liberals who want no intermediate societies between the individual and the state do not want gender by itself to be a principle of diversity; individuals must choose the male and female characteristics that make them different from each other.

The philosopher and legislator Mary Warnock, in her book *An Intelligent Person's Guide to Ethics* (p.147), proposes the following ideal for human beings:

> They are able not only to pursue the things they have learned to value highly and avoid those they have learned to hate (as laboratory rats do), but they can form pictures for themselves of the universe as a whole and the part they would wish to play in it. They can give themselves goals to pursue, which may be totally new and idiosyncratic, or which they have learned from people they have, unpredictably, met or read about, admired or loved. It is this ability to set new goals, newly invented or traditional, but, either way, taken on individually by the unique human being, which lies at the root of ethics, and remains untouched by the genetic inheritance each may have.

Mary Warnock's ideal goes back at least to Mill, whose chapter 'On Individuality' in *On Liberty* is an extended encomium upon it, and it rests upon what Isaiah Berlin, in *Two Concepts of Liberty*, called 'the "positive" sense of the word "liberty"'. This derives, says Berlin (p. 16):

> from the wish on the part of the individual to be his own master. I wish my life and decisions to depend on myself, not on external forces of whatever kind. I wish to be the instrument of my own, not of other men's, acts of will. . . . I wish, above all, to be conscious of myself as a thinking, willing, active being,

> bearing responsibility for his choices and able to explain them by reference to his own ideas and purposes. I feel free to the degree that I believe this to be true.

Freedom as 'negatively' conceived, according to Berlin, is acting or refraining from action just as you please without interference from other people, and includes choosing, like Plutarch's Gryllus, the life of a pig: it is freedom *from* something, namely constraint. Freedom positively conceived, in contrast, consists in realising to the full your human capacities: it is freedom *to* something, namely, to grow into a kind of being you personally have chosen as ideal.

The positive conception is not confined to secular liberals. Pope Leo XIII's encyclical *Libertas Praestantissimum* (1888) declared: 'In human society what is truly to be called liberty consists not in acting as you please . . . but in this: that civil laws make it easier for you to live in accordance the precepts of eternal law.'

The phrase 'eternal law' was taken to cover both natural law, as defined in Roman jurisprudence, and Mosaic law. Vatican II develops the same idea in *Gaudium et Spes* (s. 17):

> That which is truly freedom is an exceptional sign of the image of God in man. For God willed that man should be left in the hand of his own deliberation [*diaboulion*] so that he might of his own accord seek his creator and freely attain his full and blessed perfection by cleaving to him. Man's dignity therefore requires him to act out of conscious and free choice, as moved and drawn in a personal way from within, and not by blind impulses in himself or mere external constraint. Man gains such dignity when, ridding himself of all slavery to the passions, he presses onward towards his goal by freely choosing what is good.

The difference is that whereas Catholics take their ideal from the Judaeo-Christian tradition and think they can achieve it only with God's help, Mary Warnock takes hers from Mill and the Enlightenment tradition, and thinks we can achieve it by our own individual efforts.

It is obvious that no one could think in the way Mary Warnock recommends who was not the product of a fully developed culture. Berlin remarks (*Two Concepts of Liberty*, p. 46) that it is 'unlikely' that such thinking should occur among 'any but a small minority of highly civilised and self-conscious human beings'. He also points out that as a matter of history: 'integrity, love of truth and fiery individualism grow at least as often in severely disciplined communities among, for example, the puritan Calvinists of Scotland or New England, or under military discipline, as in more tolerant or indifferent societies' – societies, that is, with liberal values. That is not surprising. Diversity and originality among individuals depends upon the richness and fertility of their culture. If the only practical values in their society are the cult of diversity and choosing the sort of person you want to be, minds will be blank.

Some suspicion of this may have inspired Mill's opposition in *On Liberty* to letting schools and universities be controlled by the state. He says (Warnock ed., p. 239): 'A general State education is a mere contrivance for moulding people to be exactly like one another; and as the mould in which it casts them is that which pleases the predominant power in the government, . . . it establishes a despotism over the mind.'

Could a modern state however allow parents complete freedom to educate their children as they please and teach them as much and as little as they want? In the medieval West schools and universities were provided by the Church along with healthcare and other welfare services. Would a modern state be willing to separate education from other services it provides and entrust them to sub-societies? Copson speaks of 'the importance of the freedom of the individual *from religion*' (*Secularism*, p. 95, my emphasis). Quite apart from the risk of what is called 'radicalisation', a substantial change in balance would be needed between government and non-government spending. In these days, when the economy of a society is all intricately interconnected, many people might feel it best if all large expenditure is controlled by the government.

In Chapters 10 and 11 I pointed out that, on the essential issues of birth, death and procreation, Christian principles conflict with those of many modern Western democracies. It follows that there is bound to be conflict on the issue of education. A society cannot survive if it permits its sub-societies to educate children in principles contrary to its own. If Christianity is allowed to do that, Christian children will be taught that abortion, infanticide and involuntary euthanasia are murder, and that it should be illegal to ask other people to kill you. They will also be told that there is an important difference between men and women, that children should be produced only by two persons of opposite sexes in a stable relationship and that sex outside marriage is bad even when contraception is used. They will be taught this despite the fact that the contrary is taught in state schools and widely accepted by their peers. And if the citizens of a state all have civil rights and choose legislators, sub-societies will press for their own customs not only to be permitted –

12. Education and Multiculturalism

something that will cause friction and possibly protest and 'offence' – but enshrined in law, not out of hunger for power but because they sincerely believe them to be best on the whole for everyone.

Mill, despite having said that the state should not itself provide schools and universities, nevertheless urged that it should require 'all children, and beginning at an early age' to undergo annual public examinations in a 'gradually extending range of subjects' which include religion, politics and 'other disputed topics' (Warnock ed., pp. 240-1). The examinations on these topics 'should not turn on the truth or falsehood of opinions, but on the matter of fact that such and such an opinion is held, on such grounds, by such authors, or schools, or churches'. Beyond the acquisition of an unspecified 'minimum of general knowledge', the examinations should be voluntary, but the state 'may very properly offer to ascertain and certify that a person possesses the knowledge requisite to make his conclusions on any given subject worth attending to', to certify, perhaps, whether he (or she) deserves a vote. Mill does not say this but he lived in an age of limited suffrage.

This system of education is now in place in Britain and other Western countries. Mill's words about how children should be taught are echoed, without his misgivings about trusting the state, by Copson in *Secularism* (p. 113): 'The secular state school should teach about religions and non-religious world views in an objective, fair and balanced way, allowing no confessional instruction and actively seeking to equip children with the critical skills needed to make up their own minds.' Mill thought that schools, in addition to providing the 'religious education' he prescribes, might be allowed (*On Liberty*, Warnock ed., p. 141) to do what Copson calls 'confessional instruction' and Mill called 'teaching religion', that is, teaching the religion of a child's family; but in Mill's day England was not increasingly threatened by culturally inspired violence, a threat now countered by increasingly intrusive inspections.

Did Mill perhaps exaggerate the danger of state education? Is it establishing a despotism over the mind and moulding people to be exactly like one another? He says of his own contemporaries (*On Liberty*, Warnock ed., p. 203):

> They now read the same things, listen to the same things, see the same things, go to the same places, have their hopes and fears directed to the same objects. . . . And the assimilation is still proceeding. All the political changes of the age promote it, since they all tend to raise the low and to lower the high. Every extension of education promotes it, because education brings people under common influences.

It is for the jury to decide whether or not these words might be uttered today.

I said in Chapter 1 that, if you teach that various opinions on disputed matters were held for various reasons without giving any hint of your own views, your hearers are likely to draw the conclusion that all the disputed conclusions are false. Politicians who advocate the school subject called 'religious education', which is supposed to teach the beliefs of Christians, Muslims, Hindus, Buddhists, Sikhs and so on in this way, and who speak of 'religious literacy', a phrase meaning nothing to non-European ears, may not wish this conclusion to be drawn; they may think they would accept a society in which many religions can flourish without clashing. They have little idea, however, of what a culture is. It is far harder to understand an alien religion than to learn to speak an alien language. A grammar book and a lexicon will enable anyone to translate from one language into another, but, in order to understand another religion, it is necessary to match not words with words or grammar with grammar but one entire way of living and thinking with another. E.E. Evans-Pritchard in *Theories of Primitive Religion* (p. 15) spoke of anthropologists who 'sought, and found, in primitive religions a weapon which could, they thought, be used with deadly effect against Christianity'. For this purpose, they imagined they could learn about another country's religion by spending a few weeks there with an interpreter, or even by sitting in a university library and reading travellers' books and articles. If, however, you want to understand a society other than your own, you have to live in it for quite some time.

Trotter was no advocate of multiculturalism, but he looked forward (*Instincts of the Herd in Peace and War*, pp. 60-65) to a future in which human beings would be more specialised. He traced the social nature of human beings back to the evolution of multicellular from unicellular organisms, and he thought that evolution would next turn human societies into groups the units of which would be like bees or ants, each living solely for its contribution to the group's survival. Human beings would retain their present brainpower and add to it; but stand in relation to society rather as the various cells stand to a human body. Aldous Huxley in *Brave New World* envisages something similar, but only for the lower social classes.

Trotter thought that this evolutionary development would depend on greatly increasing the possibilities of intercommunication between individuals. He says (p. 62): 'The enormous power of varied reaction possessed by man must render necessary for his attainment of the full advantages of the gregarious habit a power of intercommunication of absolutely unprecedented fineness. It is clear that scarcely a hint of such power has yet appeared.' That was in 1915. More than a hint has appeared since. We have small portable objects, cell phones, smart phones, i-pads etc., which enormously increase the possibilities of intercommunication between individuals all over the world. Much of practical life in modern societies is conducted through these, and, wherever we go, in public transport, in streets, in restaurants, we see individuals intent upon them to the exclusion of persons and events in their vicinity. The state requires adults to transact more and more business 'on line', and children to be taught how to use the electronic devices. If this is a Trotterian process of evolution, individuals need not know that they are evolving or wish to do so. In fact, however, improved intercommunication seems to be making individuals more rather than less alike in their activities and aims.

When Dunbar worked out his figure of 150 for the largest possible number of human beings in a stable group, he was faced with two difficulties. The first was that he believed a group could cohere only if the members all engaged in social grooming of one another, and that, if 150 people did that, they would have no time to obtain food or do anything else. The solution to this difficulty, he suggested, was language. Language is a form of social grooming, and we can engage in conversation with several people at once. The blind clumsiness of genetic replication threw up genes for language, hominids started to chatter, and this enabled primitive villages to form. The other difficulty, which he did not address, is that we actually live not in primitive villages but in states containing up to a billion citizens; yet China has not fragmented, nor has the United States. Random genetic variation has recently thrown up genes that caused people like Alan Turing to build machines which enable increasingly large numbers of people to engage in intercommunication. Nevertheless, cerebral neocortices would still have to get very much bigger for there to be social grooming in societies with memberships of millions.

Speculations about evolutionary advances need not be constricted by dogmatic physicalism. Even if the evolution of multicellular organisms has an austerely physical explanation, the natural evolution of societies should depend not just on the laws of nuclear physics but on the rationality of individuals. A mass society that fits the idea of an evolutionary advance should be far more complex, not more than a palaeolithic village but more than a modern nation-state. In the last hundred years globalisation has been attended by the emergence of supra-national organisations. The League of Nations was a step in the direction of a new kind of society. It could be compared with a species that disappeared. The United Nations is another. The European Union with its Council of Ministers, its Commission and its Parliament, its forms of proportional and non-proportional representation, its separate legal and account institutions, developed in an unplanned way over many years, and shows the right kind of complexity. It does not, however, make its member states like specialised organs or their citizens like specialised cells, but it is liable to fragmentation and such multiculturalism as it derives from its constituent countries is more of a problem than a beauty.

To think that multiculturalism can be a value of any society is self-deception. 'Difference', originality and eccentricity among individuals might be a social ideal, but a plurality of cultures cannot be. Copson is right (*Secularism*, p. 113) to speak of 'the state's interest in social cohesion'. *Contra factum*, however, *non est argumentum*. Multiculturalism is now a fact, and it is the duty of our rulers to prevent sub-societies from coming to blows. In the past rulers have denied civil rights to members of sub-societies or tried to get rid of them by penalising or expelling them. That strategy would not be tolerated in the West at this moment, and has never in the past proved effective. Control of immigration is aired as a tactic, but it meets with moral objections, it damages the economy and the time for it may be past.

Perhaps the best we can hope for is that, if the state holds the ring and prevents internecine violence for long enough, then, in the words of Bernard Williams that I quoted in Chapter 4, 'The convictions that people previously deeply held, on matters of religion or sexual behaviour or the significance of cultural experience [may] dwindle into private tastes' (*Philosophy as a Humanistic Discipline*, p.133).

Liberals, of course, hope that Christian convictions will dwindle away, and the world will come to have a single culture 'asymmetrically skewed,' as Williams puts it, 'in the liberal direction'. That is not assured, however. The culture of communist China is hardly liberal and there exist today societies with a strongly Islamic culture. Simone Weil, writing in 1943 when France was occupied by the Germans, begins *L'Enracinement* (*The Need for Roots*) with a list of 'Needs of the Soul' which she claims not Nazi Germany, but Western liberal society in general before 1939 failed disastrously to meet. Her 'needs' included not only equality and security but obedience, responsibility, hierarchy, honour, risk (*risque*), private property and collective property.

Liberals fear that 'radicals', 'extremists' and 'fundamentalists' would like their particular culture to prevail everywhere but they show little fear that their own 'convictions' might evaporate and Christianity might become the culture of a global society. Christianity, they think, has

12. Education and Multiculturalism

had its turn and is now on its way out. They are not the first people to have thought that. As G.K. Chesterton points out in *The Everlasting Man*, people in the past have often said it and been proved wrong. No intelligent Greek, Roman or Jew after the execution of Christ would have thought it possible that Christianity would ever become the religion of the Mediterranean world. Yet it not only did, but Western culture remained Christian for sixteen centuries. Should that not be cause for liberal concern? Should liberals not wonder, in the words Evans-Pritchard quotes (*Theories of Primitive Religion*, p.15) from Henri-Louis Bergson, 'How it is that beliefs and practices which are anything but reasonable could have been, and still are, accepted by reasonable beings?'

Edward Gibbon wondered that in the eighteenth century, and the first volume of his *History of the Decline and Fall of the Roman Empire* (1776) offers no less than six explanations which Robin Lane Fox in *Pagans and Christians* (p. 314) praises, expands and 'adjusts'. Liberals who have not read either historian are probably content with what Evans-Pritchard (*Theories of Primitive Religion*, p. 15) calls:

> the optimistic convictions of the eighteenth-century rationalist philosophers that people are stupid and bad only because they have bad institutions, and they have bad institutions only because they are ignorant and superstitious, and they are ignorant and superstitious because they have been exploited in the name of religion by cunning and avaricious priests and the unscrupulous classes who have supported them.

The trouble with this diagnosis is that the culture Christianity superseded was very similar to that of modern liberal societies. Liberals, indeed, have often looked back wistfully to the time at the grave senators of the Roman republic before the Julio-Claudians destroyed its oligarchic republicanism, and have seen themselves as following in the tradition of Stoics like Seneca, Thrasea Paetus and Marcus Aurelius. Graeco-Roman culture allowed male homosexuality and sex outside marriage; and wives as well as husbands could give writs of divorce. Suicide was held in honour. Parents could remove by abortion and infanticide unborn and newborn children they did not want. Graeco-Roman culture was marred, indeed, by slavery but that was at a time when there were no machines, let alone robots, to do work that was too laborious or boring for people to want to do themselves. Furthermore, a point on which Peter Acton dwells in *Poiesis* (2014), his analysis of industry in Classical Greece, slaves, unlike industrial workers in the nineteenth century, were housed and fed. Clytemnestra says in Aeschylus' *Agamemnon* (1035-43) that the life of a domestic slave in a good family was not too bad. Forced labour, as distinct from slavery, is not inconsistent with liberal principles. Indeed, Mill himself says (Warnock ed., p. 230): 'If, either from idleness or from any other avoidable cause, a man refuses to perform his legal duties to others, as for instance to support his children, it is no tyranny to force him to fulfil that obligation, by compulsory labour if no other means are available.'

An affluent liberal society will provide cheap food, clothes, medical services and travel, and nobody is forced to work for anyone else. For these good things there is a price, however. The evolutionary leap envisaged by Trotter, after which the individual occupies himself entirely in 'functions beneficial to himself only indirectly through the welfare of the new unit – the herd', would be a steep price indeed, but it is hardly imminent. The danger is rather of regression into the sub-human life of Adam and Eve in Paradise, of Enkidu in the forest, of mankind generally under Saturn.

In a primitive Dunbar society, as I said in Chapter 3, the customs are not sanctioned by coercion and members who do not like them can go elsewhere. A primitive society is more or less self-sufficient. Its members know the people on whom their food depends and the local circumstances that affect its delivery. In a mass society we do not know the distant suppliers or their circumstances or the transporters. In this we are like farm animals. In a primitive society people do not spend their time working for others. They may work together at hunting or agriculture but they have the feeling of working for themselves, and when and as they like. I have been asked by inhabitants of a remote island in the Pacific how Europeans can bear having to go to work every day. We are used to it. Self-employed individuals, whether subsistence farmers, tradesmen or artists, are a small minority. Most of us work for others, and those who are best paid work long hours and get home late and tired. In that respect we are worse off than farm animals. If both parents go out to work all day and have little or no responsibility for their children, they are themselves like children. Children differ from adults partly in having no children of their own, but, at best, dolls. People in a liberal society are like children also if they have no intermediate societies for life; we recognise no intermediate societies between children and their parents or the persons running playgroups.

The concepts, social practices, doctrinal beliefs and moral principles which enter into a culture, as I said in Chapter 2, are not just an aggregate but a system. They modify and reinforce one another, and cannot easily stand alone. Christian moral principles and doctrinal beliefs have been part of European culture for the last two thousand years. Liberal principles have no concepts, practices or beliefs of their own to support them unless you count their concept of a person which I discussed in Chapter 10. Whereas the concept of a human being has a scientific basis, that of a person has none. The criteria for awarding personal status are moral or political; persons are human beings with whatever qualities make it morally correct and politically expedient to give them certain rights. In *Out of the Silent Planet*, C.S. Lewis distinguished human beings from persons to extend the notion of a person to God and to other intelligent species, and invented for this purpose the word *hnau*. The liberal concept restricts it. For those who use it, it is like the concept of a child or a priest or a policeman, the concept of a kind of social status. In Chapter 5 I interpreted it rather as a formal or second-order concept. I think of you as a person if I think you can be harmed or benefited, and act in order to do one or the other. Personhood apart, liberals have to rely on concepts, practices and beliefs they inherit from the culture of Christian Europe. These are all suffering attrition. In what follows I compare the relative chances a Christian and a secular liberal culture have of prevailing by taking them in turn. I speak of Christian culture, but what I say applies in some measure to other cultures that accept a transcendent personal god, and even to other non-European cultures that do not.

Besides giving us cheap food and clothes, our affluent societies enable us to eat the same fruit and keep our houses the same temperature all year round, and to be as well-lit by night as by day. As a consequence, we do not have the same consciousness as our forebears of the natural processes on which life depends. Town-dwellers seldom see the stars, have little idea where they are in the lunar month, and hardly notice the annual movements to north and south of sunrise and sunset. To quote Simone Weil (*L'Enracinement*, p.47):

> a man can belong to the so-called educated circles . . . without knowing, for example, that not all the constellations are visible in every season. People now believe that a country child today at a primary school knows more than Pythagoras because he repeats docilely that the Earth circles round the Sun. . . . This Sun of which he speaks in class has for him no relation with the sun he sees.

We have more scientific knowledge than our forebears of the movements of Earth, Sun and Moon, but less experience, and the concepts of light and dark and the seasons play far less practical part in our thinking. Nevertheless, the concepts of our predecessors are embedded in their literature and also in the Bible and in Christian liturgy. Liberal humanists can read the literature of Antiquity, the hymns and prayers of Christians and the poetry of Dante, Shakespeare and Milton, but the concepts of nature they find there have little bearing on their own lives and no associations with worship. Unlike Hamlet's mother and Christians today, they do not think they are 'passing through nature to eternity' (Act 1, Scene 2).

The arts were held in high esteem in the world in which Christianity arose. Jews and Greeks had history, poetry and architecture of which they were proud and, though the temple at Jerusalem was destroyed, the temples of Greece and Rome survived. They were sometimes, like the Parthenon in Athens and the Pantheon in Rome, adapted to Christian worship, and conversely pre-Christian architecture probably influenced the way in which Christian worship developed. When the Western Roman Empire collapsed and literacy seemed of little value to the local warriors and tribal chiefs who succeeded the Roman officials, Christian priests kept it alive, collected books, established schools, and wrote history. This cultural framework gave rise to the medieval universities and to the churches that were the central buildings in cities, towns and villages. It stayed in place while Europe remained Christian; its survival was part of what made Europe Christian. Today, however, cities, towns and villages are no longer dominated by churches. College chapels, which corresponded to the temples of the Muses in Plato's Academy and Aristotle's Lyceum, are not part of new universities and secular museums do not fully replace them. The anonymous religious music called 'plainsong' developed over a thousand years, and was succeeded by the music of composers like Palestrina, Bach, Handel, Haydn and Mozart. Written to add beauty to religious worship, this is now played only in concerts and heard chiefly in recordings. Liberal humanists can listen to it as they can visit basilicas, cathedrals and university chapels, but they cannot make the sense of these works that Christians can, and the dissociation of Christianity from music and the arts may well be changing popular conceptions of those arts themselves. Have the architects of the buildings that dominate modern cities the same conception of architecture as Pheidias or John James' 'builders' (*Chartres, les Constructeurs*, 1977)?

Something similar goes for education. The Christian view rested on the idea that the new grows out of the old and the old is contained within it. That was shown by the forming and maintaining of libraries. Children were introduced to the literature of the past, to Homer, Virgil and Dante,

12. Education and Multiculturalism

and were taught the whole of documented history. Now the idea seems to be that the new replaces the old. Simone Weil (*L'Enracinement*, p. 52) described 'the destruction of the past' as 'perhaps the greatest of crimes.' The teaching of history in many schools extends back no further than a few years, so people have hardly any knowledge of the past beyond what they and older people around them can remember. In many universities only the philosophy of the last twenty years is taught and its teachers are expected to imitate natural scientists in doing 'research'. Public libraries are being closed. Literacy and numeracy, so cultivated by Christianity, are less needed for the smooth running of large mass-societies. Pocket calculators save us from having to calculate ourselves, and as artificial speech develops and becomes ubiquitous we shall no longer have to read; governments will be enabled to direct everyone electronically. Liberals would mostly prefer a more liberal education, but that is hard to justify in terms of a materialistic conception of human happiness. Christianity is more help than liberal humanism to people who want to understand the concepts of the past.

As social beings we need collective public practices which have no obvious value or utility for us as individual organisms, practices which, for that reason, anthropologists used to classify as religious. These form part of a society's culture. A state will offer public holidays and spectacles to celebrate events in its own history like becoming independent, winning a war or having a revolution. It may devise ritual acts like saluting a flag or singing a national anthem. It may cause large pictures of the head of state to be publicly displayed. This is comparable to burning incense before a statue of the Emperor. No dogmatic belief need be attached to it, but it can be rationalised by saying that the state is worthy of worship in the same sort of way as the Sun. The Sun provides the physical essentials for life on the earth. It is no wonder, therefore, that societies have marked its movements with little rituals. In the absence of any concept of a transcendent God, this is a substitute for religion. Any society is the source of something essential to its members, social life. Modern affluent states claim to provide much more: justice, safety from external enemies, and health and educational services. Nevertheless, they are human institutions, imperfect, prone to corruption, easily destroyed; at best they compare badly with the Sun. Public holidays have always been sublimated by being connected with astronomical events like the solstices. China and Japan tried to present their imperial systems as part of a wider cosmic order. Christian nations valued patriotism and had rituals and pageants connected with civil offices and events, but human societies were seen as subordinate to the order of the transcendent creator, who as a person took precedence over the best human rulers. Detached from a wider background, public holidays in honour of the state may seem flat.

In addition to practices related to the state, advanced societies usually have public sports and games. Classical Greece had the Olympic, Pythian, Isthmian and Nemean Games. We have revived the Olympics, and ceremonies are emerging and vast stadia springing up everywhere for festivals of spectator sport. The Greek games, however, were actually festivals in honour of Zeus, Apollo and Poseidon, and included cultic acts. Our public sports are not connected with religion unless they are seen as forms of nature-worship. Mary Midgley suggests that Steven Weinberg wants astronomy to take the place of religion and notes in *Are You an Illusion* (p. 4) his plea that money should be spent on superconducting supercolliders because they are 'the cathedrals of our age'. Athletic stadia could be seen as temples to health and fitness. Working out in public gymnasia can be compared to churchgoing and going on solitary runs to solitary devotions like saying the rosary.

Besides national and athletic festivals, ancient societies had temples in honour of Aphrodite or the Mother Goddess, attended by priests, priestesses and sacred prostitutes. Like other ancient cults, the cult of Aphrodite was unburdened with any system of moral principles. It may have been felt, however, to provide an outlet for sexual feelings that otherwise could be disruptive, and to contribute to health. Euripides' *Hippolytus* contains a warning against abstinence: 'I smash,' (*sphallô*) says Aphrodite at the beginning, 'those who think themselves above me.' Certainly, we often hear today that it conduces to mental and bodily health to engage in sex and that it is unhealthy to suppress sexual desire or refrain from gratifying it. This sounds, indeed, a little like the comforting economic doctrine, proposed by Bernard Mandeville in *The Fable of the Bees* (1714) and reiterated by Adam Smith in his *Theory of Moral Sentiments* (1759), that the selfish pursuit of personal wealth has a trickle-down effect which benefits all members of society. However, whether or not attaching a lot of value to sexual gratification is really beneficial, modern societies do not have public buildings or festivals in honour of it. Beauty contests are permitted but deplored as sexist. Perhaps the nearest we come to the ancient cults is in filling public spaces with advertisements which rely on stimulating our sexual instincts.

Christianity has been accused of hostility to sex but in fact hostility to the body, in general, and to sex, in particular, was a principle not of Christianity but of Manicheanism, which Christians branded as heretical from the third century onwards and sometimes violently persecuted.

12. Education and Multiculturalism

Manicheanism in its medieval forms had a certain amount in common with modern liberal culture. The Albigenses were strongly opposed to procreation and considered free sex an evil lesser than marriage; they approved of suicide and Berlin's positive conception of freedom and the spirituality of Mary Warnock's ideal would have appealed to them. It is to these Manichean aspects of modern permissiveness that Christians chiefly object. They are able to offer more public celebration of sex than their critics, but they sublimate it by tying it to marriage and the family. Christian weddings are ceremonial public events involving not just a pair of lovers but their families and friends. Christians also sublimate motherhood. They replaced temples to Aphrodite and the Mother Goddess by churches in honour of Mary, Virgin and Mother. Julian of Norwich in her *Revelations* speaks both of God and of Christ as a mother.

Liberals have no distinctive new concepts or ways of meeting our need for collective activities to buttress and fuse with their practical 'values'. What of their beliefs about the whole natural order, beliefs that mirror what Julian Huxley identified (*Religion Without Revelation*, p. 137) as the core of religion, 'the reaction of the personality as a whole to its experience of the Universe as a whole'?

The modern atheist asks us to believe either that the universe has actually existed for an infinite length of time, or that it started a finite time ago, and brought itself into being. It continues to exist, we are to suppose, either because it is just in its nature to do so, or, as Mackie claimed, because earlier processes cause later. This cosmology has no basis in science (though modern science favours the view that the universe has existed only for a few thousand million years); and, as I said earlier, it faces philosophical difficulties. Analysis of the concept of infinity casts doubt on the possibility of an actual infinite. That causes are prior to their effects was Hume's idea; Aristotle insisted that the causing of a change must be contemporaneous with it. Atheistic cosmology, then, is fully as mystical as the Christian doctrine of creation; but it is considerably less cheering. The Stoics, whose pantheism was the nearest ancient approximation to it, were not a cheery lot. Christianity teaches that God created the universe and keeps it going for the benefit of the living creatures in it. This offers us what Spinoza identified as the supreme good: 'knowledge of the union of the mind with the whole of nature' (*De Intellectus Emendatione*, 13). Christianity still preserves in its worship, its literature and its art a joy in light and dark and the seasons. That is expressed in the *Laudes Creaturarum* of St Francis of Assisi with their delight in Brother Sun and Sister Moon, and even in Sister Death. It also invites us to take a share ourselves in God's creative activity, in what Jewish and Christian writers call his 'glory'. The Christian doctrine was found acceptable by the jury of the Graeco-Roman world, and liberals should not be surprised if people tomorrow prefer to believe that the universe was created a finite while ago, and continues to exist for the benefit of living creatures.

The strict physicalism professed by some liberal thinkers is no less mystical than modern atheism but more repugnant. They accept no purpose in reality anywhere, not even in human activity. Our feeling that we act on purpose is an illusion caused by physical action upon our bodies and within our brains, an illusion experienced by entities that do not really exist but the existence of which is itself part of the illusion. We are like figures projected on a cinema screen that watch themselves in mirrors. Only a handful of fanatics believe this, or imagine they believe it; nobody could act upon it.

Strict psychological egoism is a belief with which a person might live. You might believe that what looks like altruism or duty is really action in one's own interest, though possibly disguised by self-deception. Yet this is certainly not an attractive doctrine, and few liberals hold to it in practice; they act and speak as if duty for duty's sake and disinterested friendship were possible.

Liberals who trust in the trickle-down effect in economics may profess ethical egoism, but they will include in it the pursuit of objectives which in fact are intelligible only if we are essentially social beings. Hobbes in the passage I quoted in Chapter 2 (*Leviathan*, 1.13) mentions diffidence and glory as causes of war. Diffidence covers not only fear for your life but aversion to being despised, put to shame, and excluded. By 'glory' he had in mind not what is meant by the word in Bible translations which speak of the 'glory' of God, but an essentially social objective gained by power over others and victory. Ancient philosophers called it *timê* which may be translated as 'honour' or 'social status'.

How, in a modern liberal society, is honour to be achieved? High officers of state like presidents and prime ministers by that very fact have status, but there are not many high offices, and these, being distributed not by lot but, supposedly, on merit, are practically accessible only to a small minority of members. Who can believe that everyone is equally meritorious, or equally fit (if that is something different) to legislate, judge, run public services and make war and peace? Celebrity as an athlete or an entertainer brings honour, but is achieved by even fewer people than achieve high office. For many people status is proportional to wealth. Poorly paid employment like teaching brings little status;

12. Education and Multiculturalism

actions and discoveries that benefit others, unless financially rewarded, bring even less. For most people in a liberal society social goods boil down to money.

Civilisation seems to have started with agriculture, and a division soon appeared between people who did the agricultural work – ploughing, sowing, reaping and so on, and the people under whom they worked, the landowners and their managers who lived on the profits. The status of the former, the people who did the work, was lower than that of the latter. In later times this distinction became the one Justinian's jurist noted, between slaves and the free. In the Middle Ages slaves and serfs gave way to agricultural labourers, and, with the industrial revolution, the division appeared as one between industrial workers, on the one hand, who actually made the goods, built the bridges and so forth, and on the other the managers and capitalists who shaded into each other. Today that division is extending to the services providing health and education and to the sciences. The people who actually do the work, nurses, and increasingly doctors, teachers and scientific researchers, are less well paid than managers and held in lower esteem. The division is even extending through the legal and financial services. Work, which in itself might be satisfying, is deprived of giving pleasure by managerial pressure and by insecurity, and honour proportioned to pay, which unlike honesty and concern for clients is something quantifiable, goes to those who apply the pressure and can hire and fire.

Liberals call equality a 'value', but they do not want everyone to be equally rich. It is communists, not liberals, who want that, and they understand it can be achieved only by abolishing private wealth altogether. Nor do liberals want everyone to have an equal share in running society. That was the ideal of ancient Greek democrats and they tried to realise it through election by lot, but liberal societies want offices to be filled by those fittest to discharge them, and believe that can be achieved only through election by ballot. What liberals want is equality of opportunity to *compete* for office and pre-eminence in power and wealth; and to compete by rules they set.

Any competition requires rules and most competitions require judges. Competition for office and wealth is governed by laws that define legal ways of getting richer, and the procedures for attaining various offices and the powers attached to them. More generally, competition for social prizes is governed by the laws and customs of each society. In advanced societies competitors are expected to be literate and numerate, and to develop tastes and interests admired by people already rich and powerful who are to a large extent the judges able to reward competitors with offices and opportunities for gain. The prizes can be won only by a minute proportion of the populations. The liberal hope is that the 99.9 per cent who end up without wealth, power or status will realise that it is their own fault. They have only themselves to blame. They had equal opportunities; if they did not win, it was because they were lazy, a common weakness of the poor, or lacked natural ability.

Accepting this, however, will hardly raise the self-esteem of the poor, and there is the risk they should imagine they would have done better if their society had had different laws and customs. Despite the efforts in recent years by enlightened governments to give everyone equality of opportunity, it is widely recognised that inequality in wealth and status is increasing. The liberal reaction is not to question economic practices or political or moral theories but by more legislation to make opportunities more equal; that is, to try get out of the hole by more digging.

How desirable, in fact, are these prizes which of their nature can in large societies be gained only by very few?

The equal of opportunity our liberal democracies offer their subjects is, in the words of Lucretius at the beginning of Book 2 of *De Rerum Natura*, his exposition of Epicureanism:

> To compete in ingenuity, to contend in nobility,
> To strive night and day with outstanding effort
> To arrive at the summit of wealth and get control of public affairs.

Lucretius himself comments:

> O, the misery of men's minds, the blindness of their hearts!
> *O miseras hominum mentes, o pectora caeca!*

Christianity here sides with the Epicureans. It condemns ambition, and pursuit of money, the 'prize' Christ called it, of wrongdoing ('*mamôna adikias*', Luke 16:9). Following much Old Testament teaching, it urges respect for poverty, regardless of how it has come about. Concern for the poor and generous giving are not commended only by bishops or theologians; these characteristics (not economic acumen, enlightened legislation or military success) are the leading claims to sanctity of medieval kings and queens, and they are recurrent themes in secular writers like Christine de Pisan. Humility is an ideal, *tapeinôsis*, a word which primarily signifies low status itself, but also acceptance and acknowledgment of it. Mary applies it to herself in the Magnificat. Critics have accused Christians of hypocrisy here, but Christians are warned by

12. Education and Multiculturalism

Christ to watch out for hypocrisy and many Christians in the past have been honoured for renouncing wealth and privilege the better to serve God or their neighbours. The vows of poverty, chastity and obedience are such a renunciation.

The Christian ideal is to combine disinterested concern for all living things with recognition that all the originality, creativity and heroism for which we may be admired in society comes to us through others and ultimately from God through Christ. A Christian society may have more in the way of respect than a secular liberal society to offer to people who are not ambitious, competitive or particularly well-endowed either physically or intellectually. Perhaps, too, it is realistic to see ourselves not as alone and burdened with the responsibilities of creating ourselves as recommended by Mary Warnock, but dependent, and the better for our dependence.

Let me summarise these last pages. I quoted Bernard Williams' speculation that convictions now deeply held 'on matters of religion or sexual behaviour or the significance of cultural experience' might dwindle into private tastes. I pointed out that the Roman Empire in the time of Christ had a culture quite like the culture modern liberals favour and that, most surprisingly, the Roman Empire actually turned into a unicultural society with Christian values. Williams hoped that in the affluent West, or in the whole globalised world, a unicultural society would arise in which Christian values were replaced, where there was conflict, by liberal values. Since the moral principles of a society have to live in union with sets of concepts, social practices and beliefs about the world, I considered what concepts, practices and beliefs liberals could muster to support their principles. That survey makes me think that liberals might again be surprised, and that future generations might prefer Christianity to secular liberalism not only as being more cheerful and providing more inspiring ideals, but as being more rational and even more liberal.

Bibliography

Acton, Peter, *Poiesis: Manufacturing in Classical Athens* (Oxford: Oxford University Press, 2014)

Aeschylus, *Agamemnon*, ed. J.D. Denniston and Denys Page (Oxford: The Clarendon Press, 1960)

Alston, William P., 'Religion', in Paul Edwards (ed.), *The Encyclopaedia of Philosophy*, Vol. 7 (London and New York: Macmillan, 1967)

Aquinas, Thomas, for Bibliography see Kenny, Anthony, ed.

Armstrong, Karen, *Fields of Blood: Religion and the History of Violence* (London: Vintage, 2015)

Aristotle: for translations see Barnes, Jonathan, ed.

Barnes, Jonathan, 'Belief Is up to Us', *Proceedings of the Aristotelian Society*, 106 (2005-6) pp. 189-206

Barnes, Jonathan, ed., The Complete Works of Aristotle: The Revised Oxford Translation (Princeton: Princeton University Press, 1985)

Behe, Michael J., *Darwin's Black Box: The Biochemical Challenge to Evolution* (New York: The Free Press, 1996)

Bentham, Jeremy, *Introduction to the Principles of Morals and Legislation*, see Warnock, Mary (ed.), *John Stuart Mill*

Bentley, E.C., *Clerihews: Biography for Beginners* (Mineola, NY: Dover Publications Inc., 2014)

Berlin, Isaiah, *Two Concepts of Liberty* (Oxford: The Clarendon Press, 1858)

Boscovich, Roger J., S.J., *A Theory of Natural Philosophy* (Boston: The MIT Press, 1966)

Boyle, Nicholas, 'Truth Telling, the Media and Society', *New Blackfriars*, 98 (2017) pp. 19-33.

Butler, Joseph, *The Works of Joseph Butler* (Oxford: The Clarendon Press, 1826)
Butler, Samuel, The Way of All Flesh (London: Grant Richards 1903)
Carroll, Lewis (Charles Dodgson), 'What the Tortoise Said to Achilles' (1894), in *Complete Works* (London: Nonsuch Press, 1939) pp. 1104-8.
Catechism of the Catholic Church (London: Geoffrey Chapman, 1999)
Caxton, William (translator), *The Golden Legend* (London: Kelmscott Press, 1892)
Charlton, William, *The Analytic Ambition: An Introduction to Philosophy* (Oxford: Basil Blackwell, 1991)
'Trisecting the Psyche', *Philosophical Writings*, 1 (1996) pp. 92-106
——— *The Physical, the Natural and the Supernatural* (London: Sheed & Ward, 1998)
——— 'The Real Presence', *New Blackfriars*, 82 (2001) pp. 161-74
——— *Being Reasonable about Religion* (Aldershot: Ashgate, 2006)
——— 'Is the Concept of the Mind Parochial?' in R.A.H. King (ed.), *The Good Life and Conceptions of Life in Early China and Graeco-Roman Antiquity* (Berlin: de Gruyter, 2015) pp. 213-26
——— 'Natural Law, Aquinas and the Magisterium', *New Blackfriars*, 96 (2015) pp. 326-44
Chesterton, G.K., *The Everlasting Man* (London: Hodder & Stoughton, 1925)
Clark, Stephen R.L., 'Atheism Considered as a Christian Sect', *Philosophy*, 90 (2015) pp. 277-303
Clough, Arthur H., 'The Latest Decalogue', in Upton Sinclair (ed.), *The Cry for Justice: An Anthology of the Literature of Social Protest* (Philadelphia: John C. Winston Pub. Co., 1915)
Compendium: Catechism of the Catholic Church (London: Catholic Truth Society, 2006)
Copson, Andrew, *Secularism: Politics, Religion and Freedom* (Oxford: Oxford University Press, 2017)
Crane, Tim, *The Meaning of Belief: Religion from an Atheist's Point of View* (Cambridge, MA: Harvard University Press, 2017)
Darwin, Charles, *The Descent of Man* (London: John Murray, 1871)
Davidson, Donald, 'Actions, Reasons and Causes' (1963), in Donald Davidson, *Essays on Actions and Events* (Oxford: The Clarendon Press, 1980)
Davies, Paul, *The Goldilocks Enigma: Why Is the Universe Just Right for Life?* (London: Allen Lane, 2006)
Dawkins, Richard, *The Selfish Gene* (Oxford: Oxford University Press 1989)
Dembski, William A., *The Design Revolution: Answering the Toughest Questions about Intelligent Design* (Nottingham, Inter-Varsity Press, 2004)
Denzinger-Schönmetzer (DS), Denzinger, Henricus, and Adolfus Schönmetzer, *Enchiridion Symbolorum Definitionum et Declarationum de Rebus Fidei et Morum* (Barcelona and Rome: Herder, 1976)
Descartes, *Descartes: Philosophical Writings*, Elizabeth Anscombe and Peter Thomas Geach (eds) (London: Thomas Nelson & Sons, 1954)
Disraeli, Benjamin, *Vivian Grey* (1826) (Scotts Valley, CA: Create Space, 2016)
Duffy, Eamon, *The Stripping of the Altars: Traditional Religion in England, 1400-1580* (New Haven, CT, and London: Yale University Press, 1992)
Dunbar, R.I.M., 'Neocortex Size as a Constraint on Group Size in Primates', *Journal of Human Evolution*, 22 (1992) pp. 468-93

——— 'Co-Evolution of Neocortex Size, Group Size and Language in Humans', *Behavioural and Brain Sciences*, 16 (1993) pp. 681-735

Durkheim, Émile, *Elementary Forms of the Religious Life* (1912), tr. Joseph W. Swain (London: George Allen & Unwin, 1915)

Edge, Peter, and Lucy Vickers, *Review of Equality and Human Rights Law Relating to Religion or Belief*, Research Report 97 (Manchester: Equality and Human Rights Commission, 2015)

Entrèves, Alessandro P. d', *Natural Law* (London: Hutchinson's University Library, 1951)

Euripides, *Hippolytus*, in *Euripidis Fabulae* I, ed. Gilbert Murray (Oxford: The Clarendon Press, 1902)

Evans-Pritchard, Edward E., *Witchcraft, Oracles and Magic among the Azande* (Oxford: The Clarendon Press, 1937)

——— *Theories of Primitive Religion* (Oxford, The Clarendon Press, 1965)

Fabre, Jean-Henri, *Fabre's Book of Insects*, tr. Alexander Teixeira de Mattos (New York: Tudor Pub. Co., 1936)

Finnis, John, *Natural Law and Natural Rights* (Oxford: Oxford University Press, 2nd ed. 2011)

Fitzpatrick, Joseph, *The Fall and the Ascent of Man: How Genesis Supports Darwin* (Lanham, MD: University Press of America, 2012)

Freeman, Kathleen, *Ancilla to the Pre-Socratic Philosophers: A Complete Translation to the Fragments in Diels* (Oxford: Basil Blackwell, 1962)

Freud, Sigmund, *Complete Psychological Works, Vol. 13: 'Totem and Taboo' and Other Works* (London: Hogarth Press, 1986)

——— *Complete Psychological Works, Vol. 19: 'The Ego and the Id' and Other Works* (London: Hogarth Press, 1986)

Gilgamesh: see Sandars, N.K., tr.

Golding, William, *The Scorpion God* (London: Faber & Faber, 1971)

Gooch, Bernard, *The Quiet World of Nature* (London: Bodley Head, 1939)

Grisez, Germain, *Contraception and the Natural Law* (Milwaukee, WI: The Bruce Pub. Co., 1964)

——— 'The First Principle of Practical Reason', in Anthony Kenny (ed.), *Aquinas: A Collection of Critical Essays* (London: Macmillan, 1970) pp. 340-82

Hamilton, Edith, and Huntington Cairns, ed., *The Complete Dialogues of Plato including the Letters* (New York: Bollingen Foundation, 1963

Harré, Rom, *The Principles of Scientific Thinking* (London: Macmillan, 1970)

Huxley, Aldous, *Brave New World* (London: Chatto & Windus, 1932)

Huxley, Julian, *Religion without Revelation* (London: E. Benn, 1928)

James, John, *Chartres, les constructeurs*, (Chartres: Société archéologique d'Eure-et-Loir, 1977)

James, William, *The Varieties of Religious Experience: A Study in Human Nature* (London: Longmans Green & Co., 1902)

Kenny, Anthony, ed., *Aquinas: A collection of Critical Essays* (London: Macmillan, 1969)

Knox, Ronald A., *The Belief of Catholics* (London: E. Benn, 1927)

Lane Fox, Robin, *Pagans and Christians* (New York: Alfred A. Knopf Inc., 1987)

Lewis, C.S., *Out of the Silent Planet* (London: The Bodley Head, 1938)

Long, A.A., and D.N.Sedley, *The Hellenistic Philosphers* (Cambridge: Cambridge University Press, 1987)
Lumen Gentium, see *Vatican II*
Mackie, John L., *The Cement of the Universe: A Study of Causation* (Oxford: The Clarendon Press, 1974)
Melville, Herman, *Typee* (London: Folio Society, 1950)
Mill, John Stuart, *A System of Logic* (1843) (London: Forgotten Books, 2018)
——— *On Liberty* (1859), see Warnock, Mary (ed.), *John Stuart Mill*
——— *Utilitarianism* (1863), see Warnock, ibid.
Midgley, Mary, *Science as Salvation: A Modern Myth and its Meaning* (London: Routledge, 1992)
——— *Are You an Illusion?* (Durham: Acumen, 2014)
——— *What is Philosophy For?* (London: Bloomsbury 2018)
Moore, George E., *Principia Ethica* (Cambridge: Cambridge University Press, 1903)
More, Thomas, *De optimo Reipublicae Statu, deque Nova Insula Utopia* (London: Penguin, 2012)
Murray, Alexander, *Reason and Society in the Middle Ages* (Oxford: The Clarendon Press 1978)
New Jerusalem Bible, The (London: Darton, Longman & Todd, 1985)
Orwell, Gorge, *Animal Farm* (London: Secker & Warburg, 1945)
Orwell, George, *Nineteen Eighty-Four* (London: Secker & Warburg 1949)
Pestieau, Joseph, *Guerres et Paix Sans* État (Montreal: L'Hexagonie, 1984)
Plato: for translations see Hamilton, Edith, and Huntington CVairs, edd.
Pope Benedict XVI (Joseph Ratzinger), *Spe Salvi* (Vatican City: Libreria Editrice Vaticana, 2007), available online at: http://w2.vatican.va/content/benedict-xvi/en/encyclicals/documents/hf_ben-xvi_enc_20071130_spe-salvi.html (accessed 8 October 2019)
Pope Leo XIII (Vincenzo Pecci), *Libertas Praestantissimum* (Rome, 20 June 1888), available online at: http://w2.vatican.va/content/leo-xiii/en/encyclicals/documents/hf_l-xiii_enc_20061888_libertas.html (accessed 8 October 2019)
Pope Pius XII (Eugenio Pacelli), *Humani Generis* (Rome, 1950)
Pufendorf, Samuel von, *De Jure Naturae et Gentium* (1672)
Reybrouck, David van, *Against Elections: The Case for Democracy*, tr. Liz Waters (London: The Bodley Head, 2016)
Rose, H.J., 'Religion', in Max Cary (ed.), *The Oxford Classical Dictionary* (Oxford: The Clarendon Press 1950)
Russell, Bertrand, *What I Believe* (New York: E.P. Dutton & Co., 1925)
——— *The Principles of Mathematics* (London: Allen & Unwin, 1937)
Sandars, N.K. (tr.), *The Epic of Gilgamesh* (Harmondsworth: Penguin Classics, 1972)
Saunders, Edith, *Fanny Penquite* (London: Oxford University Press, 1932)
Sheldon, W.H., *The Varieties of Temperament: A Psychology of Constitutional Differences* (New York and London: Harper & Bros, 1942)
Smith, George D. (ed.), *The Teaching of the Catholic Church*, 2 Vols (London: Burns Oates & Washbourne, 1952)
Sophocles, *Antigone*, with critical notes, commentary and translation in English prose, by Sir Richard Jebb (Cambridge: The University Press, 1906)

Bibliography

Sorabji, Richard, *Time, Creation and the Continuum: Theories in Antiquity and the Early Middle Ages* (London: Duckworth, 1985)

Strang, Colin, 'Plato and the Instant', *Aristotelian Society*, Supplementary Volume 48 (1974) pp. 63-79

——— 'Tripartite Souls, Ancient and Modern', *Apeiron*, 16 (1982) pp. 1-11

Swinburne, Richard, *The Existence of God* (Oxford: The Clarendon Press, 1979)

Tolkien, J.R.R., *The Return of the King* (London: Harper Collins, 2012)

Trotter, Wilfred, *Instincts of the Herd in Peace and War* (London: T. Fisher Unwin, 1917)

Vatican Council II: The Conciliar and Postconciliar Documents, ed. Austin Flannery O.P. (Leominster: Fowler Wright Books Ltd., 1980)

Vermes, Geza, *The Religion of Jesus the Jew* (London: SCM Press, 1993)

Warnock, Mary (ed. and intro.), *John Stuart Mill: Utilitarianism, On Liberty, Essay on Bentham; Together with Selected Writings of Jeremy Bentham* (London: Fontana, 1962)

——— *An Intelligent Person's Guide to Ethics* (London: Duckbacks, 2001)

——— 'A Duty to Die?' *Nordisk tidsskrift for palliativ medisin* (2008)

Weil, Simone, *L'Enracinement* (Paris: Gallimard, 1949)

Wiggins, David, *Identity and Spatio-Temporal Continuity* (Oxford: Basil Blackwell, 1957)

Williams, Bernard, *Philosophy as a Humanistic Discipline* (Princeton, NJ: Princeton University Press, 2006)

Wilson, Edward O., *Sociobiology: The New Synthesis* (Cambridge, MA: Harvard University Press, 1975

Wittgenstein, Ludwig, *Philosophical Investigations* (Oxford: Basil Blackwell, 2nd ed. 1958)

——— *Blue and Brown Books* (Oxford, Basil Blackwell, 1958)

Woolf Institute, *Living with Difference: Community, Diversity and the Common Good*, Report of the Commission on Religion and Belief in British Public Life (Cambridge: The Woolf Institute, 2015)

Wright, L., 'Functions' *Philophical Review* 80 (1973) pp.139-68

Index

Abortion, 46, 99, 132-4, 138, 156, 162
Acton, Peter, 167
Actuality, 68-9, 116
Aeschylus, 95, 168
Al-Ghazali, 64
Al-Kindi, 64
Alston, William P., 38
Altruism 25-30, 53-5, 103, 147, 155
Ambrose of Milan, 86
Anscombe, Elizabeth, 8
Antiphon 'the sophist', 140
Aquinas, 37, 48, 49, 51, 64, 66, 73, 82, 91, 100-103, 109, 118, 139, 143, 145-8, 153-4, 156
Aristotle, 2, 7, 14, 16, 35, 45, 50, 53, 59-60, 63-4, 67, 75, 84, 94, 100-103, 117, 126, 141, 142, 145, 151, 152, 173

Armstrong, Karen, 32, 38
Atomism, varieties of, 77-8
Augustine of Hippo, 65, 89, 97, 100
Austin, J.L., 68
Barnes, Jonathan, 52
Beattie, Tina, 132
Bede, 17,
Behe, Michael J., 72-3
Belief, 3, 5, 18, 29, 39-40, 49, 54
Benedict XVI (Joseph Ratzinger), 50
Bentham, Jeremy, 1-11 10
Berlin, Isaiah, 142, 160-1
Bonaventure, 64
Boscovitch, R.J., 62
Boyle, Nicholas, 35-6
Butler, Joseph, 30
Butler, Samuel, 131
Carroll, Lewis (Charles Dodgson), 155

Catechism of the Catholic Church, 81, 84, 85, 88, 100, 139
Causality, causal explanation, 61, 62, 67, 69, 72, 79
Caxton, William, 39, 50
Charity, 50, 56, 58, 132
Chesterton, G.K., 167
Christianity and religion, 38; origin, 3, 42
Cicero, 68, 73, 142, 143, 144
circumcision, 42
Clark, Stephen, 38
common good, 33, 36
Copson, Andrew, 44, 162, 163, 166
Crane, Tim, 3, 45, 41
Creation, and causation, Chapter 6
creed, 49
culture, 22, 44, 56, 81

custom, distinguished from convention, habit, 21-2,
Darwin, Charles, 57
Davidson, Donald, 66
Davies, Paul, 73
Dawkins, Richard, 25
deism, 55
Dembski, William A., 72-3
Descartes, 62, 67, 73, 98, 151
Design, 72-4
Dickens, Charles, 29
Disraeli, Benjamin, 108
Duffy, Eamon, 50
Dunbar, R.I.M., 34-6, 165, 168,
Durkheim, Emile, 40-2
Edge, Peter, 5
Elizabeth of Bohemia, 67, 98, 94
Entrêves, A.P. d', 140, 143-6, 153
eternity, 116
Euripides, 172
Evans-Pritchard, E.E., 59, 164, 167
existence, 68
Fabre, J.-H., 76
'faith', senses of, 48-9, 58,
Finnis, John, 139, 150, 152-5
Fitzpatrick, Joseph, 17, 82
Flew, Anthony, 8
forensic reasoning, 75-7
form, and matter, 60-1, 100-103
Francis of Assisi, 173
Frege, 2
Freud, Sigmund, 28-9
Function, 147
Gibbon, Edward, 167
Gilbert, W.S., 123

Gilgamesh, 16, 17
'god', the word, 52
Golden Legend, The, 39, 50
Golding, William, 86
Gooch, Bernard, 76
good, concept of, 146
Gratian, 145
Grotius, 149, 150
Harré, Rom, 61-2
Heraclitus, 140
Hesiod, 6, 141
Hobbes, 11, 12, 13, 15, 16-17, 26, 28, 149, 150, 174
Homer, 16, 18, 34, 59, 95
humanism, 2, 38, 53, 171
Hume, David, 11, 63, 67, 72, 110, 131, 151, 153, 173
Huxley, Aldous, 164
Huxley Julian, 38, 173
individuals, 9-11
ius, 23, 150
James, John, 170
James, William, 37-8
Jerusalem Bible, The, 84
Jewish nation 4, 51, 80-81, 83, 85-7, 90, 105
Jews, 3, 5, 7, 38, 39, 41, 42, 43, 52, 53, 56, 59, 64, 95, 96, 97, 118, 132, 136, 170
Josephus, 43, 95, 145
Julian of Norwich, 173
justice, 117
Justin Martyr, 97
Justinian, 139, 143, 144, 175
Kant, 7
Knox, R.A., 51
Lane Fox, Robin, 167
Language, 4, 13-18, 21, 27, 28
law, custom and right, 23-4, 150

law, and nature, 7, 23, chapter 11
Lewis, C.S., 169
Life, societies for, 21-2, 137
Locke, 11, 12-13, 71, 149,
Lucretius, 176
MacIntyre, Alasdair, 8
Mackie, John L., 8, 67, 173
Maimonides, 64
Mandeville, Bernard, 172
Manichaeanism, 172
mass-societies, 35, 138, 158, 171
mathematics, 48, 60, 62, 63, 77, 149, 151
Mathew, Gervase, 115
Mead, Margaret, 138
Melville, Herman, 42
Midgley, Mary, 8, 55, 156,172
Mill, John Stuart, 8, 9-11, 26, 33, 72, 79, 98, 134 ,137-8, 160-1, 163, 168
Moore, G.E., 153
More, Thomas, 37
Multiculturalism, 45-7, chapter 12
Murray, Alexander, 149
Muslims, 38, 39, 41, 53, 56, 64, 132
Mutakallimum, 64
natural, contrasted custom, 23, supernatural, 41, 59, technology, 60
natural phenomena, social concepts of, 19-20
natural selection, 26-7
natural science, 2, Chapter 6,
Newton, Isaac, 65

Index

Ockham, 103
Original sin, 57, 81-2, 100
Orwell, George, 135, 159
'pagan', 39
pantheism, 53, 69-71, 141, 173
Pascal, 77, 121
'penny' catechism, 50, 69, 89, 99
person, formal concept, 53-4, 135; legal concept, 144; modern concept, 134, 135, 169; see also Trinity
Pestieau, Joseph, 16
Philo, 97
Philoponus, 64
philosophy, 2-3, 5, 7-8, 60, 62, 77, 152
physicalism, 10, 26-7, 174
Pius XII (Eugenio Pacelli), 100
Plato, 6-7, 14, 15-16, 18, 31-2, 35, 60, 62, 63, 97-8, 100, 103,105, 108, 109, 141, 146-7,147, 149, 151, 159
pleasure, pleasant sensations, 11
Pliny, 43
Pope, Alexander, 102
Popper, Karl, 2
possibility, and actuality, 68-9
primitive societies, 18-19, 22, 36, 42, 158, 160, 168,
prudence, 50, 156
psychological terms, concepts, 17-18, 22, 28, 58, 95-6,

Pufendorf, 149, 150
punishment, 121, 149-50, 152
Rahner, Karl, 4
Reasoning, deductive and practical, 24, 25, 75, 149, 151, 154-6; forensic, 69-73,
reincarnation, 107
'religion', the word, 3, 37
Reybrouck, David van, 35
rights, 19, 22-3, 124-5
Rose, H.J., 3
Rousseau, 15, 31, 38, 137
Russell, Bertrand, 8, 38, 43, 78, 107, 140
salvation, 57, Chapter 7
Saunders, Edith, 109
Scotus, 103
Secularism, 44
sex, 7, 30, 126, chapter 11
Shakespeare, William, 98
Sheldon, W.H., 31
Smith, Adam, 26, 172
Smith, George D., 108
social feelings, 28-9
societies for life, 21-2
societies, mass-, 35, 36, 138, 158, 171
societies, primitive, 17-18
Sophocles, 24, 123, 140,
Sorabji, Richard, 64
Spinoza, 66, 146, 173
Stoics, 53, 141-4, 148, 167, 173
Strang, Colin, 31, 116
Sub-societies, 3, 42-6, 137, 159
Suarez, 149, 150

Swinburne, Richard, 8, 73
Syllabus of Errors, 81
Thatcher, Margaret, 2
Thucydides, 76, 141, 150
Tolkien, J.R.R., 124
Tolstoy, Leo, 54
transcendence, 41
Trinity, Christian doctrine of, 81, 88-9, 111-12, 114
Trotter, Wilfred, 30, 33, 164, 168
Turing, Alan,165
Ulpian, 143, 146
utilitarianism, 93, 130
values, 41
Vatican Council II, 33
Vermes, Geza, 83
Vickers, Lucy, 5
Vincentius Victor, 100
vine, imagery of, 80, 87, 111
virtue ethics, 7
Voragine, 39
Warnock, Mary, 134, 160-1, 177
Warnock Report, 133
Weil, Simone, 166, 169, 171
Weinberg, Steven, 172
Wells, H.G., 120
Wiggins, David, 103
Wilberforce, William, 57
Will, faculty of, 151-2
Williams, Bernard, 46-7, 166, 177
Wilson, Edward O., 10, 25
Wittgenstein, Ludwig, 104
Woolf Institute, 1, 5
Wright, L., 147